The Big Oyster

New York in the World

A Molluscular History

THE BIG OYSTER

The Big
Oyster

—

New York in the World
A Molluscular History

MARK KURLANSKY

JONATHAN CAPE

LONDON

Published by Jonathan Cape 2006

2 4 6 8 10 9 7 5 3 1

Frontispiece: *Harper's Weekly*, 1882

First published in the United States of America in 2006
as *The Big Oyster: New York on the Half Shell* by
Ballantine books, Random House, Inc., New York 2005

First published in Great Britain in 2006 by
JONATHAN CAPE
Random House, 20 Vauxhall Bridge Road,
London SW1V 2SA

Random House Australia (Pty) Limited
20 Alfred Street, Milsons Point, Sydney,
New South Wales 2061, Australia

Random House New Zealand Limited
18 Poland Road, Glenfield,
Auckland 10, New Zealand

Random House South Africa (Pty) Limited
Isle of Houghton, Corner of Boundary Road & Carse O'Gowrie,
Houghton 2198, South Africa

The Random House Group Limited Reg. No. 954009
www.randomhouse.co.uk

A CIP catalogue record for this book
is available from the British Library

ISBN 9780224074339 (from January 2007)
ISBN 0224074334
ISBN 9780224078238 (from January 2007)
ISBN 0224078232

Papers used by Random House are natural,
recyclable products made from wood grown in sustainable forests;
the manufacturing processes conform to the environmental
regulations of the country of origin

Printed and bound in Great Britain by
William Clowes Ltd, Beccles, Suffolk

To Alvin and Barbara Mass,
two great New Yorkers

Others will see the shipping of Manhattan north and west,
and the heights of Brooklyn to the south and east.
Others will see the island large and small;
Fifty years hence, others will see them as they cross,
the sun half an hour high,
A hundred years hence, or ever so many hundred years hence,
others will see them,
Will enjoy the sunset, the pouring-in of the flood-tide,
the falling-back to the sea of the ebb-tide.

—WALT WHITMAN,
"Crossing Brooklyn Ferry," 1856

CONTENTS

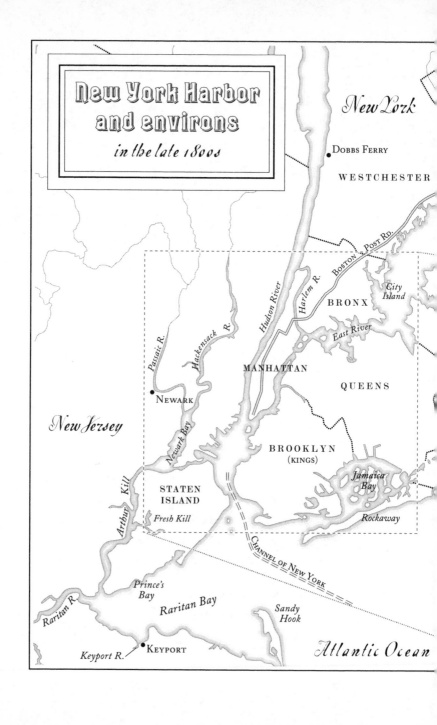

New York Harbor and environs in the late 1800s

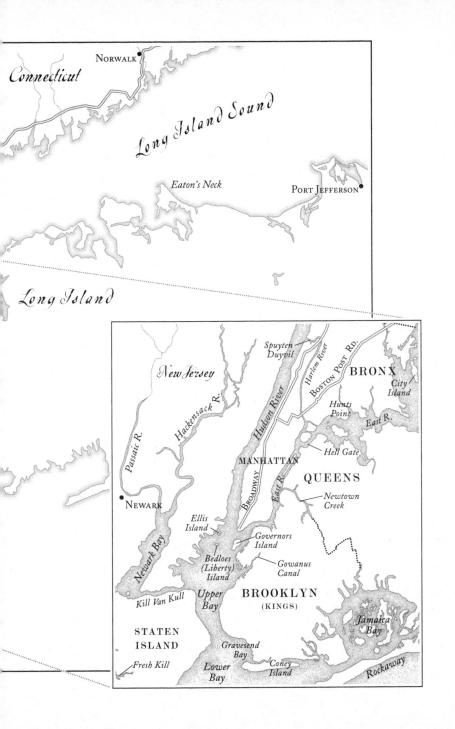

Connecticut

NORWALK

Long Island Sound

Eaton's Neck

PORT JEFFERSON

Long Island

New Jersey

Spuyten
Duyvil

Harlem River

BOSTON POST RD.

BRONX

City
Island

Hackensack R.

Hunts
Point

East R.

Passaic R.

Hudson River

Hell Gate

MANHATTAN

QUEENS

BROADWAY

East R.

Newtown
Creek

NEWARK

Ellis
Island

Governors
Island

Bedloes
(Liberty)
Island

Gowanus
Canal

Newark Bay

Upper
Bay

BROOKLYN
(KINGS)

Kill Van Kull

Jamaica
Bay

STATEN
ISLAND

Gravesend
Bay

Fresh Kill

Lower
Bay

Coney
Island

Rockaway

The Hard Shell of the City

*To me New York is the most wonderful and
most beautiful city in the world. All life is in it.*

—CHILDE HASSAM,
American Impressionist painter, 1889

To anyone who is familiar with New Yorkers, it should not be surprising to learn that they were once famous for eating their food live. The fact that oysters are about the only food eaten alive is part of what makes them a unique gastronomic experience—that and the sense that no other food brings us closer to the sea. Oysters spend their lives—a dozen years if we left them alone, but only three or four because we don't—sucking in seawater, extracting nutrients, and pumping it out again. There used to be enough oysters in New York Harbor to process all the water there, which is one of the reasons environmentalists want them back. And perhaps this is also why oysters taste like eating the sea.

New Yorkers seldom think of it this way, but they live in the estuary of the Hudson River, an expansive interconnected tidal system that also involves New Jersey and Connecticut. Damage anywhere in this system deteriorates the entire estuary.

Recently, while riding a train from Washington, D.C., to New York, I found myself along the part of New York Harbor's shoreline that some people unkindly call "the chemical coast." Many New Yorkers forget that this is part of their harbor because it is "out of town" in New Jersey. Usually when I'm returning to New York, at this point I would look homeward to Manhattan at the never-disappointing skyline of the island where I live. Otherwise I would look out at smokestacks and pipes and flames from refineries. But for some reason, this one time, I looked instead right in front of me and realized that I was in a grassy wetland—a magnificent grassy wetland where egrets and herons could live. As the grass rolled in waves and the sun reflected on narrow waterways, I saw that this could have been a northern Everglades. By what act of blind insanity did people decide to build chemical plants, oil refineries, and heavy industry in a beautiful wetland that belonged to one of the world's great waterways? Blind madness? It occurred to me that they had probably never really looked at it either.

The only thing New Yorkers ignore more than nature is history. They have a habit of not spending a great deal of time pondering the history of their city. That is because of a sense that it has always been more or less the same, or, as Edmund Wilson, one of the more venerated *New Yorker* writers of that magazine's heyday, explained his waning enthusiasm for reading history in his old age, "I know more or less the kind of things that happen."

The history of New York oysters is a history of New York itself—its wealth, its strength, its excitement, its greed, its thoughtlessness, its destructiveness, its blindness and—as any New Yorker will tell you—its filth. This is the history of the trashing of New York, the killing of its great estuary.

New York is a city that does not plan; it creates situations and then deals with them. Most of its history is one of greedily grabbing beautiful things, destroying them, being outraged about the conditions, tearing them down, then building something else even further from nature's intention in their place. What could be more typical of New York than "the Doorknob," a spot in New York Harbor that is contaminated from being used as a dumping ground for the trash created when the city tried to correct decades of neglect on the Lower East Side by tearing down the tenements to build housing projects.

One of the great New York paradoxes is that the metropolis is both unique and typical. Many of its stories are true for other cities as well. The oyster history of New York often matches that of other great oyster capitals such as Paris, and London on the oyster-encrusted estuary of the Thames. It is interesting that London, rich in its own oysters like New York, also destroyed them, whereas Paris, which was the commercial and consuming capital of oysters brought in from other regions, did more to preserve its beds.

Before the twentieth century, when people thought of New York, they thought of oysters. This is what New York was to the world—a great oceangoing port where people ate succulent local oysters from their harbor. Visitors looked forward to trying them. New Yorkers ate them constantly. They also sold them by the millions, supplying Chicago, St. Louis, Denver, and San Francisco, but also shipping to England, France, and Germany. As New York transportation improved, New York oysters traveled ever farther. In the nineteenth century the British credited New York with meeting their oyster needs when their own famous beds failed.

Oysters were true New Yorkers. They were food for gourmets, gourmands, and those who were simply hungry; tantalizing the wealthy in stately homes and sustaining the poor in wretched slums; a part of city commerce and a part of international trade.

If eating an oyster is tasting the sea, eating a New York oyster was tasting New York Harbor, which became increasingly unappealing. The oyster was New Yorkers' link to the sea, and eventually it was lost. Today New Yorkers eat not as many oysters, but still quite a few, albeit from a dozen other places, and now when they think of the sea, they think of somewhere else—perhaps the eastern tip of Long Island or New England or even Florida. Though they live by the sea, they take vacations to go somewhere else to be by the sea. Of the many odd things about New Yorkers, there is this: How is it that a people living in the world's greatest port, a city with no neighborhood that is far from a waterfront, a city whose location was chosen because of the sea, where the great cargo ships and tankers, mighty little tugs, yachts, and harbor patrol boats glide by, has lost all connection with the sea, almost forgotten that the sea is there? New Yorkers have lost their oyster, their taste of the sea. This is the story of how it happened.

A Good Time Coming

"Fruges consumere nati *[born to eat produce]*," may designate
*humanity elsewhere, but here the quotation may be out of
place, for man seems born to consume "oysters."*

—CHARLES MACKAY ON NEW YORK CITY,
*Life and Liberty in America or Sketches of a Tour in the
United States and Canada in 1857–58*

L*ife had been working out very well for Charles Mackay,*
a Scottish songwriter. Every week, from 1851 to 1855, the London
Illustrated News had published one of his songs and they were becoming a popular phenomenon on both sides of the Atlantic. The sheet
music of one tune, "A Good Time Coming," had sold four hundred
thousand copies.

In 1857, at the height of his popularity, Mackay accepted an offer
for a lecture tour of the United States and Canada. Though originally
he had enthusiastically embraced this opportunity to see North
American cities, while he was waiting in Liverpool for his ship to sail,
his exuberance was quickly fading.

The wind ripped through the harbor with such a loud eerie howl that he could not sleep at night. It was only early October and winter was already settling into Liverpool. Surely the North Atlantic in the weeks to come would be even worse. The dark, opaque sea, almost indistinct from the muddy, dark sky, churned at the mouth of the Mersey, throwing up little peaks that even in their sheltered moorings made the ships' spars swing like anxious pendulums as the rigging creaked gloomily. He thought of weeks in this rasping wooden box under blackened skies on a heaving, dark sea.

A disturbingly cheerful friend was hosting him at the Waterloo Hotel while he waited for the hour to board ship. As his friend saw him to the door, Mackay studied the rain beating against the windows. It was not just falling on the panes, it was pelting them, tiny hard beads that bounced off the glass.

His friend wished him a safe and speedy crossing and then added grandly in a voice that rose above the howling wind and pelted panes, "I envy you your trip to America."

Mackay, probably unconvincingly, attempted an appropriately jovial expression, but all he could manage to say was "And why?"

"Because," the friend answered with a joyous, beaming smile, "you will get such delicious oysters! New York beats all creation for oysters."

Two months later, writing in his diary from New York City, Mackay noted, "Mine host spoke the truth. There is no place in the world where there are such fine oysters as in New York. . . ."

PART ONE

The Beds of Eden

—

This is the land, with milk and honey flowing
With healing herbs like thistles freely growing
The place where the buds of Aaron's rods are blowing
O, this is Eden.

—JACOB STEENDAM,
Dutch settler in New Netherlands from 1650 to 1660

A Molluscular Life

—

Obviously, if you don't love life, you can't enjoy an oyster.

—ELEANOR CLARK,
The Oysters of Locmariaquer, 1959

In 1609, *when Henry Hudson, a British explorer employed* by the Dutch, sailed into New York Harbor on his eighty-five-foot ship, *Halve Maen,* with a half-British, half-Dutch crew of sixteen, he found the same thing Mackay would two and a half centuries later— a local population with the habit of feasting on excellent New York Harbor oysters.

Hudson was a seventeenth-century man in search of a fifteenth-century dream. His employer, Holland, would soon be in its golden age, offering the world Rembrandt, the microscope, and the stock exchange, but not, as Hudson and his sponsors had hoped, a river through North America leading to China.

A water route to Chinese trade replacing the long, arduous Silk Road was a great dream of the Renaissance. The only alternative ever found was in 1499 when Vasco da Gama sailed from Portugal and went around Africa to the Indian Ocean. All of the westward voyages of exploration had ended in failure, with endless landmasses standing in the way between Europe and China. Cabot was stopped by Canada in the north, Verrazano was stopped by the United States farther south, Columbus by Central America in the middle, and Magellan showed that it was a hopelessly long way around South America to the south. Only one idea still held any possibility and that was a passage through arctic waters.

And so Hudson was essentially an arctic explorer. In fact, he was a failed arctic explorer. On his first voyage for the British he sailed straight north, attempting to travel beyond the ice and down the other side of the globe. The plan was geographically astute but meteorologically absurd and he was stopped by ice. At the point he could go no farther, his seventy-foot wooden vessel was only six hundred miles short of Robert E. Peary's 1909 achievement, reaching the North Pole. His second voyage, heading northeast over Russia, was also stopped by ice. At this point his British sponsor, the Muscovy Company, dropped him.

A new idea came along. In the early seventeenth century, Captain John Smith, the ruggedly handsome legendary adventurer famous for his conquests both military and sexual, was the great promoter of European settlement in North America. He charted the coastline, reported on his findings, and pitched North America to any Englishman who would listen. He was to play a role in the promoting of Britain's two leading North American colonies, Virginia and Massachusetts. Hudson knew Smith and they corresponded in 1608, by which time four-fifths of Smith's 1607 Virginia settlers had already died. There was a growing belief that North America was uninhabitable in the winter. But Smith's contagious enthusiasm never faltered. Not only did he believe in North American settlement—this entire debate taking place as if no one was already living there—but his maps and letters to Hudson promoted an alternative to the theory that a water route to China could be found north of Canada—the so-called Northwest Passage. Smith's theory was that somewhere north of Virginia a major river connected the Atlantic to the Sea of Cathay.

This is a case of people hearing only what they want to hear. Smith's Chinese sea was presumably the Pacific Ocean, but rivers are not known to flow from one sea to another. Smith's theory was based on statements from northern tribes who trapped for fur. They talked of an ocean that could be reached from a river. They probably said nothing about Cathay, China, which was an obsession of Europeans, not North Americans. It seems likely that the North Americans were talking about how they could travel up the Hudson and follow the Mohawk tributary and with a short land portage—for a canoe—arrive at the Great Lakes. Standing on the shore of Lake Erie, one can have the impression of being on the coast of a vast sea. Furthermore, the currents of the Hudson are so multidirectional, the salty ocean water travels so far inland, that according to Indian legend, the first inhabitants came to the Hudson in search of a river that ran two ways, as though it flowed into seas at both ends. Whether such early Indian explorers existed, the Europeans came looking for exactly that.

Hudson, the out-of-work explorer, had something to sell: a possible new passage to China. The Muscovy Company had listened and voted against the project. But Britain's new and fast-growing competitor, Holland, was interested. The Vernenigde Oostindische Compagnie, or VOC, known in English as the Dutch East India Company, hired him. The Dutch were not interested in new theories from John Smith or Henry Hudson. They hired Hudson to search for the northeastern passage, a route through the ice floes north of Russia. Hudson had no faith in this northeastern theory, but the VOC gave him a commission with a new ship, and so he took it and sailed north until well out of the view of Dutchmen. Then he picked up a westerly gale and crossed the Atlantic, thousands of miles in the opposite direction of his orders, and reached the North American coast off Newfoundland.

More than a century after John Cabot's voyage, this was a well-known route. Hudson then followed the coastline south to Cape Hatteras and the mouth of the Chesapeake within miles of his friend Smith at Jamestown but, sailing in a Dutch vessel, did not visit the British settlement. Perhaps he needed to locate Smith's Jamestown to find his bearing on Smith's maps. Then he began exploring the coastline for a river to China.

In this search he became the first European to enter Delaware Bay. But seeing the shallow waters, shoals, and bars at the mouth of the Delaware, Hudson felt certain that this was not a river great enough to cut through North America to China. He continued on, viewing the forest lands of an unknown continent off the port side, seemingly uninhabited, with only an occasional bird chirp for counterpoint to the rolling surf on sandy beaches and the creaks in the *Half Moon*'s rigging.

Then, rounding a flat, sandy, narrow peninsula, today accurately labeled Sandy Hook, Hudson and his men, almost as if falling through a keyhole, found themselves in another world. The wide expanse of water, one hundred square miles, lay flat, sheltered by the bluffs of Staten Island and the rolling hills of Brooklyn. Sandy Hook on the port and the shoals of Rockaway Peninsula on the starboard, an ideal barrier furnished with several channels, protected the opening. When they looked into the water, they could see large fish following them.

This was the place. From all directions they saw rivers pouring into the bay. If there were a chasm in the heart of North America opening up a waterway all the way to China, this is what it would look like.

Hudson identified three "great rivers." They were probably Raritan Bay, which separates New Jersey and Staten Island, the opening to the Upper Harbor, and the Rockaway Inlet on the Brooklyn–Queens shore of Long Island. He had not yet sailed through the narrow opening between Staten Island and Brooklyn—not yet seen the Upper Bay, the Hudson River, the Harlem River, and the East River that connects with Long Island Sound. He had not yet seen the lush, green, rocky island of ponds and streams in the middle of the estuary.

Hudson sent a landing party ashore on Staten Island. It was late summer and the plum trees and grapevines were bearing fruit. Immediately upon landing, as though Hudson's crew had been expected, as though invited, people dressed in animal skins appeared to welcome them. These people in animal skins saw that the leader of the people who arrived in the floating house wore a red coat that sparkled with gold lace.

In what would become a New York tradition, commerce instantly began. The Europeans in red had tools, while the skin-clad Americans offered hemp, beans, and a local delicacy—oysters. The Europeans thought they were getting much better value than they were giving, but the Americans may have thought the same thing.

Hudson and his men had no idea with whom they were trading. They reported that the people in skins were friendly and polite but not to be trusted. These people the Europeans distrusted called their land *Lenapehoking,* the land of the Lenape. The Lenape thought they knew their visitors. They were a people they called in their language *shouwunnock,* which meant "Salty People." The grandparents of the Lenape who saw Hudson may have seen an earlier Salty Person, the Italian, Giovanni da Verrazano, sailing the coast with his crew for Francis I, king of France, in 1524. Verrazano had chosen to moor his ship off Staten Island, farther up than Hudson, in the narrow opening that bears his name and where Staten Island is now connected to Brooklyn by a bridge. Verrazano could see the second interior bay with its wide rivers and well-placed island and described the bay as "a pleasant lake." He named it Santa Margarita after the sister of his patron, Francis. "We passed up with our boat only into the said river, and saw the country very well peopled. The people are almost like unto the others, and clad with feathers of fowls of divers colors. They came toward us very cheerfully, making great shouts of admiration, showing us where we might come to land most safely with our boat."

But soon shifting winds forced the Europeans, with great reluctance, to return to their ship and sail on. This was probably the first sighting of Salty People by the inhabitants of the harbor, although their grandparents may also have seen Ésteban Gomez, a Portuguese explorer who passed this way. An early Portuguese map suggests that Europeans, probably either Portuguese or Basque fishermen, may have sailed to this place at the time of Columbus. Some of those who now met Hudson and his crew may have heard of or even had contact with the Frenchman Samuel de Champlain, who only a few months earlier had traveled south from what is now Canada to the lake that is named after him. Jamestown, near the mouth of the Chesapeake

Bay, was just south of the Lenapes' Delaware Bay and was already two years old when Hudson arrived in New York. By the time Hudson arrived, the Lenapes knew Salty People when they saw them. They had been coming for a long time with very little consequence.

This group stayed longer than the others. They explored the upper harbor, then chose the river west of the island and sailed up what is now called the Hudson as far as what is now Albany. From there, it must have been clear that this narrowing river was not leading to China and they left.

In the Lenape language, *lenape* translates as "the common man." Sometimes they called themselves *Lenni Lenape,* which means "we, the people." Europeans have labeled the language and the people Delaware. They were a loose confederation of populations living between the South River, the Delaware, and the North River, the Hudson. Until the twentieth century, it was believed that between eight and twelve thousand such people lived in what is today Delaware, Pennsylvania, New Jersey, New York, and Connecticut when Hudson arrived. But these low estimates were based on the count in the year 1700, which was three thousand. Starting in 1633, the Lenape had already been through at least fourteen epidemics of such European diseases as smallpox, malaria, and measles. More recently, archaeologists have concluded that as many as fifteen thousand lived in what is today New York City and possibly as many as fifty thousand others lived in the Lenape region.

Lenape villages were busy little clusters of longhouses made of bark and grass. They lived on fishing and hunting, and gathering nuts, fruit, and shellfish. They made clothes of cured deer and elk skins. In spring, coastal Lenapes set up large fishing camps. They trapped, netted, and speared shad and other river fish. They had monogamous marriages, but sexual relations between the unmarried

Lenape village drawn on a Dutch map (circa 1655–77) by Claes Janzoon Visscher.
NEW YORK PUBLIC LIBRARY

were acceptable until Europeans introduced venereal diseases. The dead were greatly mourned. Sometimes mourners would blacken their faces for an entire year. The dead, it was believed, traveled along a star path. Each star in the Milky Way was believed to be a footprint.

The Lenape believed that their history began when *Kishele-mukong*, the creator, brought a giant turtle up from the deep ocean. The back of the turtle grew into a vast island, North America. They believed they had come to the mid-Atlantic from farther west and archaeologists agree, saying they arrived at the Atlantic three thousand years ago.

There were three major groups of Lenape and numerous subdivisions within those. They had few unifying institutions except language, and even that broke down into dialects. One of the groups, the Munsey, which means "mountaineers," controlled the mountains near the headwaters of the Delaware. They also maintained hunting grounds in what is now the New York City area. It is the Munsey language that gave Manhattan and many other New York places their names. It is uncertain from which Munsey word the name Manhattan is derived. One theory is that it comes from the word *manahactanienk*, which means "place of inebriation," but another is that it comes from *manahatouh*, meaning "a place where wood is available for making bows and arrows." The even more prosaic possibility that is most often cited is that it comes from *menatay*, which simply means "island."

Lenape and *Lenni Lenape* are Munsey words. Many of the subgroups have become place names. On Long Island, the Canarsee, the Rockaways, and the Massapequas all spoke Munsey. The Raritans, Tappans, and Hackensacks, all of whom spoke Unami, a different language in the same family as Munsey, controlled different parts of Staten Island, northern Manhattan, the Bronx, and parts of New Jersey. All of these people and other locals such as the Wieckquaesgecks of Westchester, ate oysters, and some may have traveled some distance for them. The Lenape who gave Hudson his first taste of New York oysters were from what is now Yonkers.

We know that the Lenape ate copious quantities of oysters because oyster shells last a very long time and they left behind tremendous piles of them. These piles, containing thousands of shells, have been found throughout the New York City area. Archaeologists call them shell middens. The most common marker of a pre-European settlement anywhere in the area of the mouth of the Hudson are these piles of oyster shells, sometimes as much as four feet deep, sometimes buried in the ground, sometimes piled high. The early-seventeenth-century Dutch were the first to note the shell middens. One such mountain of oyster shells gave Pearl Street, originally on the waterfront in lower Manhattan, its name. Contrary to popular belief, the street was not actually paved with oyster shells until many years after it was named for a midden. The Dutch found another midden at what is now the intersection of Canal Street and the Bowery and called it *Kalch-Hook,* Shell-Point.

Another pile was found alongside a forty-foot-deep inland pond, a favorite fishing spot of the Lenape and later the English, in the marshlands of lower Manhattan. The Dutch named the pond after the pile of oyster shells, calling it *Kalck,* which is Dutch for "lime," the principal component of oyster shells. Later in the seventeenth century, when the British replaced the Dutch as the administrators of Manhattan, they, too, were struck by these shell piles. In 1692, Charles Lodwick wrote a letter back to England in which he reported, "Many shells of oysters and other shellfish are found up on high hills as well as valleys and sometimes two or three foot within the earth, but are supposed to have been brought there by the natives and fishing having served them for food, and the shell rotting serve for dung which is common in these parts now coming the Christians."

Actually, shells don't rot even for Christians, and some of them are thousands of years old. But the seventeenth- and eighteenth-century European settlers sometimes took these shells and placed them in fields, where the lime would neutralize acid soil, a technique known at the time as "sweetening" the soil. They also burned shells to render lime paste to be used in colonial construction.

The middens were simply piles of shells. No one thought to seriously study these piles until the late nineteenth century. But they had always been something of a fascination on the landscape for some New Yorkers. Daniel Tredwell, a Brooklyn writer and journalist who lived from 1826 until 1921, wrote in his diary how he and his father enjoyed exploring middens in the 1830s. He wrote in 1839: "On the way out we pass many Indian shell heaps bleached as white as snow, which they much resemble at a distance. Some of them on the banks of the creek extend from fifteen to thirty feet upon the bank, and under water, in many instances entirely across the creek. These shell heaps, long ere this, has excited our curiosity and we had proposed all manner of questioning concerning their authors. These questions my father did not and could not satisfactorily answer, and we were consequently unsatisfied, and hence there was a constantly recurring inquiry."

Many shell middens have survived. Up until the end of the nineteenth century, there were a number of them on the Rockaway Peninsula area—in the marshes of Woodmere Bay, Inwood, Hog (or Barnum's) Island, and Far Rockaway. A particularly large one was a familiar sight in the Bayswater section of Far Rockaway. The middens even survived after Rockaway was developed as a beach resort in the late nineteenth century with the help of a fifty-cent train fare from Manhattan. But in the early twentieth century, when roads were being built for new automobiles, thousands of tons of shells were hauled away to use for road fill.

Most of the middens in Manhattan, Staten Island, and western Long Island are now gone. Numerous known sites lie beneath railroad tracks, city streets, dredged landfill, highways that hug the coastline, and docks. The Hudson railroad line was built along the eastern bank of the Hudson, tearing through numerous middens in the area just north of the city without regard for their archaeological value. What little remains of the midden near the Kalck Pond is covered by federal and state courthouses and the shops and restaurants of Chinatown. Archaeologists have found shells under some of the courthouses. In the twenty-first century, archaeologists and preservationists have been battling developers along the eastern Hudson bank to save some of the oldest middens of North America. In Dobbs Ferry, locals fought to stop a forty-four-acre condominium project that threatened to obliterate the oldest midden ever found on the Atlantic coast of North America.

Shell middens have been found all along the Atlantic coast of the United States and a few even older ones have been found in Europe, notably Denmark, but the lower Hudson from Peekskill to Staten Island and east to Long Island had an unusual concentration of them.

For the first 60 miles of the 315-mile-long Hudson River, from the southern tip of Manhattan until somewhere near what is now the town of Newburgh, the water remains salty enough for oysters and many other ocean species. The exact point where this ends and the Hudson becomes a freshwater river, what is called the salt line or the salt wedge, shifts from year to year and season to season. In a drought year the salt wedge can be seventy miles up the river. A few days of heavy rain can send it down to Manhattan. But the salt water will quickly rise up the river again even though this goes against the river's normal flow. About thirty miles north of Manhattan, around the town of Peekskill, the Hudson veers to the northwest, which causes tidewaters to move toward the eastern bank, and any oyster eggs deposited in the salt water would drift there. Shellfish beds and therefore middens were clustered on that bank.

The several hundred midden sites that have been identified in the New York City area, ranging from a few square yards to several acres of dense heaps, are believed to be only a fraction of the number existing at the time of Hudson's arrival. Middens are still being discovered. A midden was uncovered on Liberty Island during construction in the 1980s. In 1988, workmen found a midden below the Metro-North Railroad track while repairing cables.

The earliest oyster species by far predate man. Fossils of tiny, barely visible oysters have been dated to the Cambrian period 520 million years ago. During the Permian period, 250 million years ago, before mammals or dinosaurs appeared, there was a sweeping shake-up in marine life that left many species extinct. Oysters, however, not only survived but became bigger and more numerous. They continued to prosper in the flowering Cretaceous period, the lush epoch when dinosaurs mysteriously vanished, from 144 million to 65 million years ago. About 65 million years ago, when humans first began developing, oysters started evolving into the species that exist today. Although modern species have significant differences from their ancestors, the fossil of a prehistoric oyster looks remarkably similar to a contemporary oyster shell.

The native shell beds of the New York area and their residents, *Crassostrea virginica,* are believed to have first appeared about 10,000 B.C. The oldest Atlantic shell midden, in Dobbs Ferry, has been carbon-dated to about 6950 B.C. give or take a hundred years—long before the arrival of the Lenape three thousand years ago. This marks the oldest evidence of humans ever found in the Hudson Valley. Numerous other middens have been dated to long before the Lenape, which means they must have been left by an earlier people. But many date to Lenape times, and the People continued to leave oyster-shell mounds into the nineteenth century.

Throughout the more than a century that the Hudson shell middens have been studied, historians and archaeologists have puzzled over an unsolvable mystery. Although it is known that like the Lenape, their aboriginal predecessors ate a wide range of shellfish available in the vast estuary that is New York Harbor, the middens almost exclusively contain oyster shells. Where are the clam and mussel shells? While the Lenape valued oysters as food, they regarded hard clams as money, especially the large ones with bluish inner shells that New Englanders call quahogs. They would make long, cylindrical blue-and-white shell beads and drill a lengthwise hole in the center, though how this was accomplished with the tools they had is not known. The beads were then strung together and traded by the string. A six-foot string, of considerable value, could have seven thousand beads. This may explain the fate of quahog shells but not what happened to the shells of other clams and other molluscs.

Adding to the confusion and mystery, when the Lenape buried their dead, they often covered them in oyster shells. They also did this when burying their dogs and numerous dog graves have been found throughout Manhattan with the animals curled nose to tail and covered with oyster shells. Was there then a religious significance to the shells? Or were they added to graves for their lime content?

Archaeologists have identified two distinct types of middens, which they have labeled kitchen middens and processing middens. The principal difference between them is that kitchen middens contain evidence of bones, nuts, and other food scraps, and sometimes tools—stone ax heads are particularly common in Manhattan kitchen middens—whereas processing middens exclusively contain oyster shells. It is supposed that a processing midden was a site in which oysters were preserved for winter provisions. The Lenape smoked and dried oysters in the same way they preserved fish. The kitchen middens, on the other hand, are thought to be places where shells were dumped after the oysters were eaten fresh. This still leaves unexplained the absence of other kinds of shells.

Also puzzling is why these people ate so many oysters. Oysters are not an efficient food source. Between 90 and 95 percent of their weight comes from the inedible shell, so gathering bags of oysters from the beds and dragging them to the middens for shucking yielded fairly little food for the effort. The Lenape approach of gathering oysters in dugout canoes, which may have also been used by earlier peoples, somewhat reduces the labor. Probably to lessen the amount of hauling, no midden has been found more than 160 feet from water. But it still was not an easy way of obtaining nutrition.

Furthermore, until the Europeans arrived, the Lenape had no way of prying open an oyster shell. No one has ever seen a stone tool capable of this task. The small abductor muscle that holds the shells closed on a living oyster exerts about twenty-two pounds of pressure. One theory is that the Lenape used a flint tool that could have been slipped in to cut the abductor muscle. But since the shells in the middens are mostly undamaged, it is thought that rather than force, some sort of heat was used to kill the oyster, which relaxes the muscle. Only about 120 degrees Fahrenheit is needed to kill and open an oyster. Some deep pits that have been found are thought to have been used for baking oysters. Indians taught the first Europeans in New York to wrap oysters in wet seaweed and throw them on hot coals until they opened. However they managed it, processing oysters is thought to have been the earliest form of year-round mass production practiced by New Yorkers.

But even given the effort, oysters do not produce particularly nourishing food. Modern nutritionists estimate that for a diet of oysters to furnish the caloric intake necessary for good health, an individual would have to eat about 250 oysters a day. One modern researcher estimated that it would take 52,267 oysters to supply the same number of calories to be had by eating one red deer.

An intriguing idea emerges. It is clear not only by logic but by the evidence of the kitchen remains that have been found that no Hudson people ever had a diet principally based on oysters. There is a tendency to think of early humans as struggling for survival and therefore eating what was nutritious, easily available, and efficiently exploited. But it seems in the case of the prehistoric occupants of the lower Hudson, exactly as did all of their successors, they supplemented their diets with oysters as a delicacy, a gastronomic treat that was eaten purely for the pleasure of it. And the delicacy was in demand beyond the immediate area of the beds. Oysters were bartered in trade with inland people such as the Iroquois.

The fifty-two thousand oysters required to equal a deer was a European calculation. Red deer, a European species, are larger than the indigenous whitetail. Europe had larger deer and smaller oysters than New York. To calculate the food value of New York oysters relative to the native whitetail deer, one would have to know whether the oysters came from the top or bottom of the midden. It is significant that the deeper archaeologists dig in a midden, the larger the shells they find. The large bottom shells are older than the smaller top ones, which shows that, contrary to popular belief, even before Europeans arrived, people were overharvesting oysters. On the bottom the very largest ones, described as "giant oysters," measure eight to ten inches. This suggests that Dutch reports of foot-long oysters were only slightly exaggerated.

This discrepancy in the oyster sizes at the top and the bottom of the middens was the first of many warnings unheeded by the Salty People about the bounteous oyster beds of New York. A *Crassostrea virginica*, like fish and unlike humans, if not taken by man or other predators, and not killed by disease, will grow larger every year of their twelve to fifteen year lives. Factors such as salinity and water temperature determine the speed of growth. But the greatest factor in the size of an oyster is age: how long it has been left to grow in its bed before being harvested. Apparently even back in the distant millennia, there was a tendency to harvest all of the older, larger oysters, and then when none was left, the oyster gatherers started taking younger, smaller ones. In fact, everywhere that oyster-shell middens have been studied, including Maryland and Denmark, the same phenomenon has been found: The biggest shells were on the bottom, indicating that the largest oysters were the most valued and consequently taken first. There is even a measurable prehistoric phenomenon that as population density increased, oyster sizes diminished. This short-sighted and uncontrolled attraction for the biggest seems to be an inherent universal human trait. Eventually this could have led to a crisis, but prehistoric New Yorkers never stretched their resource to that point.

CHAPTER TWO

The Bivalent Dung Hill

—

*No sooner was the colony once planted, than like a luxuriant
vine, it took root and throve amazingly; for it would seem,
that this thrice favored island is like a munificent dung hill,
where everything finds kindly nourishment, and soon shoots
up and expands to greatness.*

—WASHINGTON IRVING,

*A History of New York from the Beginnings
of the World to the End of the Dutch Dynasty,* 1809

The Dutch who came to New Netherlands fell in love with
the lower Hudson and especially the island of Manhattan. Beginning
with those first few days in the harbor on the three-masted *Halve
Maen*, ecstatic descriptions began to flow. One of the officers, Robert
Juet, wrote of the "pleasant" grass and flowers, the "goodly Trees," and
the "very sweet smell." On the first day they rounded Sandy Hook
and entered New York Harbor, he wrote in his journal, "This is a very
good land to fall with, and a pleasant land to see." The poet Jacob

Fort New Amsterdam published in 1651 shows the fort's location on the tip of Manhattan with both Lenape and European vessels in the harbor.

Steendam, who lived in New Netherlands from 1650 to 1660, called the area Eden. He wrote of "the purity of the air." Several other Dutch and English made similar comments about Manhattan's air, noting that as soon as a ship rounded Sandy Hook, a wind would blow a fresh breeze consistently described as sweet. There was considerable discussion of what could be the cause of this extraordinarily pleasant air.

The Dutch described the fine, tall-grassed meadows, the woodlands, fields of wildflowers, the streams, the variety of the cooing and clattering birds, the deliciousness of the native nuts, wild cherries, currants, gooseberries, hazelnuts, apples and pears, and especially strawberries. Adriaen van der Donck wrote in his midseventeenth-century *Description of the New Netherlands* that people who lived by the water could not sleep at night because of the clattering of swans and other waterfowl. He noted that the wild turkeys were so large and numerous "that they shut out the sunshine." Nicolaes van Wassenaer wrote, "Birds fill also the woods so that men can scarcely go through them for the whistling, the noise and the chattering."

The rivers and streams had so many fish—striped bass, sturgeon, shad, drum fish, carp, perch, pike, and trout—that they could be yanked out of the water by hand. The Dutch delighted in examining every fish caught to see if it was a new, unknown species. They identified ten familiar species in the Hudson and named each new one numerically. They dubbed shad *elft* for eleventh, striped bass was called *twalft*, twelfth, and drums were *dertienen*, thirteen. Like oysters and numerous other much-valued foods, the striped bass was credited with powers of sexual stimulation. Thus the Hudson was a river with a choice of aphrodisiacs. Isaack de Rasière, a New Amsterdam commercial agent, wrote of the striped bass in 1620, "It seems that this fish makes them [Indians] lascivious, for it is often observed that those who have caught any when they have gone fishing, have given them, on return, to the women, who look for them anxiously. Our people also confirm this."

The harbor was crowded with bass, cod, weakfish, herring, mackerel, blackfish, as well as frolicking, diving mammals—whales, porpoises, and seals. Bears, wolves, beavers, foxes, raccoons, otters, elk, deer, and even a few "lion," which may have been panthers or mountain lions, lived in the area. The Catskills, originally called Katzbergs by the Dutch, were named for their abundance of bobcats and lynx.

Jasper Danckaerts, a Dutchman who traveled the New York City area from 1679 to 1680, wrote, "It is not possible to describe how this bay swarms with fish, both large and small, whales, tunnies, and porpoises, whole schools of innumerable other fish, which the eagles and other birds of prey swiftly seize in their talons when the fish comes to the surface."

Sizes were enormous. Juet reported the first morning of fishing— it is not clear if his ship landed to the port on Sandy Hook or starboard at Coney Island—netting "ten great Mullets, of a foot and a halfe long a peece and a Ray as great as foure men could hale into the ship." According to van der Donck, the pears were larger than a fist, the wild turkeys weighed forty pounds, the lobsters were six feet long, and the oysters measured twelve inches. Van der Donck assured the Dutch, "There are some persons who imagine the animals of the country will be destroyed in time, but this is an unnecessary anxiety."

Most of the early European descriptions of North America share this enthusiasm and also, no doubt, a tendency toward hyperbole. Washington Irving pointed out that there were also reports of unicorns, and the missionary Hans Megapolensis reported on four-foot tortoises with two heads. Despite repeated Dutch claims of Hudson River salmon, these sightings are most likely mistaken, since such a fish has never been seen in the Hudson. Some of these claims may have resulted from a mistranslation of the Dutch words *salm* and *salmpie*, which could refer to trout. But even Robert Juet, an Englishman, reported seeing salmon in the harbor, possibly misidentified striped bass. Most of the exuberant seventeenth-century accounts of fecund nature in North America were probably true, including the enraptured descriptions of the island of Manhattan, its streams, meadows, and marshes. Any contemporary New Yorker who has ever watched nature consume an empty New York City lot might suspect as much. Lower Manhattan was a teaming wetland of grassy marshes, which the Mohawk called *Gänóno*, reedy place, filled with birds and marine life. A salty wetland extended to what is today Rivington Street. About where Center Street intersects White today, a stream left the Kalck Pond and turned northwest, flowing along what is today Canal Street across a grassy meadow and into the Hudson. A second stream flowed from the pond to the East River. In times of heavy rains these streams swelled and cut the island of Manhattan in two. Another little trout stream ran past what is now Times Square west into the Hudson. Minetta Brook, from the Dutch word meaning "little one," in what is now Greenwich Village, was also known for its trout. Teawater Spring, which fed the Kalck Pond, was known for its exquisite drinking water. The marsh where Washington Square now stands was known for its ducks. The early Europeans always praised the natural richness of the place and in their rhapsodic descriptions almost always included some mention of oysters.

The settlers wrote of how good the oysters were for stewing and frying and how "as each one fills a spoon they make a good bite." They often referred to their large size and one settler added that they found them "occasionally containing a small pearl," which is difficult to believe, since *Crassostrea virginica* is not a pearl-producing species.

Back in Holland, for all the lyrical depictions, New Amsterdam was mostly seen as a business proposition. Soon after Henry Hudson returned, Dutch traders visited the coast near the mouth of the Hudson, which led to formation of the New Netherlands Company in 1614. The charter granted rights to certain merchants to the exclusion of all others. This included the exclusive right to make four voyages within three years, beginning January 1615, to the new lands between the fortieth and forty-fifth latitudes, which, for the first time, were designated as "New Netherlands."

The purpose was trade, not settlement, which explains the short term of the contract. But voyages continued after the charter's 1618 expiration, and on June 3, 1621, the West India Company, an idea first proposed by Willem Usselinx in 1592, was established. It was given a trade monopoly for twenty-four years on the coasts of North and South America, the west coast of Africa from the Tropic of Cancer to the Cape of Good Hope, and to all places and islands westward to the eastern end of New Guinea. Within these borders the company had the right to negotiate alliances with local leaders, establish colonies, appoint and discharge governors and other officers, administer its own justice, and promote colonization. But the governor was not a colonial ruler in the British or French sense. He was an officer of the company who made decisions based on the needs of the company. There was no actual government. Anyone who wished to settle in New Netherlands placed himself under the absolute authority of the company.

The interests of the company were in making a profit, but beyond that, the Dutch government that chartered the company had a political objective. In 1562, the Dutch had begun a fight for independence from the Spanish, who had ruled them for a century. In 1618, the year the contracts of the New Netherlands Company had been set to expire, the Dutch began the final phase of their independence struggle, what was called the Thirty Years War, which lasted, as the name implies, until 1648.

In 1621, when the Dutch granted a charter for the West India Company, the fundamental idea was to attack Spain, Spanish colonies, and as many Spanish ships as possible. This failed to attract investors. So the charter was amended to include the saltworks in Punto del Rey, which attracted merchants who had interests in the Dutch herring trade. But in general, the company still failed to attract large-scale investment.

New Netherlands, located far from the Spanish Main—the Spanish land holdings in the Americas, which were principally the coastline from Panama to the Orinoco River, the Caribbean coast of South America—had limited impact on the war with Spain. But this water-laden Eden seemed to have wealth, and the mission of the company in New Netherlands was to exploit resources. It was remembered that Verrazano had speculated that the area "must contain great riches, as the hills showed many indications of minerals."

Most of the records of the Dutch West India Company, including Hudson's log, vanished in a series of fires and other calamities, culminating in an 1821 public auction of what remained in the hands of the Dutch government. New Yorkers did not even learn of this loss until twenty years later, when the legislature sent for records to refute Washington Irving's disparaging portraits of Dutch settlers as both lazy and incompetent administrators. "As most of the council were but little skilled in the mystery of combining pot hooks and hangers," Irving wrote, "they determined most judiciously not to puzzle either themselves or posterity, with voluminous records."

The few records and correspondence that remained made clear that above all, the Dutch interests in New Netherlands were beaver and otter pelts. The fur of beavers, the second largest rodent on earth next to the capybara, was from about 1550 to 1850, the more valuable. It was used primarily for hats, and the Russians, who had been the chief suppliers, had so greedily pursued this industry that by the dawn of New Netherlands, these rodents were nearly extinct in Russia and Scandinavia. Western Europeans, trying to compete with the Russians, had driven their beavers to complete extinction. The beaver hat industry was able to continue only because of North American pelts. The French had moved into the hat business with Canadian pelts, but now the Dutch had a chance to compete. Van der Donck estimated in midcentury that eighty thousand beavers were being killed annually.

Only the Russians knew how to remove the longer "guard hairs" from the fur. Alternatively, these hairs would wear off the pelt after about a year of use and therefore the beaver pelt of choice, known as a coat beaver, had been worn by an Indian for a year. Unused pelts, parchment beavers, could be sold only to the Russians until Westerners learned the technique of plucking the hairs with a thumb and a knife blade at the end of the seventeenth century, after the fall of New Netherlands.

New Netherlands included the entire land of the Lenape, *Lenepehoking*, from the South River—the Delaware—to the North River—the Hudson—north to Albany, where the Dutch established the settlements of Fort Orange and Rensselaer, to the Fresh River—the Connecticut—where they established a settlement in what is now Hartford. The capital, New Amsterdam, on the southern end of Manhattan, was a maritime people's idea of choice real estate, along the sheltered and defendable inner harbor of an immense waterway, with 770 miles of waterfront. From New Amsterdam, all of New Netherlands was reachable by water. A vessel could sail through the Narrows, out the lower bay rounding Sandy Hook, and follow the coastline to the mouth of the Delaware and up to where Philadelphia now stands. Or it could have taken the Newark or Raritan River into present-day New Jersey. Or sailed east from the harbor along the southern shore of Long Island out to sea and across the Atlantic. Or sailed up the Hudson River to Albany or up the East River to Long Island Sound, and up the Connecticut River to Hartford or beyond through the center of New England.

In 1623, a shipload of settlers sailed to New Netherlands—two families and six men to the Connecticut River, two families and eight men to the Delaware River, eight men to New Amsterdam, and the rest were shipped up the river to Fort Orange, today Albany, which was considered the most important part of the territory because it was where the furs could be acquired from the Indians. Catelina Trico, one of the Fort Orange–bound settlers, wrote years later that the Indians were "as quiet as lambs and came and traded with unimaginable freedom."

The 1624 Provisional Regulations of the West India Company stated that the colonists were free to pursue the inland trade as long as they sold the goods they collected to company agents. They were also free to carry on their own hunting, fowling, and fishing, but "all minerals, newly discovered or still-to-be-discovered mines of gold, silver, or any other metals, as well as precious stones, such as diamonds, rubies and the like, together with the pearl fishery, shall be allowed to be worked by the Company's men only. But anyone who discovers any of the aforementioned will be granted to him and his heirs one tenth of the proceeds for the first six years."

The colonists "shall not permit any strangers (whereupon are understood all persons who are outside the jurisdiction of the Company or its commissaries) coming to their shores to do any trading. . . ." They were also sworn to secrecy about anything they knew of the inner workings of the company and had to make a commitment to stay where they were sent for six years and plant what they were told. They were also required, under threat of "being rigorously punished," to honor any agreement made with an Indian.

No wonder the company emphasized the fur trade. Though they were never able to ship enough pelts to realize the profits of which they had dreamed, at least the furs were there and were valuable. Gold, silver, diamonds, precious stones, were a fantasy. As for the "pearl industry," it was a gross misunderstanding of biology that still exists today. Word had reached Holland of the tremendous oyster beds throughout the huge estuary. This was exciting news for the Dutch, whose pearl industries in Brazil and in Asia were so profitable that the word *pearl* was almost synonymous with wealth, which was why every Dutch town had a Pearl Street. Oysters abounded in the lower Hudson. And, as most everyone knows, pearls come from oysters.

The problem was that they don't.

If an irritating foreign particle, something indigestible, is sucked in by an Ostreid, a true oyster, the animal will eject it. In a few cases, a coating is built up, but it is a dull gray substance, usually applied in an irregular sphere. Several chroniclers of the time complained of the "brown" pearls. Van der Donck wrote of the local oysters:

> Some of these are like the Colchester oysters, and are fit to be eaten raw; others are very large, wherein pearls are frequently found, but as they are of a brownish color they are not valuable.

Lustrous, bright, valuable pearls are found in an animal popularly known as a pearl oyster but known in biology as *Meleagrina* or *Pintada*. While being a bivalve whose shell bears a physical resemblance to an oyster shell, the pearl oyster, which is most commonly found in tropical waters, belongs to the family Pteridae, and not the family Ostreidae. A number of animals in this family have the characteristic that if an indigestible food particle—not a grain of sand, as is commonly believed—gets trapped in the shell, the animal will build up a coating of a calcium-carbonate crystal called argonite and a protein, conchiolin, the two materials it uses to build its shell. These two ingredients, in surrounding the particle, become nacre or mother-of-pearl.

The pearl oyster and its relatives in the Pteridae family are more closely related to mussels than oysters. Pearl oysters attach to objects by extending threads, the way a mussel does, and not by secreting a substance from a foot, the way a true oyster does.

So the famously mercantile Dutch were disappointed by this new-found trove of oysters. Hard-shelled clams were more valuable to them, even though most Dutchmen preferred to eat oysters. Clamshells were money. The Dutch had adopted the Lenape currency for trade with all the American tribes and with their metal awls and drills they could make wampum far more efficiently than the people who had invented it. It was a matter of picking up clamshells and fashioning them, which cost the Dutch very little in material or labor. Some wampum was made from conch shells. They used inmates of jails and poorhouses to make wampum or to string Indian-made beads, and in time it began to look suspiciously as though the company was taking people to these institutions to make sure there was a good supply of wampum makers. But the Indians of eastern Long Island were considered the best wampum makers. The Dutch showed their acumen for economics, regulating the value of wampum and the price of fur pelts. Though they were never able to control the "money supply"—the amount of wampum in circulation—they devaluated and reevaluated wampum to the Dutch guilder like a regulated currency and also fixed the price of fur pelts in wampum. In this way they could keep the price satisfactory to induce the Indians to supply the pelts but still keep the cost of buying pelts low while the cost of the furs in Europe continued to rise.

Isaack de Rasière came to New Netherlands in 1626, at the age of thirty, as chief commercial agent for the West India Company and secretary of the province. Shortly after arriving, he wrote a letter to the Amsterdam Chamber of Commerce in which he observed that Indians allied with the French "come to us for no other reason than to get wampum, which the French cannot procure unless they come to barter for it with our natives in the north, just as the Brownists [Puritans] of Plymouth come near our place to get wampum in exchange." The Dutch had put themselves in the enviable position of being the primary producers of the currency of trade.

Upon his arrival in New Amsterdam in April 1628, the Reverend Jonas Michaëlius, the first minister of the Dutch Reformed Church to go to America, wrote of the "large quantities of oyster shells to burn for lime." But oysters were considered less a profitable resource than one of the pleasures of this Eden.

The Dutch, like the French and the British, were tremendous oyster eaters. Oysters and mussels were essential components of Dutch cuisine and a frequent subject of the great seventeenth-century Dutch still-life paintings with their complex composition and soft lighting. The Dutch invented the term *still life—stilleven.* Not only are oysters present where they would logically be expected in these paintings, such as a tray of opened oysters in a still life by an unknown artist titled *Preparation for a Feast;* Clara Peeters's still life of oysters with cod, prawn, and crayfish; Jacob Foppens van Es's *Lunch Table with Fish;* Abraham van Beyeren's *Preparation for a Meal,* showing beef innards hung by the windpipe, a plucked rooster, and both opened and unopened oysters; Frans Snyders's *The Fish Monger;* or Joris van Son's still life of seafood representing water, but oysters also whimsically appear in paintings of other subjects, such as Jan van Kessel's still life of fruit with opened oysters, Clara Peeters's pastry and cookies with opened oysters, or Jan Davidsz de Heen's *Still Life with Glass and Oysters*. All of these paintings were done during the period of New Netherlands. The mother country liked its oysters.

The only known cookbook from the seventeenth-century Netherlands, *De Verstandige Kock*, "The Sensible Cook," was first published there in 1667 with no author's name. Although it first appeared several years after the British takeover of New Netherlands, the population was still largely Dutch and the book, which clearly made it across the Atlantic, is thought to reflect and have influenced the cooking of Dutch people in America.

❧ To Stuff a Capon or Hen with Oysters and to Roast [Them]

Take a good Capon cleaned on the inside then Oysters and some finely crushed Rusk, Pepper, Mace, Nutmeg-powder and a thin little slice or three fresh lemons, mix together, fill [the bird] with this. When it is roasted one uses for a sauce nothing but the fat from the pan. It is found to be good [that way].

—DE VERSTANDIGE KOCK, *1683 edition, translated by Peter G. Rose*

The settlers of New Netherlands tried to maintain their traditional Dutch cuisine. They domesticated cattle, to have beef, which had become popular in Holland after being imported from Denmark in the sixteenth century. With cattle came dairy products because the seventeenth-century Dutch loved butter and cheese. They distrusted milk, which turned too easily, and they recommended that after drinking milk the mouth should be rinsed with honey. They also raised pigs and chickens, the longtime standbys of Dutch cooking. They raised their livestock in the English style of smaller, easier-to-maintain animals, while back in Holland, the Dutch raised enormous cattle and pigs.

The settlers also adopted the local habit of eating a great deal of wild game, an aristocrat's meal in Holland. Analysis of bones from kitchen scraps shows that in the early years in both the Fort Orange area and New Amsterdam, a large proportion of the meat that was consumed was deer. This suggests that though they tried to eat like Dutchmen, they also took advantage, especially in the early years, of the bounteous products of their new Eden. Wheat, always in short supply in Holland and imported there, grew abundantly, and along with pelts was the chief export of the upper Hudson. The settlers became avid bakers, but the company, ever mindful of the wheat shortages in the homeland, became concerned that too much baking could diminish the wheat supply. The company declared it illegal to sell bread or cookies to Indians in Fort Orange. One man was fined because an Indian was seen leaving his house with a sugar bun.

The Dutch of the seventeenth century were famous throughout Europe for their vegetables, and the early settlers of New Amsterdam quickly planted vegetable and herb gardens. Parsnips, carrots, and beets as well as lettuce and cabbage, and rosemary, chives, parsley, and tarragon became central to New Netherlands cooking. But a native influence was seen in the widespread use of corn, squash, and beans.

The Dutch drank beer, regarding it as safer than milk or fresh water because the water was boiled in the brewing process. The people of New Netherlands, unlike the other American colonies, were not Puritans and they drank openly and heavily. One of the first American breweries was built in New Amsterdam on the north side of Bridge Street between today's Whitehall and Broad streets.

New Amsterdam's first tavern, Stadt Herbergh, or City Tavern, was built in 1641. It was one of the finer buildings in the city, being two stories high with a view of the East River. It had a basement, which was unusual at the time, but was the forerunner of a long-standing New York tradition of basement food-and-drink establishments. In the nineteenth century, such underground eateries became associated with oysters and were known as oyster cellars.

The north side of Pearl Street between Whitehall and Broad started to become noted for taverns that offered good meals, local beer, and oysters. The exotic local specialty was terrapin, unique among turtles because it lives in the same brackish tidal waters as the clams and oysters upon which it feeds. While this local specialty went on to be featured in elaborate wine-sauce recipes in the famous nineteenth-century New York restaurants, it was originally prepared in these first few taverns, cooked in the native American way, roasted whole over an open fire.

Unlike the English of New England, New Yorkers did not develop a deep-sea fishing industry until the 1760s. This may have been because so much food was available to them in their shallow, calm waterways. They did not have the cod and herring of Holland, but the rivers were teaming with shad and sturgeon, and anyone could hand-line from the shore of Manhattan and land striped bass.

The estuary of the lower Hudson had 350 square miles of oyster beds. The beds were found along the shore of Brooklyn and Queens, in Jamaica Bay, in the East River, on all shores of Manhattan, tucked into the many coves of a coastline much more jagged than it has become today because of landfills. Oyster beds also prospered along the

Hudson as far up as Ossining, and along the Jersey shore down to Keyport, in the Keyport, Raritan, and Hackensack rivers, on many reefs surrounding Staten Island, City Island, Liberty Island, and Ellis Island. The Dutch called Ellis Island and Liberty Island Little Oyster Island and Great Oyster Island because of the sprawling natural oyster beds that surrounded them. According to the estimates of some biologists, New York Harbor contained fully half of the world's oysters.

Anyone in the area need not have traveled far to reach into shallow waters and pluck oysters like ripe fruit. The following recorded incident suggests the casual harvest. On December 29, 1656, a group of Dutch left Fort Amsterdam to travel by canoe to present-day Westchester, possibly New Rochelle. At Hell Gate, the crook of angry churning water where the East River meets Long Island Sound, there are treacherous rocks that they dared not attempt to pass in low tide. They pulled over to the Manhattan shore at a spot that today would be under the Triboro Bridge and, while waiting for the tide to change, gathered up oysters and ate them.

Washington Irving, in his 1809 book, *A History of New York from the Beginning of History to the End of the Dutch Dynasty*, which chronicled Dutch times with only a slightly mischievous license, also referred to this lazy abundance in a story about a shipwreck at Hell Gate that cast survivors on the shore of Mana-hata:

> The stores which had been provided for the voyage by the good housewives of Communipaw were nearly exhausted, but, in casting his eyes about, the commodore beheld that the shore abounded with oysters. A great store of these was instantly collected; a fire was made at the foot of a tree; all hands fell to roasting and broiling and stewing and frying, and a

sumptuous repast was soon set forth. This is thought to be the origin of those civic feasts with which, to the present day, all our public affairs are celebrated, and in which the oyster is ever sure to play an important part.

The Europeans had adopted the Indian custom of designating this casual harvest, taking a few oysters for dinner, as a woman's chore. In 1634, this poem by William Wood was published in London:

> *The luscious lobster, with the crab-fish raw,*
> > *The brinish oyster, mussels, perriwigge,*
> *And tortoise sought by the Indian Squaw,*
> > *Which to the flatts dance many a winter's jigge,*
> *To dive for cockles and to dig for clams,*
> > *Whereby her lazy husbands guts she cramms.*

Oysters were also harvested commercially and were served in taverns. But a 1621 diary complained that "very large oysters" were so easily picked up by the seashore that it was difficult to sell them in New Amsterdam. One New Amsterdam settler referred to "oysters we pick up before our fort . . . some so large they must be cut into two or three pieces." New Amsterdam settlers grabbed so many oysters at the nearby water's edge that in 1658, the Dutch council issued an ordinance against harvesting oysters in the two rivers immediately at the town's shore. This meant rowing out to one of the oyster islands to gather them instead.

Far upriver, it was a great treat for the oyster-loving Dutch in the Fort Orange area on the oysterless upper Hudson to receive a shipment from a friend or relative in New Amsterdam. Maria van Rensselaer, born van Cortlandt on July 20, 1645, was one of the first native New Yorkers of European stock—Catalina Trico's daughter Sarah is believed to be the first. When she was only sixteen, Maria married Jeremias van Rensselaer, director of the colony of Rensselaerwyk near Albany, a colony within the colony whose fur and wheat trade made it more prosperous than New Amsterdam. An extraordinary seventeenth-century woman, she ran Rensselaerwyk herself after her husband died. In the letters she left behind are numerous thank-you notes for oysters. She would ship apples from upstate to her brother in New Amsterdam and he would ship New York oysters back to her.

The People, the Lenape, continued to enjoy and trade oysters. They made knives from the shells, probably using them to scrape hides in their fur trade with the Salty People. Hudson had noted that the Indians had "killed a fat dog and skinned it in great haste with shells that they had got out of the water." But the few Dutch records on the subject showed other uses for oyster-shell knives. There was a complaint against a Dutchman who gave alcohol to the Indians, one of whom, inebriated, cut someone with an oyster-shell knife. In another incident, a Lenape tortured a captured Dutchman by cutting off several fingers with an oyster-shell knife.

Relations were not going well between the People and the Salty People. In truth, despite all the reports of friendliness and easy trading, from the start it had been a difficult relationship. On Hudson's third day on Staten Island, after a prosperous second day of trade, a dispute broke out in which a petty officer, John Coleman, commanding a shore party, was killed from an arrow wound in the throat. Hudson retreated, most authorities believe, to Sandy Hook, but the

Brooklyn legend is that he crossed the harbor to a safe anchorage in a narrow inlet, a place now called Gravesend Bay. The hilly strip of land along the bay was about five miles long and a half mile at its widest and it was overrun with wild rabbits or conies. The land may have been named Coney Island after the rabbits, or possibly after Coleman. A third theory is that it was named after a Dutchman named Cnyn who settled there. At the time the Dutch arrived, Coney Island was the Canarsee tribe's principal site for making wampum.

Aside from a love of oysters and a proclivity for trade, the Lenape and the Salty People had little in common. The Lenape never fully understood that Salty People operated under completely different rules. This inability to understand the intruder, not even completely grasping their desire to take power, would soon prove the end of the People.

Nothing better illustrates the lack of understanding between the two groups than the famous "selling" of Manhattan. Perhaps because nothing more quickly seizes the imagination of the New York mind than a story of a real-estate bargain, the most widely known event of the little-known history of New Netherlands is that in 1626 Peter Minuit, the newly arrived director general of New Netherlands, bought Manhattan from the Indians for twenty-four dollars. The figure of twenty-four dollars, which has remained the same through centuries of fluctuation in the value of a dollar, seems an uncertain calculation. An assortment of cloth, wampum, fishhooks, hatchets, and other goods, according to some later versions, was handed over to Lenape chiefs of a group known as the Wappinger Confederation. But there is no certain documentation of what goods were involved in the trade. The goods are often described as "beads and trinkets," but some beads were currency, and objects made of metal or glass were very valuable to a society that didn't make them. One Dutchman in 1626 estimated the value of the goods handed over to "the wildmen" to be sixty 1626 Dutch guilders. But items such as wampum and iron fish-hooks were worth considerably more to the Lenape than to the Europeans, just as beaver and otter pelts were worth considerably more to Europeans. In 1846, a New York historian calculated that sixty 1626 Dutch guilders was worth twenty-four 1846 U.S. dollars.

But the terms were also appraised differently by the two groups. Minuit thought he had purchased the land and began settling large tracts of the island. But in Lenape culture, and in most North American cultures, the concept of owning land did not exist. Land was used and a tribe could negotiate with another tribe on rights to use the land. Land was created by God and could not be owned any more than someone could buy a piece of the ocean, lay claim to the sky, or purchase a star. Perhaps this was why, although the Lenape had periodic outbreaks of violence, they never had true wars of the kind Europeans were prone to. The Wappinger Confederation accepted the tribute from the Europeans in exchange for supporting their claim to use the land. This meant that the Wappingers would defend Dutch rights in Manhattan. To them it was a treaty, an alliance. The Indians lived among a great many competing groups and alliances were a way of life.

Other sales followed. In 1630, Minuit purchased Staten Island from the Tappans for metal drill bits, wampum, and axes. Some Jew's harps were also thrown in. Kiliaen van Rensselaer bought a thousand acres near Fort Orange and established Rensselaerwyk. The same year, 1630, an island known in Lenape as Kioshk or Gull Island was bought by the Dutch and renamed Little Oyster Island. In the eighteenth century, it would be renamed after its then owner Samuel Ellis. In 1652, the Dutch bought several sections of Brooklyn, including what is now called Bay Ridge, from the Nyacks. A settlement began in the Brooklyn woods called *Vlackebos,* Dutch for "wooded plain." The name would eventually be pronounced by the English as "Flatbush." In all, twenty-two such sales were negotiated, the last being between the English and the Canarsee tribe, selling a section of Brooklyn in 1684.

The Europeans believed that they needed a bill of sale to take possession, and they were generally extremely scrupulous about this. It was not until after Minuit "bought" Manhattan that he officially began the settlement of New Amsterdam, with its thirty wooden houses and one more substantial stone building for the company headquarters, as a capital for New Netherlands. Two windmills at the tip of the island powered a lumber mill. The Dutch also dug canals and started building a little Amsterdam.

But they observed a strange phenomenon and were not certain what the best response to it should be. After the sale, the sellers never left. Manhattan continued to have a large Lenape population and many temporary visitors who camped at their customary campsites and hunted the forests and marshes, fished the streams and rivers, and harvested oysters.

The Dutch West India Company always regarded good relations with the Indians as of utmost importance. Isaack de Rasière, company agent, wrote, in a 1626 letter to Amsterdam, "I find it important that the natives are treated well, each according to his station and disposition, and that when two different nations are present one chief is not shown more favor than the other." Laws were decreed making swindling or other forms of mistreatment of Indians illegal.

Behind most wars lie cultural misunderstandings. The Dutch knew that they did not understand the People. In 1611, Dutch captains Adrieaen Block and Hendrick Christeaensen took back to the Netherlands for study, in reality kidnapped, two Indians whom they renamed Orson and Valentine.

The Dutch appeared to learn little from Orson and Valentine. Misunderstandings followed miscalculations. In 1626, the same year that Manhattan was "sold," a small group of Wieckquaesgeck, from what is now Dobbs Ferry, were traveling to New Amsterdam to sell their furs. As they approached the Kalck, the pond just north of town, a group of Europeans attacked and killed them and stole their pelts. The number of victims is unclear, but only one small boy, a nephew of one of the victims, escaped.

According to Lenape law, the boy, when he reached manhood, was required to avenge his uncle's death. He waited fifteen years. The Salty People were spreading out and taking over. The Dutch had not only settled in Manhattan but in the intervening fifteen years had spread to Staten Island and Brooklyn. Not only did they dominate the North River, the Hudson, with its connection to Fort Orange, but they were beginning to take over the East River as well. Even though no commercial pier was built in the East River until 1648, they began ferry service between Pearl Street and Brooklyn's Fulton Street. For those Lenape interested in such distinctions, it was not only the Dutch who were moving in on them. In 1642, the Dutch permitted an English settlement, Newtown, in what is today Queens, while to the east, north, and south of Lenapehoking, the land of the Lenape, the English, Swedish, and French were settling in.

After fifteen years, in August 1641, the young boy, now twenty-seven, fulfilled his obligation.

Claes Swits was well known to all the Europeans in New Amsterdam as a talkative old wheelwright. His nationality is uncertain. By the 1640s, many different kinds of settlers lived in New Amsterdam, including Catholics, Quakers, Anabaptists, and Jews. There were Dutch, English, Danish, French, Swedish, Polish, and African—both free and slave. Yet in most matters there seemed to be only two groups—Indians and settlers.

Swits leased two hundred acres in what is today Harlem to grow wheat and graze dairy cows and paid half the grain and two hundred pounds of butter every year as rent to the owner. When he grew too old to work the land, he set up shop on the Wieckquaesgeck trail. His doom may have been tied to nothing more than this choice of location. It was the road of the Wieckquaesgecks, the Indian route into New Amsterdam, along which the group had been slaughtered fifteen years earlier. The trail ran down what would become upper Broadway and past fields of wild strawberries, then cut over to the East Side and dropped down along what would become Second Avenue, veering west to a brook where the Plaza hotel now stands, through the woods to pick up the route that would be Broadway at Twenty-third Street, and followed Broadway down to the town on the southern tip. By 1641, it had become a busy thoroughfare, widened by the Dutch and very different from the quiet trail where the 1626 murders had taken place. Wieckquaesgecks and other tribes from Westchester and farther up the Hudson used it to sell goods in New York. White and black people farming the hinterlands of Manhattan used it to connect with New Amsterdam.

Swits's house and shop along the well-trafficked trail was at present-day Forty-seventh Street and Second Avenue. It was on a bay called Deutel Bay, a reference to the dowel-like shape. Today the bay has been filled in and the neighborhood is mispronounced "Turtle Bay."

The entire European community had the same view of what happened. A twenty-seven-year-old Wieckquaesgeck whom Swits knew —he knew many and this one had worked for his son—appeared with furs to trade. Swits invited him in and fed him, and as Swits bent over a chest to find goods to trade, the young man picked up Swits's ax and struck him so hard that the elderly man's head was severed.

The Europeans had forgotten the attack fifteen years earlier and were outraged by this unprovoked violence. In that summer of 1641, the director of the New Netherlands colony was Willem Kieft, an Amsterdamer who, given his family connections, might have been destined for greatness. But his only claim to immortality, aside from the fact that his cousin appears in Rembrandt's painting *The Night Watch*, is the tragedy following Swits's beheading, from which New Netherlands would never recover. There is some speculation that Kieft was picked for the New Amsterdam job because he had previously been sent to the Ottoman Empire to negotiate the ransom of Christians. By freeing only the ones who had small ransoms, he turned his task into a profitable operation, though a lot of wealthy people remained in Turkish prisons. To the company, frustrated by the unprofitable record of their North American holding, Kieft seemed the man for the job.

Kieft's response to the Swits killing was to annihilate the Wieckquaesgecks. The Dutch are a notoriously pragmatic people, and the settlers, though angry, felt this would have too many difficult repercussions. A peace conference was called in the northern stone house of Jonas Jonassen Bronck, a Swedish-born sea captain after whom the borough is named. But in 1643, against the orders of the West India Company, Kieft's troops killed about eighty Wieckquaesgeck men, women, and children and mutilated their bodies. Reportedly, children were hacked to death and thrown into the Hudson. The troops

returned with heads of victims. Nothing was ever the same again between the Indians and the settlers. The scalping of settlers and burning of farms became widespread. A decade later the province of New
Netherlands—the Dutch never called it a colony—was critically
weakened from this violence, just at the decisive moment when the
Dutch went to war with the English.

In 1653, the Dutch West India Company ordered the construction of an enormous wall to protect New Amsterdam. Most of the
physical labor was done by African slaves owned by the company. The
forty-three wealthiest citizens loaned the financing at 10 percent interest, creating both the first Wall Street financial transaction and the
first city debt. The wall was made out of fifteen-foot wooden planks
and followed present-day Wall Street from the Hudson to the East
River with two gates, one at the present-day intersection of Wall and
Pearl streets and the other where Broadway now crosses Wall Street.
The settlers of New Amsterdam no longer had open access to the rest
of Manhattan.

Today the popularly held belief is that the wall had been built to
defend the settlement from Indian attacks. Given the way Indian–
settler relations were going, this is not an illogical assumption. But in
fact the wall was conceived at the outbreak of the Anglo-Dutch War
to defend against a possible British attack from New England. Why
would a maritime people expect another maritime people to attack
their seaport from the land side? When the British attack finally
came, not surprising for the world's leading naval power, it was by sea
and the wall was a useless defense.

By this time, 1664, the one thousand settlers of New Amsterdam had spent eleven years huddled behind a wall. They threw their garbage over the wall where it was out of sight, and a huge garbage dump started to form in the marsh just below the serene Kalck Pond. Worse, the citizenry simply dumped their chamber pots and other sewage in the streets, ignoring an ordinance prohibiting this. The city had built drainage ditches and they became sewers, mostly open. Solid waste would often clog them and cause overflow. This made New Amsterdam not only a very odorous village, but an unhealthy one—a dangerous situation for a town with no hospital until 1659, when the company established one doctor in a house.

Town ordinances were preoccupied with this health risk, but no one thought about the fact that these ditches ran into the Hudson River and the East River, which flowed over oyster beds. Oysters had evolved over 500 million years from a deep-sea animal to a creature that lived in less salty water, in the sheltered coves of estuaries where seawater mixed with fresh waters. It was the rivers of the New York area that gave the oyster beds their life, and in time the rivers would kill them.

CHAPTER THREE

The Fecundity of Bivalency

—

In science nothing is trivial or unimportant.

—WILLIAM K. BROOKS,
The Oyster, 1891

I n biology, family is important. All true oysters, regard-
less of where they are found, belong to the family Ostreidae. While
the family has a number of genera with distinct characteristics and in
total about a hundred different species, Ostreidae, the oyster family,
does have its own defining characteristics, the things that make an
oyster an oyster. In biology, unlike in Tolstoy, even happy families are
not alike. Oysters, different from clams and scallops, are permanently
affixed to an object, and they accomplish this not by extended threads
like a mussel, but by secreting a substance from the foot. And unlike
clams and mussels, their two shells are different and they always rest
on the deeper, more curved one. To a scallop this would seem to be
upside down, but this distinction makes it possible for oysters to be

shipped live with the cupped side down, which keeps the liquor, the natural juice, from seeping out and keeps them alive in their shells.

Scientists have agreed to avoid clarity by calling the flat top shell the right side, and the curved bottom one the left side. Only the left side has the ability to attach, so that it is generally on the bottom unless the oyster is resting vertically, which it often is. Asymmetry, having two sides that do not match, is unusual in nature. Humans, insects, fish, and even most bivalves are symmetrical. The oyster is, too, until it attaches the left shell, which then becomes misshapen like a poorly shod foot, sagging to form a cup in which the animal can rest. Since there is a well-established principal in evolutionary science that the growth development of an individual imitates the evolutionary development of the species, this early symmetrical phase of the oyster indicates that their prehistoric ancestors were footed wanderers like their cousins the clams.

It might surprise oyster gourmets, gourmands, *feinschmeckers,* and bivalveophiles to know that all of the oysters in North America, from Louisiana and the Gulf of Mexico, up the coast of Florida, in the Chesapeake Bay, in New York City, Long Island, Long Island Sound, Wellfleet, Maine, Nova Scotia, and even beyond, are biologically identical. They are all the same family, genus, and species—*Ostreidae Crassostrea virginica.* The fact that all these *Crassostrea virginicas* along the Atlantic coast vary in size, shape, color, and taste is simply proof that with oysters, as with wine, the deciding factor is not the variety, but where it is planted and how it is grown. Water temperature is critical. Oysters grow faster in warm water, although the length of time they are left to grow is also important. Colder water tends to produce oysters that fans call more flavorful and detractors call too strong. Northerners tend to find Southern oysters large and bland and

Southerners find Northern oysters small and harsh. In addition to temperature, oysters are altered by many factors including the salinity of the water, the type of food available in the water, the structure of the seabed, and the degree of crowding.

Crassostrea virginica, sometimes called the eastern oyster or the American oyster, begins as a fertilized egg about fifty microns or two-thousandth of an inch in diameter—a creature invisible to the naked eye. A quart jar could hold the eggs for more than five billion oysters. Unlike most animals, oyster social life has the curious characteristic that males and females are physically identical. This understandably has confused those who have studied oysters, and left many doubts about their sexuality. But it does not seem to confuse oysters, and by the nineteenth century it was understood that, as songwriter Cole Porter later observed, even oysters in Oyster Bay "do it."

Though male and female oysters appear identical, at a certain point some start releasing eggs and others start releasing sperm, both of which drift with plankton. Before fertilization each egg is one of 10 million or more discharged into the water by one adult female. Today *Crassostreas* that have been specially conditioned for spawning can discharge more than 50 million eggs at one time. Spawning occurs when water temperature rises above twenty degrees centigrade, sixty-eight degrees Fahrenheit, which usually happens in New England in midsummer, and slightly earlier in New York. Discharge is stimulated by the presence of eggs or sperm in the water. In other words, a male oyster gets turned on by being surrounded by large quantities of eggs and a female gets excited when sperm are around. Since eggs are buoyant and disperse quickly, it is important for spawning that there are large numbers of adults in close proximity.

It takes only a few hours for a fertilized egg to become a swimming larva. The larva moves through the water with fast-swimming threadlike organs called cilia. The two equal shells are formed within twenty-four hours. The young oyster feeds on phytoplankton, floating masses of minuscule organisms, and after about ten days it dives to the bottom and starts crawling, looking for a place to attach itself. An empty oyster shell is an attractive surface but so are the top shell of a living oyster, bottles, cans, golf balls, old shoes, fronds of eelgrass.

It is now about six times the size of the original egg. At this point it is very similar to a clam, having two matching shells and hobbling across the ocean floor with its foot. But once it finds an appropriate surface, it drops its clammy ways, loses its swimming devices, and attaches by secreting a substance from a gland in the foot. The attaching shell starts to sag, the oyster will never again be capable of movement, and it becomes distinct from other bivalves.

The oyster that nature put on the European coast, the oyster that seventeenth- and eighteenth-century Dutch, British, and French were accustomed to eating, is a completely different animal, a different genus and species than they encountered in North America. This is not a scientific splitting of hairs. The animal looks different, reproduces differently, and is anatomically different. The *Ostrea edulis,* the European flat oyster, sometimes called belon because of the famous beds at the mouth of the Bélon River in Brittany, France, which is one of the few places that still produces them, is a rounder and flatter oyster. It is the one pictured in the seventeenth-century Dutch still-life paintings.

Oysters of the genus *Ostrea* produce fewer eggs than do *Crassostreas,* only about one million, and the eggs have three times the diameter—about 150 microns. They live in much saltier water and begin spawning when the water reaches only fifteen degrees centigrade, fifty-nine degrees Fahrenheit, which means that they do not have the southern range of a *Crassostrea,* which thrive from Labrador to Mexico. Rather than being excreted into the water, the eggs are secreted from the female gonads, then held in the female. The male releases sperm into the water and the female pumps it into her eggs. The fertilized eggs are held in the female for more than a week so that when discharged into the water, they are already halfway through their larval stage. The genus *Ostrea* spend much less time drifting with plankton and are less likely to drift away to less favorable areas. This is why they can produce fewer eggs. Nature always balances risks with fecundity.

Up until the nineteenth century, the oyster was thought to be a simple primitive creature. We like to think this of the creatures we eat, especially the ones we pop into our mouths whole and raw. But it turns out that an oyster has a brain and a nervous system. In the words of the nineteenth-century British Darwinist Thomas Huxley, "I suppose that when the sapid and slippery morsel—which is gone like a flash of gustatory summer lightning—glides along the palate, few people imagine that they are swallowing a piece of machinery (and going machinery too) greatly more complicated than a watch."

The creature is surrounded by what is called a mantle and this mantle has what appears to be a dark fringe, which is actually a battery of sensory nerve endings. The oyster at rest has its mantle fringe exposed to perceive danger. When that message is transmitted to the brain, the brain sends an impulse to the muscle, and the oyster shell slams shut.

Oysters eat mostly plankton. They feed by pumping in water with fine cilia on the surface of the gill. Like hungry young birds, they rest with their shells open, letting the water feed them. But if disturbed,

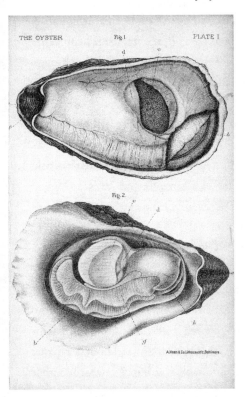

THE OYSTER Fig 1. PLATE I

The anatomy of an oyster from The Oyster, *William K. Brooks, 1891.*

Figure 1. The left side of an oyster lying in one shell, with the other shell removed. The mantle has been turned back a little, to show its fringe of dark-colored tentacles, and in order to expose the gills.

Figure 2. An oyster in the left shell, with the right shell and right fold of the mantle removed, to show the gills and the body of the oyster. *a* is the hinge, *b* is the edge of the mantle, *c* is the muscle, *d* is the pericardium, *f* is the hinge ligament, *g* the gills, *h* the lips.

they will snap shut and can remain that way for days. That is in fact what they do if yanked out of the water. When feeding, they will eject unwanted particles by snapping their shells shut to push out the water. This action for a long time was confused with a mammal's habit of closing its mouth around food. To this day, the snapping closed of an oyster is called feeding, but it is actually the opposite, the ejecting of food. Oysters cannot break down cellulose and thus reject anything with thick cellulose walls such as most plant life. Any particles larger than ten microns are ejected.

The oyster snaps its shell by means of a ligament, which it squeezes in order to close. If the animal relaxes, the ligament springs the shell open. This ligament is like a piece of rubber and is not alive. Like the shell itself, it is manufactured by the oyster from a substance it excretes. The ligament will cause the shell to open any time the oyster does not apply pressure, which is why a dead oyster has an opened shell.

The muscle that an oyster uses to squeeze its shell closed has extraordinary strength relative to its small size. Oyster shuckers sometimes refer to it as "the heart." They think of it as a vital organ, because once it is cut the oyster easily opens and so is presumed dead—stabbed in the heart. Oyster shuckers may not want consumers to know the truth. All they have done is destroy the oyster's ability to squeeze the ligament. William K. Brooks, the nineteenth-century Maryland pioneer in the study of oysters, said, "A fresh oyster on the half-shell is no more dead than an ox that has been hamstrung." If the oyster is opened carefully, the diner is eating an animal with a working brain, a stomach, intestines, liver, and a still-beating heart. As for the "liquor," that watery essence of oyster flavor that all good food writers caution to save, it is mostly oyster blood.

In 1932, at a convention of the Oyster Growers Association in Atlantic City, Dr. Vera Koehring of the U.S. Bureau of Fisheries said that it was cruel and inhuman to crack open an oyster's shell and pry the animal loose. Dr. Koehring proposed, "The oysters, before being shelled, should be given an anesthetic." She suggested several harmless ones like lactic acid, boric acid, or a light solution of carbon dioxide. She even calculated that since the anesthetized oyster would release its abductor muscle and lie open, the cost of shucking would be reduced from twenty-five cents to two cents a gallon. But the oyster growers seemed to feel that the entire subject would be best not raised with the public.

As with most creatures, the more oysters eat, the more they grow. Warmer water tends to have more oyster food, which is why it produces larger oysters in the same period of time. A three-year-old Chesapeake Bay oyster is considerably larger than a three-year-old New York oyster, but smaller than one from Florida. This is not purely a matter of food supply. The *Crassostrea virginica* grows best in water between twenty and thirty degrees centigrade, sixty-eight and eighty-six degrees Fahrenheit, and growth completely stops at five degrees centigrade, forty-one degrees Fahrenheit. Under good conditions, an oyster spawned in late spring or early summer will be larger than fifty millimeters or two inches long by midfall when the first growing season ends.

Crassostrea thrive in warm, brackish water in intertidal and subtidal areas along shorelines where there is fresh water flowing from rivers that are rich in organic matter—a perfect description of the New York Hudson estuary. Oysters of genus *Ostrea* prefer clear and cooler water of high salinity and do best in subtidal areas. New Yorkers may want to eat *Ostrea,* but the *Ostrea* wouldn't want to live there. *Ostrea* are also slower growing, requiring four to five years to reach marketable size, whereas the *Crassostrea* are usually of a marketable size, with a shell of seventy-five millimeters, three inches, and a weight of fifty grams, one and three-quarters ounces, in three years.

Oysters hibernate in the winter and resume feeding and growing in the spring as the water becomes warmer. It is then, in the first new spring, that the *Crassostrea* begins to develop reproductive cells and becomes clearly male or female. Hermaphroditism, having both sexes, is a rare but not unknown occurrence.

Crassostrea yearlings are fully capable of reproduction and, unless eaten by a predator, buried in silt from a storm, or infected with a fatal disease, will live at least another ten years. Despite the assertion of the Scottish poet Robert Burns that he envied the oyster because "It knew no wish and no fear," the oyster has a lot to fear. Predators include oyster drills, little snails that attach themselves to oyster shells, slowly cutting a round hole with a long toothy tongue and then inserting a tube with which to suck the animal out. Among other equally efficient oyster slayers are starfish, crabs, whelks, and humans. Juvenal oysters are also eaten by flatworms (*Stylochus ellipticus*).

The starfish is so deadly to oysters that centuries ago the Admiralty Court of England fined oystermen who did not attempt to kill any starfish they ran across, which some hesitated to do because magical powers, including poison, were often attributed to these small creatures. The starfish nibbles at a mollusc's shell with tiny but multitudinous teeth until, faster than an oyster drill drills, the creature is exposed and eaten. Without any royal incentives, New York oystermen of the seventeenth and eighteenth centuries would collect every starfish they found in their beds, tie them in small packets, slice the packets in two and throw the dead starfish back into the sea, where, they later came to understand, the two parts would each grow back their missing limbs, so that the oystermen were actually increasing rather than decreasing the population. Some varieties, when sensing danger, will even pull themselves into pieces, each of which will later grow into a full starfish. Starfish will sometimes move in armies, invading an oyster bed and destroying the inhabitants. Worse, they have few natural enemies. Almost no fish wish to eat starfish with the exception of cod, which will eat almost anything. The starfish did, however, have a natural enemy in the French, who ground them up, finding that the resulting fish meal made excellent fertilizer for vineyards.

Oyster populations can be decimated by epidemics, violent storms and hurricanes, oil spills, pesticides, sewage, and other pollutants. As it opens and closes its shell to pump in water through its system to absorb nutrients, the oyster is also taking in anything else that is in the water. Oysters under normal conditions feed continually, and between twenty and fifty gallons of seawater are moved through a single oyster's gills every day. Assuming the water is in fairly good condition, oysters serve a natural function, filtering and cleaning the water. It has been found that a few oysters placed in a tank of algae- and phytoplankton-laden green water will make the water clear in only a few hours. The original oyster population of New York Harbor was capable of filtering all of the water in the harbor in a matter of days. One of the formulas of the balance of nature is that estuaries overproduce plant life and depend on animals to consume it. Oysters and other bivalves play an important role in this process. In his brilliant study of the role of oysters in Chesapeake Bay, published in 1891 before the word *ecology* was in use, William K. Brooks said, "In the oyster we have an animal, most nutritious and palatable, especially adapted for living in the soft mud of bays and estuaries, and for gathering up the microscopic inhabitants and turning them into food for man."

Unlike most other bivalves that live around *Crassostreas*—softshell clams, mussels, and bay scallops—oysters are able to survive long periods out of the water because of the protection of their thick shells. They can also survive an amazing range of conditions. The American oyster, the same species that prospers along Florida and Louisiana in water that heats up to more than thirty-two degrees centigrade, or ninety degrees Fahrenheit, can live in water that seasonally plunges below freezing. They are at home in almost fresh water and water that has more than 30 percent salinity.

It took a remarkably long time, well into the nineteenth century in America, to understand that the best thing to do with oyster shells was not make wampum, burn them for lime, or use them for roadfill, but to dump them back into the oyster beds. This became clear with the study of oyster physiology. The mantle that sends out warnings to the oyster brain also creates the shell. It produces a first pearly layer of shell and throughout the animal's life constantly creates new shells, each a little larger than the one before. That is why an oyster shell looks like many paper-thin layers pressed together. The oyster shell will conform to the surface it is next to, smooth if attached to a bottle, following the contours of a rock, even molding itself to the shape of a crab claw if attached to it. Oysters can also repair their shells and mend cracks. They are able to do all this by using the lime that they extract from the water. Oysters need lime to grow, and no matter how rich the water is in nutrients, without the presence of lime growth cannot take place. Throwing the shells back into the water not only provides good material for seedlings looking for a surface to attach to, which has come to be known as *cultch*, but also enriches the growing environment of the water. The sea will break down the shell and the oyster will absorb the lime. The more lime that is available, the faster and thicker the shells will grow. The sooner an oyster has a thick shell, the more likely it is that it will survive its many enemies.

It took considerable observation to grasp this about oyster shells. But elsewhere in nature it is readily apparent. William Brooks pointed out that old dried bones in the woods invariably have wood snails on the underside and rivers that run through limestone beds are generally rich in freshwater mussels. Nature chooses estuaries that are fed by rivers running through limestone to establish oyster beds.

Sometimes the ocean beds themselves are rich in lime, which is often a decomposition of coral reefs and shellfish. This is why limestone frequently contains fossils of sea life. Limestone containing fossilized oysters, such as has been found in Kansas, reveals vanished prehistoric seas. All seawater contains lime, but the added lime of decomposing oyster shells or limestone makes the water more suitable for oyster growth.

But almost none of this was known by the seventeenth-century Dutchmen who rejoiced that their New Netherlands that did not seem to have much real wealth at least had a seemingly inexhaustible supply of very large oysters.

CHAPTER FOUR

A Nice Bed to Visit

—

In this manner, did the profound council of NEW AMSTER-
DAM smoke, doze, and ponder, from week to week, month to
month, and year to year, in what manner they should construct
their infant settlement—mean while, the town took care of itself,
and like a sturdy brat which is suffering to run wild, unshackled
by clouts and bandage, and other abominations by which your
notable nurses and sage old women cripple and disfigure the
children of men, encreased so rapidly in strength and magnitude,
that before the honest burgomasters had determined upon a plan,
it was too late to put it in execution—whereupon they wisely
abandoned the subject altogether.

—WASHINGTON IRVING,
A History of New York from the Beginnings of the World
to the End of the Dutch Dynasty, 1809

By 1654, the Dutch had lost their colony of pearls and
sugarcane in Brazil and began to think that their Eden of oysters in
North America might have to be their star New World property after

all. But it did not seem promising. A 1644 audit showed that New Netherlands had cost the company more than 550,000 guilders, while earning only about 60,000 guilders a year. Indian relations were only one of the preoccupying problems. The settlers themselves were tired of living in a company and wanted a homeland with a real government.

To try to make the New Netherlands work, the company had brought in their tough, one-legged troubleshooter, Peter Stuyvesant. A military man with a religious background—his father was a Calvinist minister—he was not known for open-mindedness, nor patience. Nor was he a son of the flowering intellectualism of his native seventeenth-century Holland. He was expelled from the university after two years, according to some accounts, for his sexual relations with the wrong person's daughter. In the Caribbean he had been a fierce and impassioned warrior in the brutal war for territory with the Spanish and the Portuguese.

While he was fighting to retake Saint Maarten, a Spanish cannonball demolished his right leg. Just before losing consciousness, he ordered the siege to continue. Then, surviving a seventeenth-century amputation, a frequently fatal operation, he became administrator of the Caribbean for the Dutch West India Company based on the island of Curaçao. In 1647, the Dutch West India Company sent Stuyvesant to New Netherlands to replace Kieft, who had become a gruesome figure associated with the killing and grisly torturing of countless Indians.

Stuyvesant was more drawn to the often noted Dutch yearning for order than the equally often invoked Dutch claim to tolerance. He immediately decreed ordinances against alcohol and mandating religious observance on Sunday. He persecuted all religious practice other than that of the Dutch Reformed Church, singling out Quakers and attempting to bar Jews from settling in New Amsterdam, serving in the militia, or owning land, saying that they were "a deceitful race." Asser Levy, a Polish Jew, and Manhattan's first kosher butcher, opposed Stuyvesant, a stance made easier when it turned out, to Stuyvesant's chagrin, that a number of officers of the Dutch West India Company were Jewish. The Dutch settlers had always been proud that their city was not like Boston, that it was an open, a diverse city. But now New Amsterdam was starting to resemble New England.

In Holland, the Dutch government did not recognize slavery, but in the Americas, the Dutch West India Company created its own law. Having come from Curaçao with its slave market, Stuyvesant bought Africans from there to build fortifications against the British in New Amsterdam. But increasingly the merchants, with their own agenda, were taking control of the city, gradually forcing Stuyvesant to allow city government instead of company rule. There were only three sizable buildings in New Amsterdam, the notoriously ill-constructed fort, the West India Company, and the City Tavern. These were the three places where public notices were posted. As the people of New Amsterdam became impatient with tyrannical company rule and the despotism of Peter Stuyvesant, the West India Company was forced to create some government institutions, and in 1652, the City Tavern became City Hall. It also doubled as a prison, and in 1656 held twenty-three Englishmen who had attempted to settle in what is now Westchester without company permission.

The little city's new government ordered the dirt or planked roads to be paved with stones. In 1658, this village of 120 houses for the first time began to designate its paths and lanes with street names. The long path through the entire length of Manhattan used by Indians delivering fur pelts was now officially called "Beaver Path." But once the path was broadened, people started calling it "Breede Wegh" or "Broadway."

Other improvements came with self-government. Residents started building brick houses. The city forbade residents from dumping animal carcasses and other garbage in the streets and each home owner was responsible for cleaning the street in front of his house. But the townspeople continued, despite a city ordinance, to toss their chamber pots into the street.

The settlement was still at war with the Indian tribes, and Stuyvesant, still in command, even ordered an attack against the Spanish who attempted settling on New Netherlands land. In 1664, British colonel Richard Nicolls sailed from England with a four-ship squadron, stopped in Boston, where the colonists showed no interest in joining the expedition, and sailed on to establish a naval blockade of New Amsterdam. When the British threatened to attack, not surprisingly from the harbor and not over the wall, few residents were interested in fighting for the Dutch West India Company and most had no objections to British rule as long as they were promised fair treatment. Ninety-three leading citizens, including his son, petitioned Stuyvesant to surrender and avoid suffering. Stuyvesant said that he would rather die, but he nevertheless negotiated terms at his farm on what is today Stuyvesant Street in the East Village. Richard Nicolls became the first governor of New York.

The British inherited a small Dutch town of windmills and canals, though not many of either. They had snidely referred to the Dutch as "Jankees," a sarcastic joining of the name John and the word cheese. Soon their own colonists would adopt the name. The Dutch accepted their conquerors. Many anglicized their names. Brugge became Bridge. Rather than the Dutch style of a first name, van, and the father's name, they began using full last names in the English manner.

The British legal system under Nicolls combined English, Dutch, and New England law, but unlike New England there were no provisions for public school, no town meetings or elected assembly. But also unlike New England there was religious freedom.

In 1681, when the British crown sent George Carteret to establish a British colony in formerly Dutch New Jersey, Carteret promised settlers, "The Bay and Hudson's river are plentifully stored with sturgeon, great bass, and other scale-fish, eels, and shellfish, as oysters, etc. in great plenty and easy to take." The new settlers who had replaced the Dutch wrote home to England about the oysters. One letter from what is today Perth Amboy said, "And at Amboy point and several other places there is abundance of brave oysters." Another said there were enough oysters "to serve all England." Another said that oysters provided them with lime for building inexpensive stone houses "warm for winter and cool for summer."

Meanwhile, New Amsterdam was being reshaped. In 1679, Jasper Danckaerts, the Dutch visitor, was still noting the sweet smell of Manhattan: "I must add that in passing through this island we sometimes encountered such a sweet smell in the air that we stood still, because we did not know what it was we were meeting." But in 1699, when the British province of New York dismantled the wall, a garbage dump was found behind it, spreading to the Kalck, the pond the English called the Collect. This pond where the Lenape once fished, where the Dutch picnicked on an adjacent hill to have a view of it, was becoming a mucky, malarial swamp, strewn with trash and festering with disease. The trashier it became, the more it was abused. Since it had become a despoiled zone, the most polluting industries, such as butchers and hide tanners, were installed there. The butchers gathered at the nearby Bull's Head Tavern, which provided pens for livestock. By 1700, the shores of the Collect was the only spot in Manhattan where slaughtering animals was allowed, and the area had an unendurable stench. An island in the middle of the Collect was used as a place to carry out executions. After a 1741 slave uprising, numerous black conspirators were brought there and hanged. Some were burned at the stake.

In the city to the south, Peter Kalm, a botanist at the University of Abbo in Swedish Finland, who was sent to America by the Swedish Academy in 1747, reported that the townspeople got so bitten up by mosquitoes at night that they would be "ashamed" to show their swollen faces. He also found New Yorkers suffering from what he called "fever and ague." This was probably malaria. Until 1748, it was not known that malaria was spread by mosquitoes. And even what medical knowledge existed at the time was seldom available in New York. After the small Dutch hospital was abandoned in 1674, New York City had no hospital until 1776, not even during the smallpox epidemic of 1727 that killed five hundred people in less than a month.

Also, the city was running out of fresh water. The drinking water came from local wells that caught the rainwater that washed down the foul streets. By midcentury, the quality of Manhattan water had become so bad that out-of-town horses refused to drink it.

Though short on drinking water, New Yorkers had no lack of oysters, which Kalm compared in quality to England's famous Colchesters. In 1748, he wrote:

The sea near New York affords annually the greatest quantity of oysters. They are found chiefly in a muddy ground, where they lie in the slime, and are not so frequent in a sandy bottom: a rocky and a stony bottom is seldom found here.

Since New Yorkers have always felt themselves different from the rest of the people in the United States, it is intriguing to reflect on what endured from Dutch culture in New York. New Jersey and part of Connecticut also were settled by the Dutch. But it was in New York that the Dutch established their ways in the midst of English colonies and that is one of the factors in making New York different. New Amsterdam was a more cosmopolitan place than Boston and other ports because, with the notable exception of Stuyvesant, the Dutch West India Company was open to most anybody settling there who would work with the company. In fact, in the seventeenth century, Amsterdam was one of the most open cities in Europe, taking in people who were not wanted in England and France, including, for a time, the Puritans who later settled Massachusetts.

English New York continued the cosmopolitan tradition. New York was less English and more diverse than any other British North American colony. It became known for its Jews. Kalm said that when he was in New York he often found himself in the company of Jews. He was surprised to find that unlike in Europe, New York Jews had full rights of citizenship. "They have a synagogue, own their dwelling houses, possess large country seats and are allowed to keep shops in town. They have like wise several ships which they load and send out with their own goods. In fine, they enjoy all the privileges common to the other inhabitants of this town and province." In 1679, Jasper Danckaerts commented on the racial integration of Broadway. "Upon both sides of this way were many habitations of negroes, mulattoes, and whites." The first black in Manhattan was an explorer named Jan Rodrigues who came on a Dutch ship in 1613 and for a number of years was the only non-Indian full-time resident of the island. By the 1630s, a free black community had been established north of the pond. By 1750, Manhattan was 18 percent black, comparable to today's ratio. However, this did not necessarily indicate progressive attitudes. British New York became far more involved in the slave trade than New Amsterdam had been, and between 1701 and 1774, 6,800 slaves were imported to New York, about one-third of them directly from Africa. By 1750, New York had the most slaves of any American city except Charleston.

Oysters were sold from street carts and this was traditionally a black job. They were also sold by boats tied up in the canals the Dutch had built in lower Manhattan, but by the eighteenth century, the canals were gone and the oyster boats had moved to the end of Broad Street.

Along with oysters often went drinking. New York was the leading American city for oyster and alcohol consumption, as well as prostitution. Sarah Kemble Knight, who at age thirty-eight became the first woman to travel by herself from Boston to New York, noted in her diary that New Yorkers "are not strict in keeping the Sabbath as in Boston and other places I have been." New York was known to be the port to land stolen goods and the place where pirates went to sell their spoils. Pirates would sell at low prices, which made their trade profitable for New York merchants who welcomed these grim, colorful characters and showed them around the streets of Manhattan. Captain William Kidd, one of the most famous of the seventeenth-century pirates, lived the life of a popular celebrity in New York. He married a wealthy New York widow and settled into what is now 119–21 Pearl Street—with the summer home that all well-off

New Yorkers must have along the East River where Seventy-fourth Street is today. He was a respectable New Yorker with a pew at Trinity Church until one day he made the mistake of sailing into Boston. Promptly arrested, he was taken back to England and hanged. Boston was never New York.

New York became British very quickly, but it retained some Dutch ways. The Dutch contribution most often cited, and a great contribution to the American language it is, is the word *cookies* from the Dutch word *koeckjes*. If it hadn't been for the Dutch, Americans today would be calling them biscuits as the British still do. In fact, in colonial times New Yorkers were the only Americans to use the word *cookies*. The first recipe book to be published in the postrevolutionary United States has two recipes for cookies, in one place spelled "cookey." The adoption of the New York word, *cookie,* may have been a conscious effort to use language differently from the British—the first American dictionary by Noah Webster intentionally created different spellings—or it may be that the author was a New Yorker. The book *American Cookery* was published in 1796 in both Hartford and Albany and there is much speculation on whether the author named Amelia Simmons was a New Yorker or New Englander. The use of *cookies* suggests she was a New Yorker, though it is forgotten that Hartford also had Dutch origins. In any event, they have been called cookies everywhere in the United States ever since Amelia Simmons published her book.

The oyster recipe she included also argues for her being a New Yorker. For it calls for an obscene quantity of oysters—and all just to cook a chicken.

❦ *To Smother a Fowl in Oysters*

Gill the bird with dry oysters and sew up and boil in water
just sufficient to cover the bird, salt and season to your
taste—when done tender, put it into a deep dish and pour
over it a pint of stewed oysters, well buttered and peppered,
garnish a turkey with sprigs of parsley or leaves of celery: a
fowl is best with a parsley sauce.

The question is What was the eighteenth-century New York concept of stewed oysters? The Albany families of van Cortlandt and van
Rensselaer left numerous handwritten recipe books. All of these
manuscripts offer oyster recipes, indicating that the tradition of shipping them up the Hudson outlasted the Dutch. There are recipes for
oyster sauces, oyster "pye," fried oysters, stewed oysters, oysters rolled
in Indian cornmeal, pickled oysters, colloped oysters, and oyster
soups. Maria Sanders van Rensselaer, who lived from 1740 to 1830 and
was a resident of Cherry Hill, Albany, handwrote this family recipe:

❦ *To Stew Oysters*

Take one pint of oysters, set them over the fire in their own
liquor with a glass of wine, a lump of butter, some salt,
pepper, and mace. Let them stew gently.

When the British took over New Amsterdam, its hundreds of miles
of natural oyster beds fell into the hands of another oyster-loving

people. British oyster shells have been excavated from the ruins of ancient Rome. The Romans, who were themselves great oyster eaters, with a fondness for the largest ones they could find, appreciated the oysters of Essex and Kent. The Roman favorites were thought to be from Richborough, near Whitstable, which they labeled "Rutupians," and from the river Colne at Colchester. Both have remained British favorites. In fact, in 50 B.C., the Roman historian and politician Sallust wrote, "Poor Britons—there is some good in them after all—they produce an oyster." In Poole, Dorset, a large shell midden has been dated to Saxon times. Anglos, Danish, Saxons, Normans—all the ancient British cultures left behind evidence of oyster eating, though Celts seemed to prefer cockles and mussels.

This recipe from an anonymous fifteenth-century manuscript is written in Middle English:

Oystyrs in grave [gravy]

Shelle oystyrs into a pott and the sewe therwith. Put therto fayre watyr; perboyle hem. Take hem up; put hem yn fayre watyr. Peke him clene. Blaunch almondys; grynd hem, tempyr hem up with the same broth: draw up a good mylke. Do hitin a pott with onyons and hole spycez and a lytyll poudyr of sygure. Boyle hit togedyr, & doo the oystres therto, & serve hit forth. & caste theryn youre dragge of hole spicys abovyn, & blaunche poudyr.

In 1699, Billingsgate, an area where shellfish and fish merchants had long hawked their goods, officially became a seafood market, greatly increasing the availability of oysters and fish. The seventeenth- and eighteenth-century English were passionate about oysters, which were remarkably inexpensive. In 1701, two hundred oysters sold for a paltry four shillings. Prices must have remained low for English oysters for a long time—at least from Chaucer, whose "Monk's Tale" expresses insignificance as being "not worth an oyster," to Dickens, whose *Pickwick Papers* equates poverty and oysters. According to the eighteenth-century author Tobias Smollett, freshness was not always the most prized aspect of these shellfish, and some oysters were deliberately kept in "slimepits" for several days covered with "vitriolic scum" until they acquired the desired greenish color.

Diarist Samuel Pepys often mentioned eating, giving, or receiving oysters for breakfasts, lunches, and dinners—in all he mentions oysters fifty times in his diaries. Dr. Johnson fed oysters to his cat, Hodge, buying them personally because he feared that if he sent servants, they would end up resenting the cat. Sir Robert Walpole, British prime minister in 1715, was noted for his program to reduce national debt, but he ran up an enormous personal bill for the barrels of oysters he had shipped to himself. Seventeenth-century English cookbooks invariably gave recipes for oysters, and not surprisingly these recipes later turned up in New York. This recipe, similar to one in the van Rensselaer manuscript in Albany, comes from *Elinor Fettiplace's Receipt Book,* an English book that was written in the first half of the seventeenth century.

To Stew Oysters

Take the water of the oisters, and one slice of an onyon, and boile the oisters in it, when they are boiled put in some butter and an oringes peel minced, & some lemon cut verie smale, and so serve it. You must put some whight wine in your stewinge.

A popular English dish of the seventeenth century that was to remain in fashion in New York into the twentieth century was the oyster pie. This recipe, from a 1694 English cookbook by Anne Blencowes, is typical of British cooking at the time, which was reluctant to cook anything without "a lump of butter," a few anchovies, always preserved in salt, and some nutmeg or the casing, which is mace. This also became the American way of cooking. Nutmeg, which the British planted in their Caribbean islands, became a reliable trade commodity for the port of New York. Pies, as in the French word *pâté*, were a way of cooking in a sealed envelope. The crust was unimportant as food and was often discarded.

Oyster Pye

Take about a quart of oysters and take off ye black fins and wash 'em clean and blanch 'em and Drayn the liquor from them; then take a quarter of a pound of fresh butter and a minced anchovie and two spoonfulls of grated bread, and a spoonfull of minced Parsley, and a little grated Nutmeg, no salt (for ye anchovy is salt enough).

Squese these into a lump, then line your Patepan with good cold crust, but not flacky, and put to one half of your mix's, Butter and anchovie etc. at the bottom; then lay your oysters two or three thick at most; then put to 'em ye other half of ye mixed Butter and anchovie etc. and pick some grayns of Lemon on ye top (and youlks of hard egg if you like 'em).

Put in two or three spoonfulls of ye oyster liquor and close it with ye Crust which should be a good deal higher than ye oysters to keep in the liquor. Bake it, and when it comes out of the oven cut up the Lid, and have ready a little

oyster Lyquor and lemon juice stew'd together, and pour it
in and cut ye lidd in Pieces and lay round it.

The leading English cookbook of the eighteenth century, *The Art
of Cookery Made Plain and Easy* by Hannah Glasse, was published in
1747 and also became the leading cookbook in the British colonies in
America. One of the most influential cookbooks ever published, the
book reflects a cuisine that used oysters, and almost everything else,
extravagantly. There are ten oyster recipes, including a soup, a sauce,
two ragouts, an oyster loaf, an oyster pie, and pickled oysters—all of
which would have been found on eighteenth-century New York tables. The fact that the oyster loaves are simply an ornament to accom-
pany an appetizer gives an idea of the quantity of food served in
prosperous eighteenth-century homes.

To Roast a Leg of Lamb with Oysters

Take a Leg about two or three Days kill'd, stuff it all over
with Oysters and roast it. Garnish with horse-raddish.

To Make Collups of Oysters

Put your Oysters into Scollop-shells for that purpose, set
them on your Gridiron over a good clear Fire, let them stew
till you think your Oysters are enough, then have ready some
Crumbs of bread rubbed in a clean Napkin, fill your Shells,
and set them before a good Fire, and baste them well with
Butter. Let them be of a fine brown, keeping them turning,
to be brown all over alike; but a Tin Oven does them best
before the Fire. They eat much the best done this way,

though most People stew the Oysters first in a Sauce-pan,
with a Blade of Mace, thickened with a Piece of Butter, and
fill the Shell, and then cover them with Crumbs, and brown
them with a hot Iron—but the Bread has not the fine Taste
of the former.

A tin oven, also called a Dutch oven, was a polished tin box into
which the food was put. One end was open and this open side was
placed close to a fire. Food would cook both from direct fire heat and
the reflected heat of the polished tin. A back door permitted basting.

❧ To Make Oyster-Loaves

Fry the French Roles as above [Take three French Roles,
take out all the Crumb, by first a Piece of the Top-crust off;
but be careful that the crust fits again the Same place. Fry
the roles brown in fresh Butter] take half a Pint of Oysters,
stew them in their own Liquor, then take out the Oysters
with a Fork, strain the liquor to them, put them into a
sauce-pan again, with a Glass of White Wine, a little beaten
Mace, a little grated Nutmeg, a quarter of a Pound of Butter
rolled in Flour, shake them well together, then put them
into the roles; and these make a pretty side dish for a first
Course. You may rub in the crumbs of two Roles, and toss up
with the Oysters.

Probably the most common fate of the eighteenth-century New
York oyster was to be pickled. Peter Kalm found this recipe in New
York City:

As soon as the oysters are caught, their shells are opened and the fish washed clean; some water is then poured into a pot, the oysters are put into it, and they are boiled for a while; the pot is then taken off the fire again and the oysters taken out and put upon a dish until they are almost dry. Then some nutmeg allspice and black pepper are added, and as much vinegar as is thought sufficient to give a sourish taste. All this is mixed with half the liquor in which the oysters are boiled, and put over the fire again. While boiling great care should be taken to skim off the thick scum. At last the whole pickling liquid is poured into a giant glass or earthen vessel, the oysters are put into it, and the vessel is well stopped to keep out the air. In this manner oysters will keep for years, and may be sent to the most distant parts of the world.

Kalm reported that oysters pickled by this recipe "have a very fine flavor." His only complaint was that they could not be fried. Fried oysters were already a well-established New York passion. He suggested a second recipe for preserving oysters that was also used by New York merchants.

They are taken out of the shells, fried in butter, put into a glass or earthen vessel with melted butter over them, so that they are fully covered with it and no air can get to them. Oysters prepared in this manner have likewise an agreeable taste, and are exported to the West Indies and other parts.

The first recipe was a more typical way of preserving oysters. Pickling is an old technique used for fish, vegetables, and meat—a way of keeping food for long journeys. Oysters, though, could also be shipped live. Contrary to popular opinion, they are not fragile and in fact are far more durable than most other food. Their shell amounts to a thick, lime-rock encasement and they can live out of the water for a number of days. Sprinkled with oatmeal for nourishment, they can live even longer.

✳ To Feed Oysters

Put them into water, and wash them with a birch besom till quite clean; then lay them bottom downwards into a pan, sprinkle with flour or oatmeal and salt, and cover with water. Do the same everyday, and they will fatten. The water should be pretty salty.

—MARIA ELIZA KETELBY RUNDELL,
*The Experienced American Housekeeper or
Domestic Cookery formed on Principles of
Economy for the Use of Private Families*, 1823

In Europe, the Dutch, English, and others had gathered oysters by wading out in low tide and picking them up or by raking, a technique that works well for gathering lunch but becomes backbreaking when used to harvest large quantities for commerce. In New York, oysters were only occasionally found in water shallow enough so that they could be picked up. The Lenape showed the Europeans how to row out in ten or fifteen or more feet of water and use tongs, a rakelike tool with a long handle and two sets of teeth to grab the shells. When

the floor of the skiff was filled, they would row back to shore and unload. In the eighteenth century, oystermen began using sail power,
often in catboats, which have a single mast planted forward and a
large open deck. A few were larger, with a cabin that slept two. But
oyster beds are close to shore and there were no long trips at sea. Sail
power allowed oystermen to harvest greater quantities of oysters and
bring them to market inexpensively.

A question of considerable interest to New York merchants in the
seventeenth and eighteenth centuries was how to convert the harbor's
oyster beds into a profitable commodity of trade. Without refrigera-
tion and given the traveling time of horses and sailing ships, this was
a difficult problem, but it was the logical next challenge for a plentiful native New York product.

New York was rapidly becoming a leading North American port.
After 1664, when British colonial government replaced the rule of
the Dutch West India Company, New York's economy evolved from
one based on hunting to one based on agriculture and fishing. In
1686, the last of the wolves in Manhattan, the only remaining feared

RAKING FOR OYSTERS.

Tonging.

BALLOU'S PICTORIAL DRAWING-ROOM COMPANION, 1850S

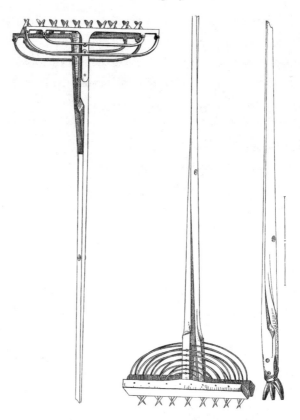

Oyster tongs and nippers, from Ernest Ingersoll's 1881
study of the oyster industry.

predator, were killed. The flour barrel replaced the fur pelt as the most valued cargo, and remained so for more than one hundred years. In 1678, the colonial government required the sifting, "bolting," of flour for export to be done at the port, thus facilitating inspection and quality control. As a result, port trade increased. In 1678, 3 ships, 8 sloops, and 7 boats came to New York. Only sixteen years later, 60 ships, 62 sloops, and 40 boats came. Between 1714 and

1717, an average of 64 ships cleared the port of New York in a year. By 1721, the average was 215 ships.

By 1770, New York had grown to be the fourth largest port in arriving tonnage after Boston, which was closely challenged by Philadelphia and Charleston. The New England region had a far larger population than the area around New York and consequently Boston received more goods. And while New York frivolously became a center for piracy, Boston was securing serious contracts trading salt cod, agricultural products, and manufactured goods. New Yorkers even received their British goods from Boston until the 1740s, when New York slapped a duty on Boston's English products.

The competition between New York and New England, between the ports of New York and Boston, was brutal and coarse. Boston merchants earned hard silver currency from New York, shaved it down, and bought New York wheat with the whittled money, saving the excess silver for other trade. They also refused to buy flour, insisting on whole wheat, which they milled themselves inexpensively and undersold New York flour in the West Indies.

New England, New York, and Pennsylvania all had the same problem. Under the rules of colonialism they were to sell what they produced to the mother country, but they all produced more than England could buy. The solution was to sell their lumber, flour, salted fish, and pickled oysters to the West Indies and Southern Europe. With the resulting income, they could buy more British products. New York products were sold down the Atlantic coast, in the West Indies, and in Southern Europe, and very little in England itself. New York, like Boston, provided the food of the British West Indies, allowing the slave islands to use all their cultivable land for sugarcane. They provided not only pickled oysters but wheat, rye, corn, salted pork and beef, apples, peas, and onions. The New York ships returned with molasses for rum and, more important, credits for New York merchants to buy manufactured goods in England. Eventually, they sailed to Africa and traded rum and manufactured goods for slaves, and traded the slaves along with pickled oysters and other food in the West Indies. The British ignored this illegal trade because it was earning New York merchants the money and credits to buy British manufacturing goods. New York's imports of British goods grew every year, whereas its exports to Britain remained steady. In 1715, £54,600 worth of British goods entered New York and £21,300 worth were exported from New York to Britain. In 1740, the exports to Britain were about the same, but the value of British goods entering New York had more than doubled to £118,800. It seemed that Britain was steadily increasing its balance of trade with its colony, which was what was supposed to happen with colonies. But this ignored the growing trade that the colony was having with everyone else. In truth, Britain had an ever shrinking participation in the economy of such colonies as New York and Massachusetts. In time, this led to greater economic independence, making political independence a potent concept.

Like Boston salt cod, New York pickled oysters were a by-product of the ports' involvement in the slave trade. Salt cod had a considerable commercial edge, since far more could be caught and the product yielded far more protein both per pound and per dollar and that was what slave owners were looking for in food. But still, New Yorkers had a profitable pickled-oysters trade with British West Indies slave plantations. New York merchants were paid for the pickled oysters six times or more what they had paid local harvesters for the fresh ones.

In the fall, the oysters would be pickled and shipped out. Although New Yorkers ate oysters all year long, it was believed that the

oysters in the months without *Rs*—May, June, July, and August—
were of inferior quality and so they waited for the better oysters to
come in the fall. This is an ancient and somewhat mythological belief.
In 1599, William Butler, a contemporary of Shakespeare, wrote, "It is
unseasonable and unwholesome in all months that have not R in their
name to eat oysters." The myth has an element of truth in the case of
New York. Oysters take their cue to begin spawning when the water
warms up, which is in May, and it is true that spawning oysters tend
to be thin, translucent, and generally less appealing. Some argued that
letting the beds rest during spawning season was a good conservation
measure. Summer oysters are, however, perfectly healthy unless
spoiled in the market by summer heat.

Between eating oysters and pickling them for trade, Manhattan
had more oyster shells than ever. Kalm wrote:

> On our journey to New York we saw high heaps of oyster
> shells near farmhouses upon the seashore, and about New
> York we observed the people had scattered them upon the
> fields which were sown with wheat, noted with surprise that
> rather than grinding them up for fertilizer the local farms
> would simply plough into the soil whole shells.

The European botanist did not think much of this practice, believing that limestone worked better. But New Yorkers needed to find
a use for their growing heaps of oyster shells. Since New York City's
oyster trade grew up side by side with the larger New York State
wheat trade, the two always had connections, often sharing markets

and even containers. In the late nineteenth century, the colonial habit of packing oysters in flour barrels was still common.

The population was growing and New York was building. The city was not only paving streets but lining them with trees. Affluent New Yorkers were now building two- and three-story brick structures with tiled roofs and gables, often with a balcony on the roof from which to view the harbor or the town or Brooklyn across the East River. Families passed pleasant summer evenings on their balconies. Several stone churches were built, the grandest of these projects being Trinity Church, an Anglican citadel to compete with the newly constructed Dutch Reformed church.

All of this building required mortar, and mortar required lime paste, which could be made by burning oyster shells. Trinity Church was formed by a royal charter in May 1697, and by that August had already put in its order for "oyster shell lime." Burning oyster shells for lime was such a common activity that private homes in the New York area built their cellars with one side open for burning shells when household repairs were needed.

The smoke of burning lime was thick and acrid, and an increasing number of New Yorkers believed that it could not be healthy to be breathing it. On June 19, 1703, the New York provincial government passed an act that prohibited both the distilling of rum, a growing economic activity as the port became involved in the Caribbean slave and molasses trade, and the burning of oyster shells within the city limits or within half a mile of City Hall. The royal governor, Lord Edwind Hyde Cornbury, in urging passage argued that "These industries contributed to the fatal distemper" in New York the summer before. But Lord Cornbury was a dubious leader, infamous for not paying his debts—it was alleged that people hid from his wife because she borrowed dresses and jewelry and never returned them. An attempt to repeal the law in 1713 failed, and on March 24, 1714, a tougher city ordinance was passed "that no oyster shells or lime be burnt in the Commons of this city on the south side of the windmill commonly called Jasper's Windmill."

But no ordinances were passed to deal with the mosquitoes that came out in summertime or the garbage in the swamp.

New York oysters remained plentiful and large. Kalm wrote, "About New York they find innumerable quantities of excellent oysters, and there are few places which have oysters of such size." The size was significant because it meant that the number of oysters taken was still a small enough percentage of the total to leave oysters growing many years before picking. New York was still an Eden where resources could be used with extravagance. Gowanus Bay in Brooklyn was particularly known for large oysters. In 1679, Jasper Danckaerts, the Dutch traveler, and his companion Peter Sluyter stayed at the home of Simon Aerson De Hart near Gowanus Cove. Danckaerts wrote:

> We found a good fire half way up the chimney of clear oak and hickory, of which they made not the least scruple in burning profusely. We let it penetrate thoroughly. There had already been thrown upon it to be roasted, a pailful of Guanes oysters, which are the best in the country. They are large and full, some of them not less than a foot in length.

In truth nobody really wanted to eat a foot-long oyster. In the nineteenth century, British novelist William Makepeace Thackeray complained that eating an American oyster was "like eating a baby," which presumably was not an endorsement. At the De Hart residence on Gowanus Cove, the largest oysters were pickled and shipped to Barbados.

Apparently oysters were plentiful enough and easy enough to harvest that they remained inexpensive. A notice in December 1772 advertised "in the different slips of the harbor, no less than 600,000 oysters for sale." Kalm not only noted the profit made on buying fresh oysters and selling them pickled abroad, but he noted that the poorest people in Manhattan lived all year on "nothing but oysters and bread." In 1763, a restaurant opened in a dark and unfavored location, the basement of a building on Broad Street, the old oyster-selling street. This working-class basement oyster bar was New York's first oyster cellar.

On November 22, 1753, an article in the *Independent Reflector* contended that no country had oysters of the quality of the city of New York. "They continue good eight Months of the Year and are, for two months longer, the daily food of our poor. Their beds are within view of the town, and I am informed, that Oysterman industriously employed, may clear Eight or Ten Shillings a Day."

But all was not well in Eden. In the late seventeenth century, New York and New Jersey started passing conservation measures. As early as 1679, the Long Island town of Brookhaven had passed an ordinance restricting to ten the number of vessels allowed in the Great South Bay, a huge natural oyster bed between Long Island and Fire Island. The European settlers in Brookhaven quickly realized the potential of Great South Bay oyster beds. In 1767, the town negotiated an arrangement recognized by the king of England in which the town, in exchange for control over the oyster beds, agreed to give the crown's recognized owner William Smith and his heirs forever half of all "net income accruing to the town from the use of the bottom of the bay."

Oyster beds are very different from fishing grounds because the oyster permanently attaches itself to the bed. For that reason and because oystering was recognized as valuable, the new New Yorkers were fighting over ownership of underwater land—a notion that the Lenape would have found even more absurd than the concept of fighting over abundant dry land.

In 1715, the colonial government, as a conservation measure, banned oystering in the months without *R*s, May 1 to September 1, because it was the egg-laying season. The measure also reduced harvesting by barring slaves and servants from taking or selling oysters. The law was aimed at New Jersey residents who shared with Staten Island Raritan Bay and Arthur Kill, both rich in natural oyster beds. Nonresidents caught working Staten Island beds had their vessels and equipment seized. In 1719, the colonial assembly of New Jersey retaliated with an act "for the preservation of oysters in the province of New Jersey." The act closed all New Jersey beds from May 10 until September 1 and also stated "that no Person or persons not residing within this province" shall directly or indirectly "rake, gather up any Oysters or Shells within this Province, and put them on board any Canow, Periauger, Flat, Scow, boat or other vessel" and that any nonresident caught would have his vessel and equipment confiscated. By 1737, Staten Island officials were also becoming concerned about the survival of their beds and they barred oystering for anyone other than Staten Island residents.

In colonial times, such laws depended on local citizens for enforcement. Oystermen caught working beds off season would claim they were harvesting clams, and the local enforcers lacked the expertise to argue the point. This ineffectual system of citizens' arrests on the oyster beds continued into the nineteenth century.

By the mideighteenth century, warnings were already being voiced of the possible destruction of oyster beds in the New York area. New Jersey passed a 1769 law to further contain avaricious neighbors. The practice of raking up oysters simply to burn for lime was banned. One of the reasons behind stricter enforcement was concern that oysters remain a cheap source of food and available means of income for the poor. The 1719 law argued that preserving the oyster beds "will tend to great benefit of the Poor people." But a 1769 law stated that the 1719 one "hath not been sufficient to preserve the oysters" and that:

> Practices are made Use of, not provided against by the said act [of 1719], which, if permitted to continue, will in a short Time, destroy the Oysters in the Rivers and Bays of this colony.

Jamaica Bay, named not after the Caribbean island but from the Canarsee name Jameco, was rich in oysters, clams, and crabs, especially on the northern side, which is dotted with islands that appear only at low tide. The residents of Rockaway attempted to regulate oystering in the bay as early as 1704, when nonresident oystermen found working the bay were arrested. In July 1763, a proclamation stated:

> Whereas diverse persons, without any right or license to do so, have of late, with sloops, boats and other craft, presumed to come in to Jamaica Bay and taken, destroyed and carried away

quantities of clams, mussels and other fish to the great damage of said town, this is to give warning to all persons who have no right or liberty that they do forbear to commit any such trespass in the bay for the future, otherwise they will be prosecuted at law for the same by Thomas Cornell Jr. and Waters Smith by order of the town.

In 1791, it was ruled that anyone taking oysters in Jamaica Bay had to pay the town of Rockaway one shilling for every thousand oysters. The penalty for failing to do so was forty shillings.

Around the New York area, local governments were feeling increasing pressure to bar outsiders, even neighbors, from local beds. Apparently the oystermen who worked the beds could see that even Eden had its limits. While Manhattan above the waterline still had enough spare land to hunt, and walk in the woods, and throw out garbage, ownership of the land under the shallow brackish sea was being contested.

It was not necessary to leave Manhattan for a trip to the country. A well-known house in rural Manhattan called the Union Flag had a tavern with twenty-two acres of open land, a wharf, and landing. The tavern offered drinking, cockfighting, and gambling, which was illegal. With seventeenth- and eighteenth-century transportation Manhattan was a large island. Danckaerts described Harlem as a village three hours from the city. New Yorkers journeyed up the East River to Turtle Bay. In 1748, a visiting English clergyman, Reverend Burnaby wrote:

The amusements are balls and sleighing expeditions in the winter and in summer going in parties upon the water and fishing, or making excursions into the country. There are several houses, pleasantly situated up the East River, near New York, where it is common to have turtle feasts. These happen once or twice a week. Thirty or forty gentlemen or ladies, meet and dine together, drink tea in the afternoon, fish and amuse themselves until evening, and then return home in Italian chaises [the fashionable carriage of the time] a gentleman and a lady in each chaise.

For in-town recreation, the common was a place for lawn bowling and cricket. Americans won a famous match against the British in April 1751.

More and more taverns opened. They were not only for drinking but also places of business and politics. In 1766, 282 taverns were operating in New York. By 1773, the number had risen to 396. Drinking was cheap. New York rum had to compete with New England rum called "Kill-devil" that was only twenty-five cents a gallon and cheap young New Jersey applejack called Jersey lightning. Alcoholism was a growing problem. It was sometimes claimed that alcohol was a substitute for the increasingly foul New York drinking water, which came from wells and natural streams until the first pipelines were installed in 1799.

Prostitution remained a New York trade, though Griet Reyniers, said to be Manhattan's first prostitute, married a pirate, that other not-uncommon Manhattan-based trade, and the two had enough money to move to Long Island and become wealthy landowners there. In 1770, reportedly five hundred prostitutes were working in New York, a city of slightly over twenty-one thousand people.

The city was growing, the port was prospering, money was being made. The rich lived in brick houses with a view of the harbor or the rivers and roasted oysters in cozy fireplaces. The poor lived in wooden shacks, near the garbage-strewn pond, the Collect, and ate oysters in basements. A city of pirates, entrepreneurs, and the struggling poor— New York was well on its way to being the city that is known today. And then came a catastrophe.

CHAPTER FIVE

Becoming the World's Oyster

—

In point of sociability and hospitality, New York is hardly
exceeded by any town in the U.S.

—NOAH WEBSTER,
in a letter on leaving New York, 1788

o American city suffered more, or gained more, from the
American Revolution. When it was over, New York was a port that
could supply a new, vigorous, and growing nation. But during the war
it was an occupied city, under hostile military rule, its commercial and
social life shut down, its connections to the rest of America cut off, its
population dwindled to those who had not wanted or had not managed to escape.

Poet Walt Whitman argued for years that August 27 should be
celebrated with pomp equal to July 4. On August 27, 1776, the British
began a battle through the fields and farms of Brooklyn. One of
Whitman's great-uncles was among the many dead that day, the beginning of a five-day engagement then called the Battle of Long Is-

land, or Nassau Island, as it was usually known in the eighteenth century. But today it is more precisely pinpointed as "the Battle of Brooklyn." It was the largest battle of the American Revolution.

Looking for a port as a base of operation, the British military chose New York City, which had been their headquarters and home to many British officials until the war broke out in 1775. They unleashed a three-month campaign to take it back and hold it. In the meantime, from the loyal northern colonies, Canada, a military force would take Albany and the upper Hudson. After New York City was secured, the British would control the Hudson and New England would be cut off from the other rebellious colonies.

New York was the town the British called home, the town they liked, where they did not have to follow an austere Puritan frontier existence. There they had urban pleasures and weekends in the country and good taverns and, not least for eighteenth-century Englishmen, good oysters. New York was the only one of the thirteen colonies that had a permanent British military presence during most of the colonial period. They were there to guard the port and to keep an eye on the Iroquois. New York City was their command base— their city. The heads of the British command, General William Howe and Admiral Richard Howe, liked America and Americans. Massachusetts had built a statue of their older brother, who had commanded in the Seven Years' War. The Howes were convinced that most New Yorkers were Loyalists and would happily hand over their city.

But apparently they were not completely convinced of this because the force they brought to New York was the largest invasion force ever assembled by Great Britain until the World Wars. This included 420 ships carrying thirty-four thousand soldiers, at a time when the total New York City population was about twenty-four thousand. General George Washington was defeated in five disastrous days. The British then spent the rest of the summer chasing and battering the Continental Army, but failing to encircle and capture them, which would have ended the Revolution. Instead they achieved their initial goal, taking Manhattan and New York Harbor, and settled in for a much longer war.

New York City did have more Loyalists than any of the other rebelling colonies. In fact, the New York delegation chose to abstain on the vote on the Declaration of Independence and did not sign. And before the Howes had arrived, a plot by more than seven hundred New Yorkers, including the mayor, David Mathews, to kidnap Washington and trap the Continental Army on Manhattan was uncovered.

If many New Yorkers were Loyalists, Staten Island oystermen went back and forth. They were not as concerned about the British as they were about the New Jersey oystermen on the opposite shore. When the New Jersey oystermen were Loyalists, they became revolutionaries. But when their New Jersey counterparts took up the revolutionary cause, Staten Islanders were Loyalists. Their war was with New Jersey, not the British. In 1700, the provincial government had tried to resolve the issue by drawing a boundary line through Raritan Bay that gave about half the beds to each side. But the conflict continued and the Revolutionary War provided the means to make it an armed conflict.

In Manhattan, an active minority of revolutionaries rioted, pulled down the statue of George III, and, according to legend, melted the metal into musket balls. They were able to stage enough such events to make the British feel unwelcome. The British responded with both brutality and corruption. Occupied New York became an example of the worst in British rule. New Yorkers anticipated this. In June, when Admiral Richard Howe sailed into New York Harbor and General

William Howe landed and encamped a large force on Staten Island, both carrying a conciliatory message to the locals, New Yorkers began to evacuate their occupied city. Many of Manhattan's houses were dark and empty.

Under colonial rule the city had established a fairly effective fire department. The first fire engine was imported from England in 1731, and by 1737, New York had an organized volunteer fire department. In 1740, they were issued new leather helmets designed to let water run down the back or, reversing the headgear, shield the face from the heat of flames. Now the 170-man fire department fell into disarray, and the Royal Navy attempted to replace them as firefighters. A series of fires in a pattern suggesting arson swept through lower Manhattan, destroying 493 houses—about a third of Manhattan. Two years later, in 1778, another fire destroyed more than sixty buildings along the East River. While the city's population dwindled to only twelve thousand, large numbers of blacks, escaped slaves, were flowing in believing that the British, despite their history of slavery and their brutal sugar colonies in the Caribbean, would be more likely to grant their freedom than would the new Americans.

Manhattan remained a charred, half-empty city until the British withdrew in 1783. There was no trade in wheat or pickled oysters or anything else. The harbor was used for mooring the British fleet and for mistreating prisoners of war on prison ships docked off Brooklyn and in the Hudson and East River. Eighty percent of the prisoners held on those ships in New York Harbor died.

New York served the British military as a military, not a commercial, harbor. As it turned out, it was not a particularly good one. A series of sandbars close off the lower harbor between Sandy Hook and Brooklyn. This protects the harbor, and experienced navigators find the trenches between the sandbars. But this means that a large fleet becomes bottled up when it needs to sail out quickly, which kept the great British navy from being available for numerous engagements during the war.

In 1783, after the British surrendered, revolutionary New Yorkers returned to the city, many finding that their homes had been occupied by Loyalists who were now fleeing with the British. The black population also fled, believing that when they reached the Loyalist colony of Nova Scotia they would be set free. But once they arrived in Nova Scotia, few were set free and the British sent most of them back into slavery on sugar plantations in the West Indies, one of the cruelest fates for an African slave.

New Yorkers returned to a nearly destroyed city. The unused wharves, having seen no commerce, were covered with seaweed and barnacles. Most of Broadway between Wall Street and Bowling Green had been ruined by the two fires. George Washington's thirty-four-year-old son, Philip, was placed in charge of redistributing the abandoned and confiscated Loyalist-held properties. There was little law enforcement, commercial activity, or even sources of revenue. But once the last British ship left in autumn 1783, New Yorkers displayed tremendous excitement about the future of their port and the new republic it could supply. The city's first hero's welcome was to George Washington and the troops of the Continental Army as they entered the city from the Bronx, marched down Manhattan to the Bowery, and paraded through the city to the Battery. The Union Jack was taken down and the new thirteen-starred American flag raised. The burned-out city celebrated for ten days.

There was a daunting list of things to be done. The city needed new buildings, a sewer system, a fire department, laws, courts. It began widening and paving streets, including one, now vanished, called Oyster Pasty Lane. They built a jail and an almshouse, and in 1784, a garish red structure resembling a Chinese pagoda was added between them. This was the gallows, where the convicted were sent for a rapidly lengthening list of capital crimes including treason, murder, rape, forcible detention of women, forgery, counterfeiting, robbing a church, housebreaking if the house was occupied, robbery, arson, and malicious maiming. The gallows was used with regularity. In 1789 alone, ten executions were carried out, five on the same October day. For lesser crimes, a whipping post and stocks were installed nearby.

A process, not entirely planned, of Manhattan increasing its land and narrowing its waterways had begun. Discarded trash would start to fill in around the piers and merchants, rather than cleaning it out, would extend the docks farther out and finish filling in the trash area with landfill until they had added several blocks to lower Manhattan at the expense of the East River, the harbor, and the Hudson. After nearly eight hundred people died in the yellow-fever epidemic of 1798, affluent New Yorkers fled downtown and settled in a newly landfilled area that became known as Greenwich Village.

New York had lost its leading market, including its leading oyster market, because the British barred the new nation from trading with their empire. But there was always the local market, as more and more people settled back in Manhattan. In 1785, John Thurman, a local merchant, wrote a description in many ways familiar to today's New Yorkers:

Many of our new merchants and shopkeepers set up since the war have failed. We have nothing but complaints of bad times. . . . Yet labor is very high and all articles of produce very high. Very small are our exports. There is no ship building, but house building in abundance, and house rent remains high. Law in abundance, the Trespass Act is food for lawyers—yet we say there is no money. Feasting and every kind of extravagance go on—reconcile these things if you can.

New York, which created North America's first bar association, became and has remained a city of lawyers. From 1700 to 1712, the number of lawyers doubled. Among the abundant new laws were several dealing with sanitation. Every Friday between May and December, every home owner was to gather the dirt, garbage, and refuse from around his house and pile it near the gutter before 10 A.M., when the city would pick it up. But many did not bother to put their trash out early in the morning.

The city's sewage system consisted of a long line of black slaves carrying pots of sewage on their heads late at night to dump into the rivers, on top of the oyster beds. There were still some open ditches of sewage running to the rivers, as did the canal that had been covered over by the Dutch to build Broadway, leaving the waterway as a sewer underneath it. All of the dozen or so streams and brooks of the island of Manhattan were eventually turned into sewers and covered over. The landfill around the edges of lower Manhattan that expanded the area by more than sixty acres did not have proper drainage. Such waterfront neighborhoods as Water Street and Pearl Street frequently had flooded basements and sewage would back up and flood the yards. Houses had to keep their windows closed to keep out the smell. Finally, in 1796, at the insistence of the city health officer, Dr. Richard Bayley, the city's first underground sewer pipes were laid.

New York officials avoided discussion of these issues in 1789 when the city was in competition with a new District of Columbia to become the permanent capital of the United States. However, a notice in the *Daily Advertizer* on December 19, 1789, called upon New Yorkers to be more civic-minded about their trash disposal:

AWAKE THOU SLEEPER, let us have clean streets in this our peaceful seat of the happiest empire in the universe. That so our national rulers and their supporters may with convenience and decency celebrate a Merry Christmas and a happy New Year.

The New York argument, as in Hudson's time, was the sweetness of the air and the healthiness of the city. It was pointed out that the Congress had met in New York for a three-month session and only one member had been sick in all that time. Dr. John Bard argued that New Yorkers were unusually healthy, and stated as one of the reasons the variety of fresh seafood that was available.

New York is justly esteemed one of the healthiest cities of the continent. Its vicinity to the ocean, fronted by a large and spacious bay: surrounded on every side by high and improved land covered with verdure and growing vegetables, which have a powerful influence in sweetening and salubrifying the air and which often in their season salute the inhabitants settled on the west side of the Broadway with fragrant odors from the apple orchards and buckwheat fields in blossom on the pleasant banks of the Jersey shore . . .

All of this may have been a bit too much of a sales pitch. In August of that year, during a heat wave, twenty New Yorkers dropped dead. But it was certainly as accurate as the opposing side, the District of Columbia promoters, who were claiming—with shades of John Smith and Henry Hudson—that the Potomac River connected with the Ohio and thus provided a waterway through the continent.

Six years after Washington said farewell to his troops in a war-scarred and rebuilding New York, he was inaugurated president and

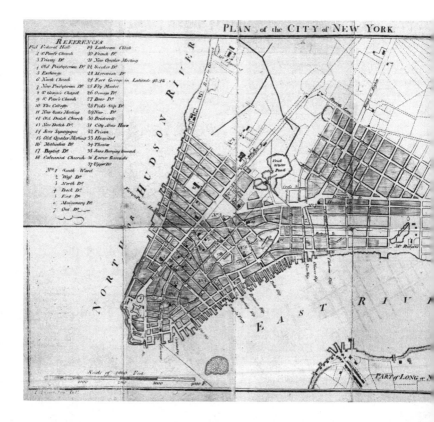

New York was a thriving commercial city, well on its way to becoming the most important port in the new country. The tip of Manhattan had four thousand houses and twenty-nine thousand inhabitants, more than double its wartime population. Trinity Church had not yet been fully restored and the landmark Lutheran church on Rector Street and Broadway was still a blackened ruin, popularly known in acidic New York humor as the Burnt Lutheran Church. Not surprisingly, the first insurance company, founded with the help of Alexander Hamilton in 1789, specialized in fire—the Mutual Assistance Company Against Fire.

There were six food markets in lower Manhattan where oysters and fresh fish from the harbor, local fruit and produce, and meat were sold. The oldest was the Fly Market, started in 1699 on Maiden Lane between Pearl and Water streets. Soon all of these markets would be gone and replaced by newer ones. But these older markets had had very exacting government-enforced quality and health standards. In the nineteenth century, courts ruled that such market codes were an unlawful interference with free enterprise. An 1843 decision virtually ended consumer protection in New York City for one hundred years.

The city had an increasing number of taverns and oyster houses. In fact, the Bowery village, a suburb just north

This map was included in the city directory of 1789, the third such directory. These books would be published annually until the twentieth century creation of telephone books. This was the first city directory in the United States to include a street map. The map shows the completion of Greenwich Street, a fifty-year landfill project along the Hudson River and also shows the Collect, marked "Fresh Water Pond."

COLLECTION OF THE NEW-YORK HISTORICAL SOCIETY

of the city where Peter Stuyvesant's farm had been located near East Tenth Street, used an oyster house as its village post office.

The city did not become the capital of the new nation; it did not even become the capital of the state, losing out to Albany in 1797. But it continued to grow, and in the same year that it lost its seat to Albany, it became the leading port of the United States, surpassing Boston and Philadelphia.

Robert Fulton is often credited with having invented the steam engine, which he did not, and never remembered for inventing the submarine, which he did. That is because he was never able to sell the submarine, whereas his steamboats changed New York City.

The first steam-powered vessel in New York City was built by a man from Bristol, Connecticut, named John Fitch. In 1790, Fitch had built and operated a steam-powered ferry service between Philadelphia and Trenton. The venture had lost money, as did all his subsequent ventures, in part because he could not attract substantial investors. Few had been excited about the commercial possibilities of Fitch's somewhat reduced crossing time from Philadelphia to Trenton and the service had never made a profit and had left many convinced that steamboats were not commercially viable. His last project was a steamboat with a screw-type propeller that in 1796 he demonstrated on the Collect, lower Manhattan's increasingly defiled pond. Among the passengers aboard the experimental vessel were Robert Fulton and Robert Livingston, Fulton's future patron. No one expressed interest in backing Fitch's boat and it was never used. Fitch committed suicide.

Robert Fulton's life, too, defies logical biography. He died at the age of fifty-one from not tending to a cold. He grew up in Lancaster, Pennsylvania, where he studied art but became a gunsmith. Then, still only seventeen years old, he moved to Philadelphia, where he became a painter of portraits and landscapes. When the forgotten Fitch was building steamboats, Fulton was painting portraits. It was while studying art in England under Benjamin West that he became interested in engineering, the master gunsmith in him emerging again. He worked on canal projects.

In 1796, he went to Paris at the invitation of Joel Barlow, a former chaplain of the Continental Army and passionate booster of all things American. Barlow was in Paris convincing a group of Frenchmen to immigrate to Ohio. In France, Fulton became fascinated, obsessed according to some accounts, with underwater warfare. He designed submarines that fired torpedoes. In 1801, he demonstrated his prototype, which stored fresh air in a copper globe, to the French Admiralty. Although the vessel managed to stay under the water in Brest Harbor for more than four hours, the French government declined to develop such a weapon.

Then he visited Robert Livingston, with whom he had several years earlier steamed across the Collect. Livingston had been a deputy to the Continental Congress, law partner of the first Supreme Court chief justice, John Jay, and a native New Yorker who was serving as the U.S. ambassador to France. Fulton could not interest Livingston in his submarine either. Livingston had a long-standing interest in steamboats, though, which was why he had been on board Fitch's invention on the Collect. Being from New York City, Livingston immediately grasped the significance of Fulton's idea for using the steam engine. The engine Fulton wanted to use had been developed by James Watt, a Scot who is also sometimes credited with inventing steam engines but had not—Thomas Savery did in 1698—

to drive two paddle wheels and power a vessel. Livingston contracted Fulton to build a boat with steam-powered paddle wheels that would work the Hudson River between New York City and Albany. Their first prototype in 1803 sank in the Seine. The French were nevertheless impressed with the theory. But Fulton and Livingston were not theorists, they were a new breed of American pragmatists in search of commercial success.

They returned to America, and Livingston secured a monopoly from the New York State legislature for all steam-powered vessels on New York rivers. On the East River, the site of numerous shipyards, they built the *Clermont,* a 130-foot vessel with two 15-foot-diameter side paddle wheels and two masts flying square canvas sails for added power.

In August 1807—historians disagree on the exact day—the *Clermont* steamed from Manhattan to Albany, 150 miles up the Hudson, in thirty-two hours. Along the way the forty-one-year-old artist-engineer-inventor-entrepreneur at last found the time to propose marriage to Harriet Livingston, a relative of his partner. He made it back downriver to Manhattan in thirty hours. The state monopoly had been on condition that they could produce a steamboat that traveled at least four miles an hour. They had averaged five miles an hour. "The power of propelling boats by steam is now fully proved," Fulton wrote Joel Barlow. Immediately following this successful demonstration, Fulton and Livingston began regular service between Manhattan and Albany. The fares were high, seven dollars one way to Albany, and yet the boats were packed with eager customers. Fulton and Livingston had shown that steam travel was profitable and that is what changed New York and the world and probably why Robert Fulton is erroneously remembered as the inventor of the steamboat.

The travel time was reduced even further and the ability to travel between New York and Albany in half a day instead of a week had tremendous commercial implications not only for passenger traffic but also for freight. It meant that Hudson Valley produce could be shipped out of New York and around the globe, and goods could be brought in from around the world and quickly delivered to be sold in the Hudson Valley. This held special promise for New York City producers of perishable goods, and near the top of such a list were oyster producers.

Not everyone was pleased. The *Clermont* burned pine and belched black smoke and spit bright sparks, but this was the beginning of the nineteenth century, an age when some feared technology and others pointed at black smoke with pride as a sign of progress. One observer called the *Clermont* "the horrible monster which was marching on the tide and lighting its path by the fire that it vomited." The operators of the old river sloops took every opportunity to attempt to scuttle or block the *Clermont*. The state legislature passed a law specifically against injuring the *Clermont* or other steamboats.

But the possibilities were apparent, and not only to oystermen. On October 2, 1807, the *New York Evening Post* ran an article reporting on "Mr. Fulton's Steam Boat" that concluded: "Yesterday she came in from Albany in 28 hours with 60 passengers. Quere would it not be well if she could contract with the Post-Master General to carry the mail from this city to Albany?"

New Yorkers fell in love with the technology, which led to reckless steamboat races down the Hudson. At least fifty passengers died in 1845 when the *Swallow*, racing two other steamboats, rammed into a rocky island and caught fire. More than sixty people were killed, including Nathaniel Hawthorne's sister in 1852, when the *Henry Clay*, also racing, caught fire near Yonkers and was run aground.

Fulton turned to the ferryboat. Of what are today the five boroughs of New York City, only the Bronx is situated on the mainland
of North America. Today the boroughs are interconnected by bridges
and tunnels, but from the time of the Dutch, and possibly the
Lenape, to the late nineteenth century, the only connection was by
ferryboats. Until Fulton, these ferries were powered by teams of
horses walking in a circle on the boat deck, turning a pole that was
the driveshaft to the paddle wheel. At the speed these boats traveled,
even a trip across the East River became a voyage. In 1812, Fulton
began producing steam-powered ferryboats to connect Manhattan
with New Jersey and with Brooklyn. Fulton also invented the pon-
toon dock, which enabled the loading dock to rise with the water and
always remain level with the ferry deck for bringing vehicles on and
off, a system that is still in use.

Fulton was interested in establishing steam service between New
York and Connecticut as well, but the route, Long Island Sound, was
still subjected to hostile British warships. It was not until after the
War of 1812, with the Treaty of Ghent in 1815, that hostilities finally
ended and steam service was established between New Haven and
New York. Soon after, the New Haven ferry went on to Providence,
altering forever the character of southern New England by joining it
to New York as much as or more so than with Boston. A steamboat
to the Raritan River in New Jersey connected New York to Philadelphia.

New York was now shipping enormous quantities of fresh oysters
upstate and to Europe and, not producing enough for all its markets,
was buying up Long Island, Connecticut, and New Jersey oysters. In
1807, the city suspended the law that had barred letting oysters enter
the city in the summer months. In 1819, the first cannery opened in
New York City for canning oysters and codfish, providing another

way to trade New York oysters over long distances. And another new idea was about to change New York and the New York oyster trade.

The Lenape, the Iroquois, the Mohawk—many of the inhabitants of what was to become New York State—had had myths that the great North River flowed through from another sea to the Atlantic. Now the Salty People were going to make that true. It wasn't a water route to China, but for the New Yorkers of the nineteenth century it was something much better—a waterway to the growing American West.

Both Fulton and Livingston strongly believed the future of America was on Western waterways and they tried to establish steamboat service on the Mississippi and other Western rivers. But the governor of New York had a different idea.

In 1808, after steam service to Albany proved to be a success, New York assemblyman Joshua Freeman introduced to the assembly a resolution to consider building a canal connecting the Hudson River to the Great Lakes. Freeman was from Salina, a salt-producing area between Lake Erie and Albany, and salt producers wanted to move their very bulky product by water to New York City and foreign markets and to the Great Lakes and Western markets.

Steamships had shown how transportation could build New York. In the early nineteenth century, one-sixth of the population of the United States lived in the New York area and with the help of steamships, New York City handled about a sixth of the nation's commerce.

But not everyone was enthusiastic about the canal idea. New York City was still agricultural, even Manhattan was still two-thirds farmland, and Manhattan farmers did not want to compete with the goods that could be brought in from upstate. Many New York City merchants initially opposed the canal because they believed that it would devalue New York products. New York City's most influential politician, Governor DeWitt Clinton, from a famous and well-connected family—his father James was a Revolutionary War hero and his uncle George served as vice president under both Jefferson and Madison while the canal project was looking for sponsors—was the canal's greatest champion. Work began in 1817 and was not completed until 1825 at an estimated cost of five dollars per inhabitant of New York State.

The first canal boat, the *Seneca Chief,* sailed into New York Harbor with two kegs of Lake Erie fresh water, which were dumped into the Atlantic near Sandy Hook. Also on board were Great Lakes whitefish, still fresh, a canoe made by Lake Superior tribesmen, and potash from the upstate saltworks. The city fathers sailed out on a steamer and hailed the *Seneca Chief,* "Whence come you and where are you bound?"

The reply recorded for posterity was "From Lake Erie bound for Sandy Hook."

The Erie Canal connected New York Harbor to the Great Lakes and the rapidly expanding northern Midwest. Its success led to other canals, like the Ohio Canal that linked the Great Lakes to the Ohio River, which ran into the Mississippi. Soon New York City was connected by water to a considerable part of the North American continent, opening its products to the West.

By the time the canal was completed, New York Harbor was handling more than a third of U.S. commerce. This was in no small part due to the Erie Canal. The most important New York State export was flour. New York shipped inexpensive flour all over the world. But it was also shipping fresh oysters. Before the canal was even completed, advertisements started appearing in western New York newspapers for fresh oysters. Once the Erie Canal was completed, steamboats and even sailing sloops would go to Albany to unload. Some days there would be forty New York oyster boats unloading in Albany, where the oysters were put on canal barges or on wagons to be sent to other New York State destinations such as Lake Champlain.

Since the Hudson froze over in the winter, the oyster sloops would take one last order for winter supplies along the Hudson in December. By choosing thick-shelled oysters and carefully packing them with the deep cup side on the bottom, the New York City dealers ensured the oysters would last through the winter. They even attempted to train the bivalves to keep tightly shut while out of the water. Producers discovered that oysters are educable. The grower would choose plump, large oysters and replant them closer to shore where they would be exposed for a few hours a day in low tide. After a few days, they would move the oysters a little farther up so that they were exposed for a few minutes longer in low tides. Producers continued the process, moving them every few days. The oysters learned to take a long hard drink before the water retreated and eventually would hold the water the entire time they were exposed.

New Yorkers were not unique in training oysters for shipment. The French, before shipping oysters to Paris, would spread them out in the water and every day tap each oyster with an iron rod, instantly causing the bivalve to close tightly. A nineteenth-century American observer quipped that a French oyster was trained "to keep its mouth shut when it enters society."

With money coming fast into the great port city, New York was able to expand, pave streets, build sidewalks, and extend roads farther up into Manhattan. Three months after the first steamboat to Albany went into service, the city experimented with its first fire hydrant, on the corner of Liberty and William streets. As the city grew, the plan for a street grid in Manhattan provided for east–west streets spaced closer together while the few north–south avenues were farther apart because the city planners were certain that the bulk of traffic would be east–west between the two waterfronts, the Hudson and the East River.

Despite the prosperity, the city offered not one first-class restaurant. According to legend, New Yorkers first noticed this situation in 1825, when the first Erie Canal boat was greeted in New York Harbor by Governor DeWitt Clinton and Mayor Philip Hone. There was no restaurant, they realized, good enough for a celebration. But that was not the worst of it. Nothing will stir a second look at the hometown restaurants like a visit from a beloved Frenchman. Actually, thirty years earlier, an exiled Jean Anthelme Brillat-Savarin, later to become one of the all-time most celebrated French food writers, had passed two years in New York, escaping the French Revolution by eking out an existence as a French teacher and violinist. He had found the food pleasing. But he was impressed with the bounty of products in the market, the value of good food simply prepared in homes. He described shooting his own wild turkey in Connecticut and having his hosts roast it. He had no restaurants or cuisine to write about. In 1825, a far more famous Frenchman with even more names, Marie-Joseph-Paul-Yves-Roch-Gilbert du Motier, Marquis de Lafayette, the French officer who at the age of nineteen had resigned his commission to come to America with his troops and fight for the Revolution, returned for a visit.

The sixty-eight-year-old marquis had imagined a quiet sojourn, but from the start he was met with canon salutes and cheered by large crowds. Even the seas around the city seemed to mark the occasion. Suddenly there was an explosion in the population of a particular variety of sea drum fish, ever after known to New Yorkers as Lafayettes.

The city's leading citizens wanted to throw not just a dinner for the marquis but a series of banquets, and among the taverns and oyster cellars, there were no establishments that they felt were fine enough in the mile between the Battery and City Hall that was New York City. Considering that New York had been under military occupation during his last trip, he may not have been in the least disappointed by the current arrangements, but a sense of municipal mortification set in.

At the time, Swiss-born Giovanni Delmonico was a wine merchant. In 1818, when he was only thirty years old, he had been the commander of a three-masted schooner trading a profitable route between New York and Havana. He picked up tobacco in Havana, sold it in Cádiz, Spain, where he bought wine that he sold in New York, where he picked up lumber to sell in Havana. In 1824, he took his considerable savings, anglicized his name to John, and established himself in New York, using his connections to buy French and Spanish wines in bulk and bottling them himself. According to some, he was among the first to respond to this appalling lack of restaurants, but according to others, he was simply anticipating the likely growth of the city because of the canal. It was probably the combination that he saw as an enormous opportunity. He went back to Switzerland to gather his older brother, Pietro, a successful pastry maker in Berne. They sailed back to New York, Pietro now Peter, with sea chests filled with, according to their nephew, Lorenzo, $20,000 in gold pieces. New York has always loved its rags-to-riches stories, and for years it was said that the Delmonicos arrived penniless and raised their money selling peanuts on the street. The truth was a lesser story, but a far better way to get started in New York.

Since one was a wine merchant and the other a pastry maker, they opened a café, the first place in New York to offer French pastry, in a two-story brick house at 23 William Street in the heart of the business district, and called it Delmonico. It was a simple place with six pine tables. Playing to their expertise, they sold pastries, cakes, coffee, wines, and Cuban cigars. Another first for New York was cups of thick and foamy hot chocolate. Initially, most of their customers were Europeans, of which there were many, most of whom had written home about the barbarous state of New York food and rejoiced in the new café. For the Americans, the initial curiosity was the first female cashier they had ever seen, a new concept, entrusting women with money. The woman, in fact, was Peter's wife.

Delmonico's introduced New York to what would become one of its basic institutions, the business lunch. They sent for their nephew Francesco, and in a break with family tradition that forecasted the direction the business was going, he Francofied rather than anglicized his name to François. By 1831, they were no longer advertising themselves as "Delmonico & Brother, Confectioners" but as "Confectioners and *Restaurant Français*."

They had competitors, such as a café on Broadway between Pine and Cedar owned by a Frenchman, François Geurin. But it was largely the success of the Delmonicos that caused a major shift in New York culture. Up until then, despite the Revolution and the War of 1812, New York cooks, when they wanted to excel, had aspired to cook the best British food, using recipes copied from British cookbooks or British cookbooks themselves, which were still in common use. Also, a number of supposedly American cookbooks were written by British cooks. *American Domestic Cookery,* published in the early 1800s in both England and the United States, was written by Maria Eliza Ketelby Rundell, who was actually British.

But toward the middle of the nineteenth century, fine dining in New York, led by Delmonico's, developed French aspirations. In fact, as Delmonico's became the most celebrated restaurant in America, French dining, with greater or lesser degrees of success, started to become synonymous around the country with "fine" dining.

In 1834, the Delmonicos bought a 250-acre farm in Williamsburg, Long Island, which later became a section of Brooklyn. They did this not only because as successful New Yorkers they needed a country home, but because they wanted farmland to grow produce not available in the New York markets. Many of these items were French or Italian, but the Delmonicos were also innovative with native American products. At a time when tomatoes, known as love apples, were just becoming popular as an ornamental plant to brighten gardens, the Delmonicos introduced New Yorkers to cooking with them.

By the 1830s, a discriminating diner could survive in Manhattan. Several alternatives to Delmonico's opened, including the Astor House, a five-story hotel on Broadway between Vesey and Barclay streets. An 1837 Astor House menu listed many French dishes but also two lingering vestiges of English cooking: "boiled cod and oysters" and "oyster pie."

At Delmonico's, the trendsetter, the emphasis was always on the French, who by the nineteenth century favored oysters raw on the half shell, served as an appetizer. It was not enough to have French dishes and French ingredients and, where possible, French chefs and

French maître d's, but the service was also to be French. French words, *mots,* were to be dropped as often as possible. The service was to have a French style, and to a large degree, the menu was to be written in French. All this was not only the pride of many affluent New Yorkers, but it pleased a considerable New York population of Frenchmen. Louis-Napoléon, nephew of the emperor and future ruler of France, was a Delmonico's regular while in exile, dining with a handsome young actor named James Wallack, with whom he returned to France. The Prince de Joinville was another Delmonico regular in 1840 when his command, a frigate named *Belle Poule,* was in port.

Not everyone was pleased by this turn to that always slightly suspect affliction, Francophilia. Philip Hone, the self-made, outspoken ex-mayor wrote in his diary in 1838:

My wife, daughter Margaret, Jones and I dined with Mr. and Mrs. Olmstead. The dinner was quite *à la française.* The table, covered with confectionery and gew-gaws, looked like one of those shops down Broadway in the Christmas holidays, but not an eatable thing. The dishes were all handed round; in my opinion a most unsatisfactory mode of proceeding in relation to this important part of the business of a man's life. One does not know how to choose, because you are ignorant of what is coming next, or whether anything more is coming. Your conversation is interrupted every minute by greasy dishes thrust between your head and that of your next neighbor, and it is more expensive than the old mode of shewing a handsome dinner to your guests and leaving them free to choose. It will not do. This French influence must be resisted.

Both the steamboat service to Albany and the Erie Canal were destined to be swiftly fleeting marvels, eclipsed by the next idea. Only seven years after the *Seneca Chief* brought whitefish to New York Harbor, the city's railroad age had begun. The New York and Harlem Railroad began service from Union Square to Twenty-third Street. But soon there were rail connections in and out of the city to Boston, across New York State to the Great Lakes, down to Washington, out to the growing West. As with the other innovations, not everyone was happy about this new idea, especially the city farmers. New York City milk producers were convinced that the Erie Railroad would be their ruin and warned New Yorkers that the city was going to be flooded with inferior milk.

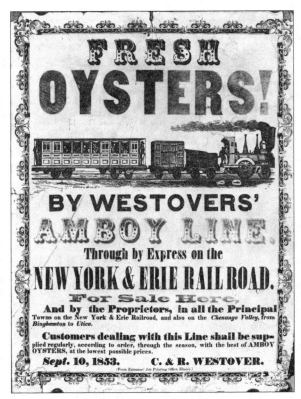

1853 advertisement
COLLECTION OF
THE NEW-YORK
HISTORICAL
SOCIETY

They were right about the quantity but not the quality. In 1842–43, the Erie Railroad brought three million quarts of milk into New York City. By the end of the decade, that amount had tripled.

Midwest newspapers advertised the arrival of New York City oysters and their competitor, Chesapeake Bay oysters. Since oysters grow faster in warmer waters, the Chesapeake ones had the advantage, in an age when size mattered, of being much larger. But Northern oysters had a reputation of being more durable for travel. Oysters on ice followed the rail lines to Buffalo, then Cleveland, then Cincinnati. In 1852, the Michigan Southern Railroad brought the first East Coast train into Chicago. Soon it was on to St. Louis. And all these trains carried New York oysters. As a young politician in Springfield, Illinois, Abraham Lincoln threw oyster parties at which hundreds of oysters were consumed.

Oysters were cheap. New York City oyster houses often offered the Canal Street Plan, which was "all you can eat," raw on the half shell, for six cents. At the same time, fashionable restaurants were offering off-season strawberries from the Mediterranean for fifty cents a berry. For most nineteenth-century diners, "all you can eat" was a considerable quantity of oysters. Who would dream of stopping at a half dozen? A few dozen was a nice appetizer. Midnineteenth-century recipes called for enormous quantities of oysters and usually specified that they should be large ones. Eliza Leslie, a Philadelphian whose *Directions for Cookery* had sixty editions between 1837 and the posthumous 1870 edition, sometimes called for hundreds of oysters or several quarts shelled. Her recipe for pickled oysters begins, "Take a hundred and fifty fine large oysters. . . ."

❧ Oyster Soup

Season two quarts of oysters with a little cayenne. Then take them out of the liquor. Grate and roll fine a dozen crackers. Put them into the liquor with a large lump of fresh butter. When the grated biscuit has quite dissolved, add a quart of milk with a grated nutmeg, and a dozen blades of mace; and, if in season, a head of celery split fine and cut into small pieces. Season it to your taste with pepper.

Mix the whole together, and set it in a closely covered vessel over a slow fire. When it comes to a boil, put in the oysters; and when it comes to a boil again, they will be sufficiently done.

Before you send it to the table put into the tureen some toasted bread cut into small squares, omitting the crust.

—ELIZA LESLIE,
Miss Leslie's Directions for Cookery,
1851 edition

The combination of having reputably the best oysters in the world in what had become unarguably the greatest port in the world made New York City for an entire century the world's oyster capital. The only question now, and only a few had the insight and bluntness to raise it, was whether there were enough oysters in New York Harbor to feed the world.

CHAPTER SIX

Eggocentric New Yorkers

—

*This is New York: skyscraper champion of the world where
slickers and know-it-alls peddle gold bricks to each other
and where the truth, crushed to earth, rises again more
phony than a glass eye.*

—BEN HECHT,
Nothing Sacred, 1937

A curiosity in the development of marine biology is that little is learned about a species until it is faced with extinction. As early as 1810, the oyster beds of Staten Island, where oystering was a leading economic activity, were showing signs of exhaustion. By the 1820s, most New York beds had been overharvested and could no longer keep up with the growing demand for New York oysters. Some were nearly barren, with only the occasional oyster on a stripped ocean floor.

It was at that eleventh hour that scientists stepped in.

Most of the oyster families, genera, and species had not even been identified at the time. Fortunately, the European *Ostrea* had troubles of its own, which in turn led a scientist to some ideas about what to do about it.

Cultivating oysters was an ancient European concept. Although none of the commercial producers bothered with it very much until North American and European beds started to show signs of permanent exhaustion in the nineteenth century, the idea had been under contemplation for a very long time. Long before anything was understood about the reproductive process of oysters, the possibility of seeding artificial beds was discussed. Aristotle noted that fishermen had taken natural oysters and moved them to a more favorable spot in a current where they "fattened greatly" but did not reproduce. An artificial bed had been created, but to maintain it, the bed would have to be replanted regularly with more oysters.

The seafloors of the ancient Aegean and Mediterranean were littered with both whole and broken pottery from shipments of wine and olive oil lost in storms. So much pottery was lost at sea that in some spots divers today still regularly run across both whole and broken pieces. By chance it was discovered that oysters seemed to like to attach themselves to this material. Would not scattering broken pottery over a suitable area create an ideal artificial oyster bed? Oysters from somewhere else could be deposited there.

The Romans were interested in such questions because they associated oysters with wealth and even created a coin in their currency, the *denarius,* which was supposed to be worth the value of one oyster. They also developed a love of gluttony. According to Edward Gibbon, the great eighteenth-century chronicler of the fall of the Roman Empire, a calamity not entirely disassociated from this turn toward gluttony, Vitellius, a first-century A.D. Roman emperor, ate as many as one thousand oysters at a sitting. The Romans ate oysters both raw and cooked. Apicius, who lived in the time of Vitellius, recommended them raw with sauces such as this mayonnaise:

> For oysters: pepper, lovage, egg yolk, vinegar, garum
> [a sauce of salted fermented fish], oil, and wine.
> If you wish, add honey.

But he also offered this cooked "Baian stew" recipe:

> Into a pot put small oysters, mussels, jellyfish, chopped
> roasted pine nuts, rue, celery, pepper, coriander, cumin,
> passum [raisin wine], garum, date, and oil.

Sergius Orata, a son of first-century B.C. Rome and its epicurean excesses, cultivated the European flat oyster, *Ostrea edulis,* in brackish lakes near Naples. These lakes have the kind of soft, black, muddy bottoms in which oysters sink and suffocate. But he placed at regular distances piles of rocks. He planted oysters from Brindisi on these rock piles and left them permanently to spawn at will. He surrounded each pile with a circle of stakes connected by rope above the water and then hung twigs from the ropes. When the breeding oysters discharged their fertilized eggs, the eggs were immediately attracted to the twigs as a place to attach themselves. The cultivator could regularly lift the twigs out of the water, pulling off the oysters of desirable size and lowering the twigs back with the smaller ones still attached to continue growing.

Orata made a fortune selling these oysters, or so said Pliny, but he also used them to feed the sea bream he was attempting to farm for commercial use. "Oyster-fed sea bream" was a great marketing concept in a Rome that loved wastefully exotic gourmetism, which is why the fish, in Italian, was named after him, *orata*. He cultivated more and more oysters in these lakes that were supposed to provide luxury bathing for the rich, until finally he was sued by bathers reluctant to share space with bivalves. The complainant quipped that even if Orata was stopped from growing his oysters in the lake, he would grow them on "the tiles," which some have translated as roofs and others the tiles of his shower baths. Orata would grow oysters anywhere he could. But while it was true that growing oysters was one of his preoccupations, baths were another. Orata had considerably improved the facilities by inventing the pipe-heated floor and the shower, from the marketing of which he was said to have earned yet another fortune.

In the nineteenth century, French naturalists such as Jean Jacques Marie Cyprien Victor Coste, professor of embryology, took up the subject of oyster culture not because oysters were running out in Staten Island and the East River, but because the beds of France from Normandy to the Arcachon near Bordeaux were looking bare. In France, the oyster tradition is no doubt as old as in Britain, with both tracing back to at least Roman times. The earliest-known French recipe collections include oysters, and though by the time of Coste the French had come to disdain oysters eaten any way but raw, these early French oyster dishes were generally cooked. This one, from *Le Mesnagier de Paris*, a guide to household management written by a fourteenth-century Frenchman to his child bride, is similar to English oyster soup recipes of the same period, and would probably be appalling to later Frenchmen:

Oysters are first washed in warm water, then boiled until their flavor is left in the broth, it must not froth up. Take them out and, if you wish, fry them and add a few of them to the soup bowls and serve the rest on a platter.

When Coste began, at the request of the French government, to contemplate the French oyster problem, he first looked at the work of Orata in Naples, work that was still well known in Europe. Without learning anything more about the animal, medieval Europeans had imitated Orata's practices, so that by the nineteenth century, replanting oysters was commonplace. Usually this was done because the ideal environment for reproduction and the ideal environment for growth were not the same.

New Yorkers understood this. In the early eighteenth century, when townships started laying exclusive claim to their own parts of Long Island's Great South Bay, it became clear that not all of the bay was equal. Young oysters prospered in the east bay while in the west bay they were decimated by oyster drills. But those that survived the west-bay oyster drills would grow far plumper at a much faster rate than the east-bay oysters. The east bay, completely cut off from the ocean by Fire Island and fed by numerous rivers, had a low salinity. The west bay, exposed to the open Atlantic, was far saltier. The east bay did not have enough salt for the oyster drill. But it also didn't have enough salinity for optimum oyster growth. The solution was to raise the oysters in the east bay until big and tough enough to survive and then replant them for growth in the west. Such operations had been carried out all over the world for centuries. Orata had found that oysters developed very well in Brindisi up to a point, but when transferred to his lakes would grow much faster.

Oyster growers had learned some things. They had learned that an oyster is fairly discriminating about what it will attach to. Pottery works well, oyster shells work better. Clean surfaces are preferable. Silt is death. The French had for centuries been raising oysters in *claires,* artificial ponds constructed above sea level so that the sea-water would only flow in at high tides.

But for oyster cultivation to have the kind of large-scale efficiency that was required for the hungry nineteenth-century market, the oysters would need to be collected and moved at a far earlier stage, when they were tiny swimming creatures. Coste understood that by providing favorable and plentiful attachment material, an oyster farmer could considerably improve on nature's survival rate and raise large quantities of oysters.

Others had quietly taken an early lead. The Japanese and even some in the Naples area had managed to collect seed oysters, as had the Chinese, with woven bamboo. Meso-Americans in coastal Mexico had solved the entire problem years, possibly centuries, earlier using tree branches to collect the tiny swimming young oysters. New York oystermen called these minuscule swimmers spats because they referred to spawning as spitting and they had been spat.

But no one in Paris or New York had noticed what Meso-Americans did with spats and it would take centuries for the French, completely independently, to settle on the same technique. Throughout the nineteenth century, as knowledge of the oyster grew, the ability to raise them artificially became increasingly sophisticated. In 1853, M. de Bon, the French-government marine commissioner, was ordered to restock some of the depleted beds and by chance discovered that oysters could also reproduce in places where none had been before. This led to experiments trying to capture the young free-swimming oysters, the spats, and plant them. De Bon devised a system of planks on the ocean floor covered with twigs. It was a variation on Orata's method eighteen hundred years earlier. De Bon never actually collected spats this way, but Victor Coste did. Coste received a government commission to attempt spat collecting on a large scale. Three million oysters were delivered to him by a fleet of small steam-powered vessels. He prepared a bed, spreading the seafloor with oyster shells. After the oysters were planted, bundles of sticks were anchored to the floor on a rope floating a foot above. At the end of one season, they hauled up the twigs and they were covered with small oysters. One bundle had twenty thousand oysters attached to it. In 1863, he obtained 16 million oysters of marketable size from half of a single one-thousand-acre bed. The government began granting sea-

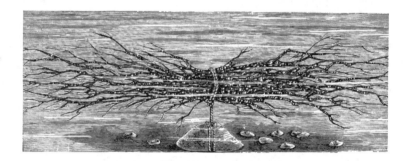

FIG. 3.

Illustrations from William K. Brooks's 1891 book shows the technique to farm seed oysters.

bed land to oystermen. Lots of 492 acres within a few years were yielding oyster harvests valued at $8 million.

With typically French administration, the government regulated the fishery by dividing the entire coastline into five arrondissements, thirteen sous-arrondissements, and sixty quartiers. A two-tier system was established. Where there were natural beds, they were dredged. The beds were maintained by cleaning them out and putting down tile or other cultch for larvae to adhere to. In this way a breeding stock was maintained. Some of the larvae would be placed in artificial beds, shallow-water locations, where tiles, sticks, string, or other objects were placed to catch them. When they grew into spats, the centimeter-long flakes were kept in mesh cages until they developed thick hard shells and then they were planted in the beds to grow and fatten.

Throughout the nineteenth century, more and more was learned about oysters so that man's proclivity for destroying them was countered by the ability to re-create them. Such newfound powers were making humankind giddy with science's magical ability to withstand its own foolish excess.

The first natural beds in New York City to be exhausted were those around Staten Island. By 1820, with the city's population and demand for oysters rapidly growing, the Staten Island beds were barren deserts from both overharvesting and suffocation from silt washed down the Raritan River. New York oystermen knew that, like Sergius Orata, they could replant their beds with oysters from elsewhere. They planted small young oysters from Arthur Kill and the Raritan River, but these took two or three years to reach a marketable size. They also tried Long Island oysters with slightly more success. With production declining, the market for oysters in New York City was growing. As early as 1816, Chesapeake Bay oysters were being sold in New York. Chesapeake oysters had the advantage that, having been reared in warm water, even transported to New York they had a faster first growing season than a native New Yorker. Small young Chesapeake oysters, seed oysters, two inches or smaller, planted in Staten Island beds would reach a marketable size—not the giants of New York legend but a suitable eating size—in only one year.

In the spring of 1825, Chesapeake spats for the first time were brought up by schooner and planted in Princess Bay, Staten Island. In the fall the oysters were collected and profitably sold in the city. Numerous schooners with a captain and a four-man crew began doing the same thing from Princess Bay, and from the New Jersey side out of Keyport and Perth Amboy. These crews could import hundreds of thousands of seed oysters each year. It took thirty-five to forty hours for a schooner to sail from Raritan Bay to the rivers of the lower Chesapeake. In two days they could load between 2,500 and 3,500 bushels of seed oysters with 400 to 500 little oysters in each bushel. Soon other mismanaged oyster regions on Long Island, Connecticut, Rhode Island, and Wellfleet in Cape Cod, Massachusetts, were doing the same thing. It was a simple transfer from one *Crassostrea virginica* bed to another.

When the schooner returned to Raritan Bay with the seed oysters, they hired an additional twelve men, often local farmers, to shovel the seeds overboard while the schooner sailed back and forth over the bed. They learned to control the density so that the bed would not be crowded—750 bushels per acre seemed the ideal formula.

Where France was an administrative society and cultivation was promoted by a government plan, the United States, and especially New York, is legalistic and needed the right laws in place before oyster cultivation could become widespread. U.S. law regarded a natural oyster bed in much the same way the Lenape had regarded all land. It could not be owned, and anyone had the right to harvest it, just like picking berries in a wild forest or fishing in the ocean. In the eighteenth century, territorial rights came into play. To harvest oysters in a particular area required residency. Any resident was entitled to the oyster beds. But planting was something different. Someone had invested labor and capital to plant spats in an empty bed. A planter would mark off his area with green saplings, the leafy parts sticking out plainly visible above the waterline.

But by the midnineteenth century, the issue had become more complicated. Some New York oystermen without the means to sail down to the Chesapeake and buy spats claimed that the Chesapeake spats had been planted in natural beds that still had wild oysters, and they had a right to collect oysters in these beds. The courts ruled that oystermen did have a right to file claims for beds they wanted to plant. No one but the state could own a sea bed, but an individual had the right to lease an underwater area from the state, provided no natural beds were within the area, and the lease granted exclusive rights to the shellfish harvested from that bed. Leases were issued by the states of New York and New Jersey for little or no fee.

This arrangement, by assuring the cultivator that he owned all the profits from his labor and investment, provided the necessary incentive to develop an extensive cultivated oyster industry in New York and New Jersey. Organizations such as the Richmond County Oyster-planting Association in Staten Island were formed to patrol the beds and guard against poachers.

Oystering in natural beds had required relatively little capital or risk. But cultivating oysters was a different kind of business. The investment in labor—buying, transporting, and planting spats and maintaining beds—was substantial. Each spat had a less than one-in-a-million chance of surviving predators, storms, and other maritime conditions. But at least, after the law was passed, no one else could harvest the planted oysters. Cultivation rapidly increased following the passage of this legal guarantee. Soon more than one thousand men were directly employed cultivating oysters in New York City waters.

Sturdy oak-splint bushel baskets became a standard unit of measure, though a bushel might contain as few as 250 and as many as 350 oysters. A new trade, oyster-basket making, was founded, bending splints of oak or maple to molds.

By the 1830s, oystering, the single most important economic activity on Staten Island, employed about one thousand people, basket makers and spat shovelers included. Oystermen started coming north with the spats to plant them. Many of these Maryland oystermen were free blacks. But even as free men and women, they found things different in New York.

New York had never been progressive on the slavery issue, but it had made substantial progress since 1735 when a man named John van Zandt had whipped his slave to death because he had stayed out at night. The coroner's jury had ruled that the cause of death was not the brutality of the owner but a "visitation from God." Immediately following the end of the Revolutionary War, New York and New Jersey were the only Northern states that did not abolish slavery or establish a program for gradual abolition. Staten Island and Brooklyn, along with Ulster County, had been particularly vehement in their opposition to the abolition of slavery. But slave labor was being replaced by immigrant labor, which was legally less complicated and just as cheap. After 1799, New York law automatically granted freedom to children born of slaves. By 1820, only 518 slaves lived in New York, mostly in agricultural areas. Finally, a law was passed abolishing slavery in New York State after July 4, 1827. Free blacks moved into an area in northern Manhattan, calling it Seneca Village, where they lived, along with remaining American Indians, in shacks and even caves. But most lived in the poorer sections of Manhattan along with mostly Irish immigrants. Seneca Village was bought up by the city in the 1850s to create Central Park.

Maryland was still a slave state, but it had an unusually high population of free blacks. The slave-owning establishment believed this population was a threat to the institution of slavery, and so the state passed laws restricting the rights of free blacks. A black oysterman was not allowed to own his own sloop or even captain a sloop unless a white man was present. On the other hand, if he wished to move to an unknown corner of West Africa called Liberia, he would be paid a stipend.

Restrictions against free blacks owning land in New York had been abolished in 1809, though blacks were still required to own at least $250 worth of property in order to vote. The property requirement had been removed for white people in 1825. In Maryland, free blacks could not own land, they could not own oyster beds, but could only be laborers working on them. In Staten Island, they could work their own oyster beds. They settled into a small community of freed New York blacks, on the far southern tip, the island's poorest land, in its most rural township. It was part of Westfield, one of the original four Staten Island townships, which had been settled by Dutch and Huguenot families, many of whom had been oystermen. Though the loam was laced with sand and clay, Westfield had farms and freed New York blacks went there for farmwork and oystering. The part of Westfield that Maryland blacks settled in was uncleared wooded land, inexpensively purchased. Though this area lacked the rich soil of the rest of the island, the blacks found the sandy soil well suited to growing strawberries. Originally called Harrisville, then Little Africa, by the 1850s it was called simply Sandy Ground, which is one of the prerequisites for growing strawberries.

The location was next to the oyster grounds of Arthur Kill on the north side and a short walk to Prince's Bay to the south. Prince's Bay oysters were particularly valued in Manhattan. Increasing numbers of blacks from the Maryland and Virginia oyster trade migrated to Sandy Ground. At first it was a poor community. The men worked for white oystermen and the women cleaned and did laundry for white families in Prince's Bay and Rossville. The black families lived in one-room shacks and built lean-tos for additions when they had children. In the summers they ate the produce from the gardens and in the winter they ate mostly oysters that they raked up from the forgotten deep recesses of Arthur Kill. Oysters are a food that loses charm when it becomes a staple.

But the little community became increasingly prosperous. Cultivation of strawberries continued, but oystering provided an economic base by which the blacks could thrive with their own shops and craftsmen and churches, becoming completely self-sufficient. They began to own their own boats. Some became basket makers, splitting the local white-oak saplings into strips they soaked and wove into bushel baskets. Others became blacksmiths, making tongs, rakes, and other equipment for oyster skiffs. Farms added to the strawberry crop such Southern foods as collard greens, sweet potatoes, and mustard greens. A boat left New Brunswick, New Jersey, every morning, steaming down the Raritan River and through the Arthur Kill, stopping in villages along the way, including Sandy Ground, picking up produce to be sold at the Washington Market in downtown Manhattan.

Some Sandy Ground oystermen operated skiffs collecting oysters with the long tongs of Lenape design or oyster rakes. Some earned enough money to buy single-masted sloops. The more affluent oyster families paved one road along the Arthur Kill, Bloomingdale Road, with crushed oyster shells. Starting in 1849, prosperous black oystering families built large, handsome, brick country homes along this road. Some of them traded oysters for bricks to build their homes.

As one of the first free black communities in New York, Sandy Ground became well known as an African American center. Black New Yorkers moved there from Manhattan at such a rate that despite the Maryland immigration, according to the 1860 census, the majority of Sandy Ground residents in the 1850s had been born in New York City or at least in New York State. It was a prosperous self-sufficient community. Esther Purnell, a woman from one of the Maryland families, established the community's own private school. It was also a stop on the Underground Railroad that moved escaped slaves north to freedom. Congress, meeting in Philadelphia in 1793, had passed the Fugitive Slave Act, making it a crime to help a slave escape or give him refuge. To the anger of many New Yorkers, the law was further strengthened by Congress in 1850. The skiffs and sloops of Sandy Ground oystermen were regularly searched for runaway slaves.

But the Staten Island oyster industry was largely integrated. Some white families made their homes in Sandy Ground, and even during the Civil War years, when New York City race relations, never good, grew particularly ugly, with numerous lynchings, the people of Sandy Ground enjoyed a peaceful relationship with the white communities that surrounded them.

Of all the oyster areas in New York Harbor, the East River was considered the place with the most advanced cultivation techniques. The first commercial practice of seeding a previously prepared bed, planted before spawning season with artificial reefs of oyster shells, occurred in the 1830s in beds surrounding a small East River island in the Bronx, City Island. On a map, the East River appears to become Long Island Sound after the two bodies meet at the narrow opening of Hell Gate, which is why the waters are so rough at this spot. But, by tradition, the narrow eastern stretch with the Bronx on one side and Queens on the other—an area today running past La Guardia Airport and the Throgs Neck Bridge as far as Norwalk, Connecticut, on one side, and Port Jefferson, Long Island, on the other—was considered part of the East River. This was a prime oystering area. Charles Mackay wrote of City Island in the 1850s: "In City Island, the whole population, consisting of 400 persons, is employed in the cultivation of oysters. The City Islanders are represented as a very honest, peculiar, and primitive community, who intermarry entirely among themselves, and drive a very flourishing business. The oyster that they rear is a particular favorite."

The City Island practice of seeding came from the observation, to quote Ernest Ingersoll's 1881 government study of the oyster industry, that "any object tossed into the water in summer became covered at once with infant oysters." Clearly, something could be placed in the water in summertime to collect large numbers of floating young oysters, fingernail-size flakes, which, at very little expense, could be transferred to a bed ideally suited for growing. A variety of objects were used to attract the young swimming oysters, which could then be deposited on oyster-shell beds.

But the success of the first experiments could not be repeated. The number of attached oysters became fewer and fewer until the oystermen understood that oysters would attach only to certain surfaces. Smooth was all right. They liked bottles. But slimy was unacceptable and slime grew very quickly. Oyster shells at the bottom of the East River became slimy in a matter of days from vegetable matter in the water. To avoid slime the oystermen learned to wait and not spread shells in the beds until the spawning was actually in progress. Instead of planting shells in May in order to be prepared, they did not place them until July. They also looked for fast-running tideways to establish beds because sliming was much slower in such areas. They learned that if they spread the shells with shovels over the side of the skiff rather than just dumping piles overboard, the oysters would grow better.

By early fall, the East River oystermen would rake up a few shells and look for small flakes on them. Those were the new oysters. At the end of the first and second year, smaller oysters were removed to give larger ones growing space. By the second year they would be the size of a half-dollar, as they used to say when they still had half-dollars. A few third-year oysters were considered small but tender delicacies. Then, after four years, the oysters would be collected. Whether the bed was successful or not, it had to be cleared before it could be used again because the old shells would be too dirty for oysters to attach to them. The oyster dredge, a new and controversial tool, was introduced.

The fact that there was so much controversy over the oyster dredge demonstrates that the New York oyster fishery, poor as its management was, was far ahead of most fisheries. Virtually the same technique, stern dragging, was raising comparatively little controversy in the fisheries targeting cod, flounder, and other bottom fish until the midtwentieth century. The crisis of overfishing became apparent in oyster beds more than a century before it became apparent in fish stocks.

Dredging and bottom dragging were first done under sail, but it was the steam engine that made them dangerously efficient. An oyster dredge dragged a heavy bar along the bed with a netting basket behind it. Immediately it was seen that such a device could clear out the ocean floor. Victor Coste vehemently opposed oyster dredges. In an 1858 report to the French emperor Napoléon III, he stated, "Six weeks of daily dragging would be enough to denude the whole coast of France." The French started calling the oyster dredge the "oyster guillotine."

In New York and New Jersey, oystermen regarded dredging, as they did most new technology, with considerable suspicion. In 1820, a New Jersey law in Monmouth County barred taking an oyster on the Navesink River by any means other than "wading in and picking up by hand." The same year the oyster dredge was completely banned from New Jersey. But by 1846, planted beds were exempted from the ban. Only sail-powered dredging was allowed in Raritan Bay and Sandy Hook Bay until the 1960s. In the East River, dredges were favored because they broke up the oyster-shell mounds and clusters and cleaned out the area, making it ready to plant more clean shells. In 1870, a law prohibited dredging in Long Island's Great South Bay, but as holdings got larger, in 1893 the law was repealed. Designed as conservation measures, dredge-limiting laws lingered on even after culti-

vation eliminated the risk of overharvesting because they had a sec-
ondary effect of making oystering inefficient and therefore unattrac-
tive to big business. In this way oystering was kept a local artisanal
industry.

In the early nineteenth century, growing demand and declining
production in New York City created an opportunity for nearby oyster beds. The Great South Bay, a sheltered body of water about
twenty miles long and approximately forty-two miles miles wide, was
covered with natural oyster and clam beds and was only sixty-five
miles from Manhattan.

In the 1840s, two Dutchmen, Cornelius De Waal and his brother-
in-law Cornelius Hage, with wives and four children each, went to
New York with the intention of moving to the Michigan frontier,
where other Dutchmen had already gone. Pamphlets advertising rich
virgin farmland in America had been circulating among the oystermen of the increasingly unproductive natural beds of the Dutch–
Belgian coast. The De Waals and the Hages were comforted by what
they found to be the Dutchness of New York—Manhattan's brick
mansions with gables and what seemed to them the Dutch style of
Brooklyn farms. They were directed to a hotel on Manhattan's
Greenwich Street run by a Dutch Jew. Traveling Dutchmen are always joyous on the rare occasions they find people who speak their
language. They talked and talked and heard a rumor that the nearby
Great South Bay was full of oysters. Being from Bruinisse in Zeeland, where they had worked in the oyster business, they were excited
by this news, and they got directions to Hunter's Point to catch the
Long Island Rail Road.

At the time Long Island was populated mostly on the North Shore and East End by the descendants of seventeenth-century Puritans who had migrated from Connecticut. They had prospered in fishing and commerce on Long Island Sound, which had kept them clustered around the North Shore. Because the railroad, started in 1835, was built with the intention of connecting to Boston with the help of a ferry from the North Fork to Connecticut, it did not service the Long Island population but cut through the center, through flat woodlands with names such as the Barrens.

The South Shore was sandy and marshy, not especially good for farming, but it did offer a short sea route to New York City's markets. Hage and De Waal chose Oakdale, where they could live off the Great South Bay on flat, sandy shoreland that reminded them of home. By 1865, friends and relatives from Holland came and they formed their own community of West Sayville. They cut down trees and started farms and small industry. But the economic heart of the area was the Great South Bay and selling oysters to New York City's market. That market was so insatiable that the harbor's huge beds, even with cultivation, could not keep it fully supplied.

Supplying oysters to the great market only about sixty-five miles away was heavy and dangerous work. The oysters were transported by schooners and wagons. A schooner would carry about seven hundred bushels, about fifty thousand pounds, through Fire Island Inlet at the most dangerous times of year, the R months. The Long Island Rail Road reached Sayville in 1868, and by 1870, some oysters were being shipped by rail. From around 1900 until World War I, the Long Island Express Company had four express oyster trains a day, a seventy-five-minute ride, at 9 A.M., 11 A.M., 2 P.M., and 5 P.M. The oysters were shipped as half shells, three bushels to a barrel, or as "shucked" meats in gallon and three-gallon cans.

The bay oystermen continued to use the traditional tongs. Each sixteen feet long, they crossed at the end and had metal teeth that worked the bottom in a scissor motion, gathering up oysters, clams, rocks, etc. and depositing them in the baskets attached to each tong. An hour of tonging produced a bushel of oysters. This was the principal activity of the "baymen" along with clamming and fishing for "mossbonkers."

In midcentury, the Great South Bay was providing 75 percent of all the clams consumed across the country as well as a large catch of mossbonkers, New York City menhaden, to be ground up and used as fertilizer. This was something that had been learned from the Indians. The Indian word for fertilizer was *munnawhatteaug,* abbreviated by most white men as menhaden, except for New Yorkers, who, from some affliction of articulation, insisted that they were called mossbonkers. After a few years of mossbonker fertilization, the soil on Long Island, Staten Island, and other places it was used began showing signs of deterioration. Also, people in the area complained of the stench of fish and invasions of green flies. Fruit and other produce on which these flies landed were said to acquire the fishy smell.

Great South Bay oysters were highly valued in New York City, especially after 1817 when they acquired the label Bluepoints. A good marketing name is never unimportant in the oyster business. According to oystering legend, the first oysters sent to the New York market as Bluepoints were shipped by Joseph Avery, a veteran of the War of 1812 who returned home to the Great South Bay in 1815. Typical of baymen of the time, he did some fishing, carted seaweed, sold cordwood to New York City by way of the Fire Island Inlet, and did some oystering. Avery is credited with being the first to plant seed oysters off of Blue Point, his childhood home. He sailed a sloop to the Chesapeake and brought back a load of seed. According to family lore, during the two years in which he waited for the oysters to grow to a marketable size, Avery patrolled his bed with a loaded musket. He labeled his harvest Bluepoints after his native town by the Islip–Brookhaven line. The town, a traditional oystering center, was named by the oystermen who worked the beds on skiffs and claimed that the point was often seen through a blue haze. Bluepoints became such a successful brand name in New York City that soon any large oysters from the Great South Bay were called Bluepoints.

By the midnineteenth century, the Great South Bay was also running out of oysters and many baymen began planting Chesapeake spats. Once the Dutch started cultivating, using the two sides of the bay, the fresher side for planting and the saltier side for growing, West Sayville became more of an oyster center than Blue Point. But the oysters, shipped to New York City, were still called Bluepoints because New Yorkers loved Bluepoints.

New York City's booming oyster market was always looking for a new oyster from a new cove with a new name. If Bluepoints were hard to get, the city hungered for Prince's Bay oysters. Then, in 1827, an unusually high wind and strong tide left almost bare a reef in the East River known as Saddle Rock. The site is actually part of Norwalk Harbor. The name Saddle Rock came from a dubious claim that the reef resembled an English riding saddle. During this particularly strong tide, for the first time in memory oyster beds became visible at the base of Saddle Rock. Saddle Rock oysters were so large that 25 instead of 250 would fill a bushel basket, and yet the oysters were tender and were said to have a particularly fine flavor. New York being

New York, everyone in town was now crazy to have Saddle Rock oysters on their tables and ready to pay unheard-of prices for them.

The popular way to serve Saddle Rocks for home cooks and street vendors was by roasting them.

⚜ Oysters Roasted

Wash the shells perfectly clean, wipe them dry, and lay them on a gridiron, the largest side to the fire; set it over a bright bed of coals, when the shells open wide and the oyster looks white, they are done; fold a napkin on a large dish or tray, lay the oysters on their shells, taking care not to lose the juice: serve hot.

When oysters are served roasted at supper, there must be a small tub between each two chairs, to receive the shells, and large coarse napkins called oyster napkins. Serve cold butter and rolls or crackers with roasted oysters.

—MRS. T. J. CROWEN,
The American System of Cookery, 1864

It took about five years for every last Saddle Rock to be eaten, and by the time Mrs. Crowen wrote her popular cookbook, the oysters from Saddle Rock were long gone. But New York merchants continued to refer to a number of other varieties as Saddle Rocks because it had become a valuable marketing name. They would sell for as high as thirty cents each, which was an enormous price for a New York oyster. Eventually, a "Saddle Rock" became any large New York oyster that did not already have a good name like a Rockaway or a Prince's Bay. There was always a new oyster.

The discovery of a new natural oyster would be covered in New York newspapers with all the excitement of a medical breakthrough. In September 1859, five oystermen from Darien, Connecticut, realized they had drifted off their course and dropped their oyster dredge as an anchor. They found themselves off of Eatons' Neck at the opening to Huntington Bay, Long Island, some thirty miles from City Island. Getting their bearings, they hauled in the makeshift anchor and found it full of oysters. They quickly filled their boat and, the oysters being unusually large, as would be expected from an unexploited natural bed, agreed to keep secret the new location. But once they started bringing these large oysters to New York City markets, New Yorkers became curious. It took $500 to persuade one of the five to break the silence. The headline in the October 1, 1859, *New York Daily Tribune* was THE GREAT OYSTER PLACER: MILLIONS OF DOLLARS' WORTH FOUND: GREAT EXCITEMENT ALONG SHORE.

Connecticut, City Island, and Long Island oystermen from Oyster Bay to the west and Port Jefferson to the east, and even Brooklyn oystermen from Greenpoint across from Manhattan on the lower East River, learned of the spot. Since no one owns natural shellfish beds, what the *Tribune* called "an immense fleet" turned out in Huntington Bay. A reporter at the scene wrote that "so closely were they together that one could scarcely make out the separate sails." The *Daily Tribune* correctly predicted that unless the bed turned out larger than was currently reported, it would be exhausted in a matter of days.

Adding further to the arrogance of human beings, it was discovered in the nineteenth century that man could make a better oyster than nature. This is unusual. Fish farming and the domestication of animals, to the thinking of most epicureans, produces an inferior product. This is because farmed animals, including fish, have been penned into a sedentary way of life and are being fed food rather than foraging in the wild. This is not the case with the farmed oyster. In its natural life the wild oyster is barely more active than a plant, and the cultivated oyster lives the same life and feeds on the same nutrients in the same way as did its wild predecessor.

If a fish market in the right Manhattan neighborhood today could get hold of "wild native oysters" and market them as such, because this is how New York operates, it would probably be able to charge astounding prices and have *New York Times* readers, after the article on wild oysters came out, gladly paying the price. Or at least, until they saw the oysters. For they would be large and misshappen and irregular. A dozen would represent twelve different sizes and shapes. And for all that, they would taste like the cultivated ones.

In the small, neglected museum of the Staten Island Historical Society, there is in a showcase both the left and right shells of a wild Staten Island oyster from centuries past. It was not saved for that reason, but because someone had painted an oystering scene on the interior of the shells. The shells are more than six inches long, not much more than an inch in width, and curved like a banana. Now and then other old wild shells are found in middens or under the water and they, too, are large and have odd, usually skinny, shapes. Eighteenth-century scientific illustrations of the *Crassostrea virginicus* depict it as a long, thin, broad-bean-shaped shell.

In natural beds, all of the oysters find the most ideal spot and crowd onto it. They crowd so tightly that as they grow they do not have room to lie down but grow vertically or at odd angles. The competition for space in a natural bed is so acute that some oysters man-

Illustration from William K. Brooks's 1891 book shows oysters attached to a shoe.

age to grow in strange configurations determined by the available space and others, becoming blocked, cannot open their shells to breathe and feed, and these die. Often in a cluster of oysters the smaller ones would be dead and larger survivors would be attached to the shells of the unsuccessful oysters.

In a cultivated bed, the oyster's life has one difference from a natural bed: Since they are planted by man, they are carefully laid out at a comfortable distance so that the shells have room to grow in a round and ample shape. Not only that, but the cultivator chooses the size. The oysters could grow quite large if left ten, twelve, or more years. It would not be profitable to raise a product that took fifteen years of growth before harvesting. Two to three years' growth is a more economically viable time for *Crassostreas*—the European flat oyster takes longer—and this produces a size that most people find agreeable. A three-year-old New York oyster is not as big as a three-year-old Chesapeake oyster, but it is a size that most people find pleasing and a few dozen could be served and all be more or less the same shape and size. Most people do not want to eat an oyster the size of a plate.

The important difference with cultivation was that New Yorkers now had an endless supply of oysters and they could almost make them to order. The technology would become increasingly refined, until by the midtwentieth century, scientists could artificially insem- inate an oyster—as though an oyster's life wasn't dull enough already.

PART TWO

The Shells of Sodom

—

The city hums with its constant, insatiate, hungry roar.
The strained sound, agitating the air and the soul, the ceaseless
bellows of iron, the melancholy wail of life being driven by the
power of gold, the cold, cynical whistle of the Yellow Devil
scare the people away from the turmoil of the earth burdened
and besmirched by the ill-smelling body of the city.

—MAXIM GORKY,
1907

CHAPTER SEVEN

The Crassostreasness of New Yorkers

—

"It's a very remarkable circumstance, sir," said Sam, "that
poverty and oysters always seem to go together. . . . Blessed if
I don't think that vena man's wery poor, he rushes out of his
lodgings, and eats oysters in reg'lar desperation."

—CHARLES DICKENS,
The Pickwick Papers, 1836

"Fifty years ago New York was little more than a village,"
wrote Captain Frederick Marryat, the popular British author of maritime adventures, in 1838. "Now it is a fine city with three hundred thousand inhabitants." By the 1830s, Manhattan was a fast-growing metropolis. In 1835, 250,000 people lived there, mostly between the Battery and Bond Street, which is in today's East Village. "Trees are few," observed Edgar Allan Poe in 1844, "but some of the shrubbery is extremely picturesque."

Pigs still wandered the streets eating garbage that would otherwise have remained on the pavement. "Ugly brutes they are," wrote Charles Dickens after a visit to New York. The city was expanding rapidly north. The Harlem line provided railroad service to northern Manhattan. While many merchants still lived above their downtown stores, those who had become wealthy were joining the nouveaux riches, buying or building houses in new neighborhoods farther up the island at prices that astounded the middle class, while the old-money families were still installed along the Battery and on Broadway.

George Templeton Strong, a leading New York lawyer from one of the old families, who kept a diary between 1835 and 1875, wrote in 1840, "I took a walk up to Eighth Street and down again. It's a pity we've no street but Broadway that's fit to walk in of an evening. The street is always crowded, and whores and blackguards make up two thirds of the throng. That's the one advantage of uptown; the streets there are well paved, well-lighted, and decently populated."

Ten years later, in 1850, he wrote, "How this city marches northward! The progress of 1835 and 1836 was nothing to the luxuriant, rank growth of this year. Streets are springing up, whole strata of sandstone have transferred themselves from their ancient resting-places to look down on bustling thorough fares for long years to come."

As the city grew, the water supply became an increasingly serious problem. In 1828, the city did not have enough water to contain a major fire. In 1832, European trade brought with it to Manhattan a cholera epidemic. The principal cause of death in cholera cases is dehydration, and in New York in 1832, there was not enough uncontaminated water for the patients to drink. The last week of June and first week of July that year, Bellevue Hospital received 556 cases, of which 334 died by the first week of August. On the Fourth of July, former mayor Philip Hone wrote:

It is a lovely day, but very different from all the previous anniversaries of independence. The alarm about the cholera has prevented all the usual jollification under the public authority. There are no booths in Broadway, the parade which was ordered here has been countermanded, no corporation dinner and no ringing of bells.

Cholera victims were literally begging for clean water. By October, five hundred New Yorkers had died. The city responded with a ten-year project, damming the Croton River, a tributary of the Hudson, creating a reservoir, and building an aqueduct. With the project's completion in 1842, the city announced that water needs had been secured for the next one hundred years. By the 1860s, the city was expanding the reservoir to meet additional needs.

Cholera was not the only bug to arrive through the port. Once the Croton Reservoir system was built, it became apparent that New York had at some earlier point been invaded by the German cockroach, *Blattella germanica.* Now the cockroaches, dubbed Croton bugs, found a new transportation system through the wet pipes that serviced the city, thereby revealing their best secret—it is not food but water that cockroaches seek.

A huge holding tank to the Croton Reservoir was located in the newly expanded area of the city up on Fifth Avenue and Fortieth Street where the New York Public Library now stands, and with its walls and promenades it became a city park. Edgar Allan Poe wrote:

When you visit Gotham, you should ride out the Fifth Avenue, as far as the distributing reservoir; near Forty-Third Street, I believe. The prospect from the walk around the reservoir is particularly beautiful. You can see from this elevation,

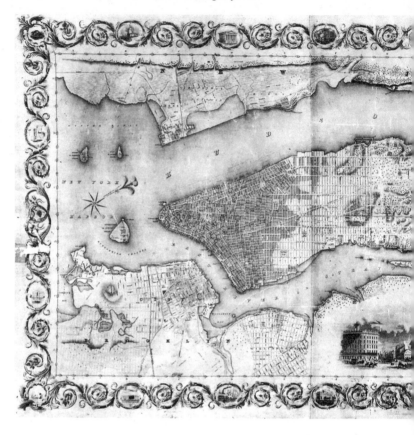

the north reservoir at Yorkville; the whole city to the Battery; with a large portion of the harbor, and long reaches of the Hudson and East rivers.

Philip Hone, on the other hand, wrote in his diary for October 12, 1842:

Nothing is talked of or thought of in New York but Croton water; fountains, aqueducts, hydrants, and hose attract our at-

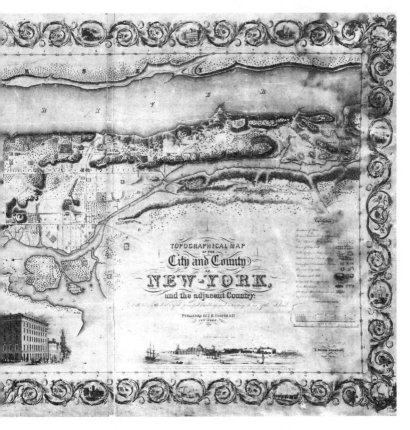

*This 1836 map shows that most of Manhattan above 12th Street
is still countryside with streams, marshes, woods, and swamps.*
COLLECTION OF THE NEW-YORK HISTORICAL SOCIETY

tention and impede our progress through the streets. Political spouting has given way to water-spouts, and the free current of water has diverted the attention of people from the vexed questions of the confused state of the national currency. It is astonishing how popular the introduction of water is among all classes of our citizens, and how cheerfully they acquiesce in the enormous expense which will burden them and their posterity with taxes to the latest generation.

Hone continued in this vein for some time afterward, referring to political rhetoric as "a great spouting" and generally regarding an urban water supply as a superfluous luxury.

Manhattan grew so rapidly that New Yorkers had not thought to provide the transportation for what was becoming more than a short walk. Charles Mackay wrote in the 1850s, "The New Yorkers consider themselves and are considered by others a fast people; but they have no Hansom and, indeed, no cabs of any description. They have not yet advanced beyond the old hackney-coach with two horses, which disappeared from the streets of London more than twenty-five years ago."

But even New York's fiercest critics agreed that the city had two good things, oysters and Broadway. Even British visitors Fanny Trollope and Charles Dickens, who praised little about America, praised Broadway. Charles Mackay, who praised much about America, wrote, "There is no street in London that can be declared superior, or even equal, all things considered, to Broadway. Broadway monopolizes nearly all the good pavement as well as cleanliness of New York."

Broadway was fine, but nearby, that once sylvan setting, the Collect, was becoming infamous. Abandoned was the proposal of Pierre L'Enfant, the engineer who designed Washington, D.C., who wanted to clean up the pond and landscape the surrounding area so that as the city expanded it would have a central park.

Manhattanites had their vision set farther uptown. Arguing that it would give the city the international panache of a London or Paris, in 1853 the wealthy merchants of Manhattan convinced the state to give the city authority to take over more than seven hundred uptown acres and build the first landscaped public park in the United States, Central Park.

The idea of making the pond the center of a canal from the Hudson to the East River had also been rejected. The prospering city would have had the funds to clean up the Collect, but they decided on what they thought to be a more cost-effective solution. In 1807, the city council spent five cents a load, a total of $3,095.92, on hauling dirt to the Collect and filling it in. By 1813, the pond had been completely filled in and the neighboring hilltop once favored by picnickers was leveled. Not for the last time, the city's solution was to level the neighborhood and turn it over to real-estate speculators. Those who had industries around the Collect hung on to their land. The reasoning was that as Manhattan expanded north, anyone who owned an empty lot ready for development in the middle of the city could eventually sell it for a fortune. Wealthy leading Manhattan families also invested in the area. But while the wealthy were eager to invest, they did not want to live there. No one really did, because it was associated with dampness, filth, and disease. The engineers had dried out the land where the pond had been, but the earth remained moist and muddy and houses would shift and even tilt. The slightest rain or snow could flood all the basements in the neighborhood. Mosquitoes and disease still bred in the dampness. All that was left of the waterway was an open sewer that ran to Canal Street.

The island at the center where executions had taken place was turned into a prison, nicknamed the Tombs, because the building was modeled after a drawing of an Egyptian tomb. The first execution at the Tombs took place in 1839. A man had married a Hot Corn Girl, as the famously beautiful corn venders on the streets of the Collect were called. Because of their beauty, they were reputed to earn a good living hawking corn. But after marriage it turned out the earnings of this beautiful Hot Corn Girl were not what her new husband had expected, and so he killed her, which became the first capital crime in the short-lived prison, which soon was replaced because it began to sink in the landfill.

The landlords had built wooden buildings two or two-and-a-half stories high in the Collect, suitable for shops and a shopkeeper's apartment above. But only people who had no other choices moved into the neighborhood. By 1825, with the immigrant population of New York City a little more than 10 percent, the Collect—it was still called the Collect for years—was one-quarter immigrants and another 15 percent free blacks. Then, in 1845, a blight struck the potato crop of Ireland, a nation so impoverished that potatoes were the population's principal food source. Hundreds of thousands starved to death, and between 1847 and 1854, 1.6 million Irish, about a fifth of the population, moved to the United States. By 1855, 51 percent of New Yorkers were foreign-born. The Collect was 72 percent foreign-born.

The immigrants went to the Collect and the landlords, finding that the neighborhood needed more but cheaper apartments, broke up their two-and-a-half-story houses into numerous small, one-room apartments, some even without windows. The landlords did not maintain the buildings because the taxes on new, well-cared-for housing were considerably higher than on dilapidated buildings with many apartments—tenant houses or tenements as they became labeled in the 1840s. According to newspaper accounts, tenement apartments were barely furnished. Few tables, chairs, or even beds were to be found. The tenants slept on piles of dirty rags or straw. There was a great deal of outrage about the discovery of men and women together in various states of undress and horror that whites, blacks, and Asians were all mixed together. "White and Black, Black and White, all hugemsnug together," in the words of one of the first of many tourists to go slumming in the Collect, Colonel Davy Crockett. Crockett, giving New York street toughs their due, also wrote, "I thought I would rather risk myself in an Indian fight than venture among these creatures after night."

As more moved in, spaces got smaller, a phenomenon familiar to many New Yorkers. But these tenements were carved up so that some rooms did not have a high enough ceiling for a man to stand erect. Up to a dozen people could be living on the floor in one small, window-less room. Some lived in basements, which were especially unpleasant because outhouses were overused and the waste often flooded base-ments in a strong rain. According to the *New York Tribune*, in 1850 the Sixth Ward, which was mostly made up of the Collect, had 285 base-ments with 1,156 occupants. Doctors working in the neighborhood said they could immediately spot cellar dwellers by their pale skin and a musty unpleasant smell that they could never lose.

The most infamous street in the infamous quarter was Little Water Street, a short passageway to Cow Bay. Cow Bay was a small open space that had been a cove in the Collect where cows drank. Little Water Street was at least six inches deep in waste and lined on both sides with clapboard tenements, one called "the Gates of Hell," another "Jacob's Ladder" after the decrepit outdoor stairway that was its only entrance. The tenements were connected by underground passages where robberies and murders were committed and, it was said, the victims bodies' concealed. An 1854 book called *Hot Corn* ad-vised anyone who went to Cow Bay to "saturate your handkerchief with camphor, so that you can endure the horrid stench."

Along with poverty and squalor came prostitution. In the 1830s, Anthony Street between Centre and Orange had more houses of pros-titution than any other block in Manhattan, and that was saying some-thing, because nineteenth-century Manhattan was to a far greater extent than most New Yorkers cared to recognize an island of prostitution. In the 1820s, New York had an estimated two hundred brothels. By 1865, according to police reports, there were more than six hundred. Reform-minded doctors, studying the health conditions in the tenements of the Collect and adjacent neighborhoods, found five hundred brothels there alone. Prostitutes would sometimes service men on the floors of tenements where others were trying to sleep. Feeding the public's outrage, the prostitution, like everything else in the neighborhood, was integrated. Black and white women worked the same brothels and both serviced black and white customers.

Sometimes men rented out their wives and daughters for added income and used the family home as a brothel. Women who had been abandoned by their husbands or widowed without money would survive through prostitution. Daughters, even those who were barely teenagers, would sometimes work along with the mothers. Merchants would rent out their top floor to prostitutes. If they were liquor merchants, they would even throw in some refreshments.

The area along the East River, with its all-night ferries to Brooklyn and all-night food markets, was also a well-known prostitution district. Catching a late-night ferry could be a respectable cover for a man arranging a tryst.

The leading theaters of downtown New York—the Bowery, Chatham, Olympic, and Park—like their London counterparts, allowed prostitutes—of a better class than in the slums—in the third tier, where they were on display for any interested theatergoers. Some prostitutes were New York celebrities, turning up at the best parties. Julia Brown was one of the most famous midnineteenth-century prostitutes. A fabled predecessor, Eliza Bowen Jumel, born in 1775 to another well-known prostitute, grew up in the trade and was even briefly married to Aaron Burr.

Articles started appearing in New York newspapers about the deplorable conditions in the Collect. A letter to the editor on the neighborhood in the *Evening Post* dated September 21, 1826, concluded:

> Something ought to be done for the honour of the city, if for no other reason than to render the place less disgusting and pernicious, it being the resort of thieves and rogues of the lowest degree, and by its filthy state and villainous smells keeps respectable people from residing near it.

There was a growing outcry to simply raze the neighborhood, which in 1829 the press started referring to as "Five Points" after a five-pointed intersection where Anthony Street intersected Cross and Orange. Today it is where downtown meets Chinatown, the area at the foot of Pearl, Mulberry, and Mott Street below Canal Street. The idea of slum clearance was born. The fate of the Collect began a pattern that was to be repeated over the years throughout New York. A beautiful place is allowed to fall into disrepair, becoming the home of the poor and immigrants, who are the only ones willing to live there. Ignored and abused, it becomes an infamous slum and then there is an outcry to just level the terrible place and build something else.

Along with Davy Crockett, Charles Dickens, the phenomenally popular British novelist and inveterate slummer, was one of the early Five Points visitors. On his 1842 trip to America, already a literary star and just turning thirty, barely looking that old, he visited the slum.

It is usually said that Dickens came to America bearing a grudge because American copyright laws failed to guarantee him the enormous sums that his popularity in the United States should have earned him. But his account, *American Notes,* was certainly no more grumpy than *Domestic Manners of the Americans,* the journal that launched the literary career of Fanny Trollope on her disastrous 1827 trip to build a utopian community in America. The mother of the future novelist Anthony Trollope observed that "The Americans have certainly not the same *besoin* of being amused, as other people; they may be the wiser for this, perhaps, but it makes them less agreeable to a looker-on."

She also explained:

> Their large evening parties are supremely dull; the men sometimes play cards by themselves, but if a lady plays, it must not be for money; no ecarté, no chess; very little music, and that little lamentably bad. Among the blacks, I heard some good voices singing in tune; but I scarcely ever heard a white American, male or female, go through an air without being out of tune before the end of it; nor did I ever meet any trace of science in the singing I heard in society. To eat inconceivable quantities of cake, ice, and pickled oysters—and to shew half their revenue in silks and satins, seem to be the chief object they have in these parties.

Some visiting Brits even criticized the oysters themselves, most notably Thackeray in his comparison of eating an oyster to eating a baby. Frederick Marryat said that the oysters were "very plentiful and large," but he didn't like their taste. Charles Mackay, as he had been promised, did:

> The stranger can not but remark the great number of "Oyster Saloons," "Oyster and Coffee Saloons," and "Oyster and Lager Beer Saloons," which solicit him at every turn to stop

and taste. These saloons—many of them very handsomely fitted up—are, like the drinking saloons of Germany, situated in vaults or cellars, with steps from the street; but unlike the German models, they occupy the underground stories of the most stately palaces of that city. In these, as in the hotels, oysters as large as a lady's hand are to be had at all hours, either from the shell, as they are commonly eaten in England, or cooked in twenty, or perhaps, in forty or a hundred different ways. Oysters pickled, stewed, baked, roasted, fried, and scolloped; oysters made into soups, patties and puddings; oysters with condiments and without condiments; oysters for breakfast dinner and supper; oysters without stint or limit—fresh as the fresh air, and almost as abundant—are daily offered to the palates of the Manhattanese, and appreciated with all the gratitude which such bounty of nature ought to inspire.

Dickens's *American Notes* was regarded as an insult by most Americans in part because he chose to examine and criticize at length slavery, the prison system, and even an asylum for the mentally ill, which he, not always a reliable reporter, identified as being "on Long Island, or Rhode Island: I forget which." He said that American men spit and that they pirated books, both of which were true. He thought the press was abominable and the prairie not as good as Salisbury Plain and also lacking a Stonehenge. But the ill-feelings of Americans may also in part stem from what the Frenchman Alexis de Tocqueville, in probably the best of the nineteenth-century European books on America, *Democracy in America,* identified as an American trait: an unyielding resentment of any criticism from abroad. *American Notes,* in fact, has many favorable things to say about New York. For that matter Fanny Trollope loved New York, was one of the first to declare it the leading American city, and found it pleasantly different from the rest of America:

New York, indeed, appeared to us, even when we saw it by a soberer light, a lovely and a noble city. To us who had been so long traveling through half-cleared forests, and sojourning among an "I'm-as-good-as-you" population, it seemed, perhaps, more beautiful, more splendid, and more refined than it might have done, had we arrived there directly from London; but making every allowance for this, I must still declare that I think New York one of the finest cities I ever saw, and as much superior to every other in the Union, (Philadelphia not excepted,) as London to Liverpool, or Paris to Rouen.

In *American Notes* Dickens wrote:

The tone of the best society in this city, is like that of Boston; here and there, it may be, with a greater infusion of the mercantile spirit, but generally polished and refined, and always most hospitable. The houses and tables are elegant; the hours later and more rakish; and there is, perhaps, a greater spirit of contention in reference to appearances, and the display of wealth and costly living. The ladies are singularly beautiful.

Of course Dickens also wrote that these beautiful American women fade at an early age and were not very shapely. But it was not "the best society" that most intrigued him. He ventured into Five Points, which he did not treat with his customary affection for London slums. "All that is loathsome, drooping, and decaying is here."

For all his criticism, Dickens made it fashionable to visit America's worst slum as the great writer had. Small groups under police escort would wander the streets to ogle the poor, stare at alcoholism and debauchery, be voyeurs in what *New York Tribune* writer George C. Foster called "the great central ulcer of wretchedness."

Despite the notable lack of *besoins* among Americans, they did have a good time in Five Points—those who were willing to risk exposure to muggers and gang warfare. Dance halls were open all night and throbbed to fusions of Irish fiddles and African drums. Dickens complained of the lack of amusement in New York. "What are these suckers of cigars and swallowers of strong drinks, whose hats and legs we see in every possible variety of twist doing, but amusing themselves," Dickens wrote. But once he found Almack's, a black-run dance hall on Orange Street at the heart of Five Points, his sourness abruptly changes to goofy elation. He noted a "corpulent black fiddler, and his friend who plays the tambourine, stamp upon the boarding of the small raised orchestra in which they sit, and play a lively measure. Five or six couples come upon the floor, marshaled by a lively young Negro, who is the wit of the assembly and the greatest dancer known." Dickens excitedly described the dancing as giving "new brightness in the very candles."

What especially thrilled him was a sixteen-year-old boy named William Henry Lane from Rhode Island. He had come to New York as a youth and moved to Five Points, where he pursued an African tradition of competitive dancing, imitating and outdoing other street dancers. He was called Mister Juba. His wild and rapid leg movements became so famous that in 1848, Mr. Juba performed in London. His blend of Irish jig and the African American shuffle is thought to be the origin of tap dancing.

Another pleasure of Manhattan slums that was seldom missed by tourists once Dickens discovered it was oyster cellars. A few years after the Dickens trip, William Carlisle, a British aristocrat, wrote in his *Travels in America,* "I cannot refrain from one, I fear rather sensual, allusion to the oyster cellars of New York. In no part of the world have I ever seen places of refreshment as attractive."

These New York restaurants ran the gamut from luxurious to sleazy. Some of the same clients visited both. Oyster cellars were situated in that nearly unique location, the halfway-underground, street-level cellar, a normal enough site in a city where many people lived in basements. Manhattan, a city that never wasted space, had a lot of basements.

Like bordellos, oyster cellars catered to different clientele depending on the neighborhood. Also as with bordellos, the menu was always similar, but the atmosphere and presentation greatly varied. Henry James mentions an oyster cellar in his novel *Washington Square,* as does Willa Cather in her short story "Coming Aphrodite." In the Cather story, Hedger, the solitary Washington Square painter, walks with his dog to an oyster restaurant.

> Behind the Square, Hedger and his dog descended into a basement oyster house where there were no tablecloths on the tables and no handles on the coffee cups, and the floor was covered with sawdust. . . .

Hedger, admittedly an oddball, ordered steak, which was available in some oyster cellars, along with raw, stewed, and a variety of other oyster dishes. The many oyster cellars on Canal Street originated "the Canal Street plan." This peculiarly American all-you-can-eat formula lent credence to the contention of Fanny Trollope and many other Europeans that Americans seek to eat "inconceivable quantities." Nineteenth-century New Yorkers took advantage of the six-cent

Canal Street plan to gobble down several dozen oysters at a sitting. If they ate too many, the management would give them one that had its shell loosely open in the hopes that after a few minutes, the avaricious client would be eating nothing for several days.

There is no record of how the denizens of rough dance halls and dark oyster cellars reacted to Dickens, the baby-faced young English visitor, but there is a clear record in *American Notes* that Dickens was smitten by both. He wrote that oyster cellars were marked not only by a red balloon, but also a sign that read OYSTERS IN EVERY STYLE, and added that "They tempt the hungry most at night, for then dull candles glimmering inside, illuminate these dainty words, and make the mouths of idlers water, as they read and linger."

A balloon made of bright red muslin stretched over wire or rattan and lit by a candle was always hung over the steps leading down to the cellar, which might be dank and forbidding or might be sumptuously decorated. It is not by chance that oyster cellars were marked by a red light, the traditional sign of prostitution. While some oyster cellars were highly respectable gathering places for downtown businessmen, others reflected the ancient link between sex and oysters. Dickens was rumored to have both consumed a great many oysters and enjoyed the services of the famous Julia Brown. Only the first of these two rumors comes with any documentation, but to the thinking of many New Yorkers at the time, the two went hand in hand.

Dickens's reputation is more difficult to account for than that of the oyster, which, like the author, is notoriously fertile but unlike him, has a somewhat erotic appearance. Romans regarded oysters as aphrodisiacal and included them on the menu at orgies. Of course they were also on the menu at dinners with more humdrum endings. Marcus Aurelius's doctor, Galen, suggested eating oysters to remedy a waning sex drive. Byron asserted the "amatory" power of oysters in

Don Juan. Giovanni Casanova, the Venetian adventurer and notorious seducer, believed in the power of oysters and was said to eat some fifty before breakfast. In Samuel Johnson's eighteenth-century dictionary and in English literature for several centuries earlier, including Shakespeare, *oysterwoman* or *oysterwench* could mean either a woman who sells oysters or a woman of low moral character. Oysters are credited for various acts deemed virile. Napoléon always ate them before going into battle, or so it was rumored by his enemies. In modern times it has been found that oysters are rich in zinc, one of the building blocks of testosterone. Prostitution and oysters, often found together, were the two most famous New York experiences. In 1850, George G. Foster wrote this description of oyster cellars:

The oyster-cellars, with their bright lamps casting broad gleams of red light across the street, are now in full tide, and every instant sees them swallow up at one entrance a party of rowdy and half-drunken young men, on their way to the theater, the gambling-house, the bowling-saloon, or the brothel—or most likely to all in turn—while another is vomited up the other stairway, having already swilled their fill of oysters and bad brandy, and garnished their reeking mouths each with an atrocious cigar, which the barkeeper recommended as "full-flavored." If we step down one of these wide entrances, we shall see a long counter gorgeously decked with crystal decanters and glasses, richly carved and gilt and the wall ornamented with a voluptuous picture of a naked Venus—perhaps the more seductive from being exquisitely painted. Before the long marble bar are arranged some dozen or score of individuals, waiting their turns for liquor—while on the other side a man with his shirt sleeves rolled up and his face in a fiery glow, seems to be pulling long ribbons of julep out of a tin cup. At the other end of the room is a row of little stalls, each fitted up with its gasburner, its red curtain, its little table and voluptuous picture, and all occupied with busy eaters. In the rear of these boxes is a range of larger apartments called "private rooms," where men and women enter promiscuously, eat, drink and make merry, and disturb the whole neighborhood with their obscene and disgusting revels, prolonged far beyond midnight. The women of course are all of one kind—but among the men you would find, if you looked

*A Five Points
oyster cellar as
depicted in
George Foster's*
NEW YORK BY
GASLIGHT, 1850

curiously, reverend judges and juvenile delinquents, pious and devout hypocrites, and the undisguised libertines and debauchees. Gamblers and Fancy men, high flyers and spoonies, genteel pick-pockets and burglars, even sometimes mingle in the detestable orgies of these detestable caverns; and the shivering policeman who crawls sleepily by at the dead of night, and mechanically raps his bludgeon upon the pavement as he hears the boisterous mirth below, may be reminding a grave functionary of the city that it is time to go home to his wife and children after the discharge of his "arduous public duties."

The women were "all of one kind," but the oysters came in a variety of types. Bluepoints, Saddle Rocks, Prince's Bays, City Islands, Spuyten Duyvels, Rockaways or Jamaica Bays, and Canarsees were considered some of the best. For the oyster aficionado there were smaller subdivisions. Just among Great South Bay oysters, any of which might be called Bluepoints, there were Fire Island Salts and Gardiner Salts, both of which were thick-shelled and salty tasting. New York merchants also bought various varieties from Cape Cod and the Chesapeake Bay.

The city turned to Downing's, the most celebrated oyster cellar, to cater Dickens's introduction to twenty-five hundred of New York's elite. Because of the author's nickname, Boz, the event was popularly known as "the Boz Ball." As a youth, Dickens had given one of his younger brothers the nickname Moses, and ridiculing the nasal way the child pronounced it, Dickens took to saying "Boses," which led to his own nickname, Boz.

Downing's at the time was *the* caterer of official events. When a company opened, a ship was launched, a steam-powered vessel first crossed the Atlantic, the Erie Railroad was extended north of the city, a bank or insurance company elected its board members, Downing's catered. When Philip Hone, the self-made man who had risen from poverty to be mayor, learned of his unprecedented catering bill of $2,200 for the event, he referred to Downing as "the great man of oysters."

The Boz Ball had thousands scrambling through what Hone called "Pickwickian" decorations to get to Downing's oysters. The crowd, as Mrs. Trollope might have predicted, was consumed with what Hone termed "the unintellectual operation of eating and drinking" and the dance floor was so crowded that the dancing was described by one participant as "like dancing in a cane break."

Hone, a keynote speaker for the event, who later described Dickens as "a small, bright-eyed, intelligent looking young fellow," wrote:

> The agony is over; the Boz Ball, the greatest affair of modern times, the tallest compliment ever paid to a little man, the fullest libation ever poured upon the altar of the muse, came off last evening in fine style.

But not for Boz was the agony over. Four nights later was the banquet in his honor at the premier hotel, City Hotel, occupying an entire block of Broadway between Cedar and Thames, with food by Gardiner's, reputedly the city's most elegant caterer. The first three of the extensive five courses included oysters. The first course consisted of three soups, including oyster "potage," and fish—trout, bass, and shad—all products of the Hudson River. The second course offered six different cold dishes, including oysters in aspic, as well as roasted sirloin, saddle of mutton, goose, veal, turkeys, and capons—note the plural—and a choice of five boiled meats, including boiled turkey with oyster sauce and stewed terrapin. At last the entrées arrived, which included a total of nineteen dishes including "Oyster Pies." Next was the game course, all from New York's woodlands: wild turkey, canvasback ducks, venison, and bear. This was followed by the fourth course, twelve desserts and six decorative pyramids. The last course was nuts and fruit. The soups came out at seven and the nuts at midnight and Dickens left a half hour later. Americans had again lived up to their reputation for eating fast and copiously.

The menu listed the soups in French, the fish, the cold dishes, roasts, and boiled meats in English. The main courses were in French translated into curious English—a *timballe* became a tamball. The French was also curious and in spots misspelled. Seventy years later, Julian Street, a magazine writer, would comment, "Broadway eats French better than it speaks it." Gardiner's charged the City Hotel $2,500 for the dinner serving 237 people, slightly more than Downing's had charged for oysters and hors d'oeuvres for 2,500 people at the Boz Ball.

On February 4, 1842, ten days before the Boz Ball, when Boz was still in Boston, George Templeton Strong had written prophetically:

The Bostonians are making horrid asses of themselves with Mr. Charles Dickens, poor man. He'll have his revenge, though, when he gets home and takes up his pen again. How people will study his next productions to see if they can find any portraits! However, we shall be fully as bad, with our Boz Ball.

That was exactly what happened with Dickens's next two works, *American Notes* and the novel *Martin Chuzzlewit,* neither of which required careful study to find the attacks. He described oysters disappearing down "gaping gullets—a solemn and awful sight to see. Dyspeptic individuals bolted their food in wedges, spare men with lank rigid cheeks, unsatisfied from the destruction of heavy dishes, glared with watchful eyes upon the pastry. But there was one comfort. It was over soon." As for Downing's and Gardiner's costly cuisine, the most celebrated food in New York, Dickens wrote that Americans ate "piles of indigestible matter." And this was from a man whose wife—Hone described her as "a little fat English-looking woman"—had penned a cookbook under a pseudonym in which she offered such refutable delights of digestion as suet dumplings and batter pudding.

As for the young, diminutive Boz himself, he made clear that he would rather be in the intimacy of an oyster cellar in Five Points.

At other downward flights of steps, are other lamps, marking the whereabouts of oyster cellars—pleasant retreats, say I: not only by reason of their wonderful cookery of oysters, pretty nigh as large as cheese plates . . . but because of all kinds of eaters of fish, or flesh, or fowl, in these latitudes, the swallowers of oysters, alone or not gregarious, but subduing themselves, as it were, to the nature of what they work in, and copying the coyness of the thing they eat, do sit apart in curtained boxes, and consort by twos, not by two hundreds.

Thomas Downing had been born to a free Virginia black family in 1791 and was to become one of the most respected black men in

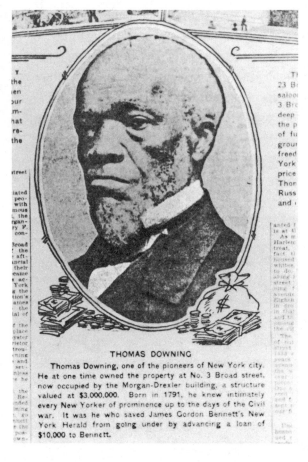

THOMAS DOWNING

Thomas Downing, one of the pioneers of New York city. He at one time owned the property at No. 3 Broad street, now occupied by the Morgan-Drexler building, a structure valued at $3,000,000. Born in 1791, he knew intimately every New Yorker of prominence up to the days of the Civil war. It was he who saved James Gordon Bennett's New York Herald from going under by advancing a loan of $10,000 to Bennett.

pre–Civil War New York, or as George Templeton Strong put it in 1854, a "venerable Ethiop." His parents had been freed because a traveling preacher had convinced the leading landowner of their area, Captain John Downing, that no one could be a member in good standing of the Methodist Church and a slave owner at the same time.

Like some of the blacks who settled in Sandy Ground, Downing came from Chincoteague, Virginia, Chesapeake oyster country, and he was an experienced oysterman when he moved to New York City in 1819. Chincoteague is an island village on an Atlantic inlet just south of the Maryland state line. During his youth, Downing had worked the small plot of land his parents had bought, dug clams, and caught terrapin, and he raked oysters. He loved eating oysters. He probably went to New York to be in the thriving city oyster trade.

But it was more than just his oyster background that drove him to the oyster-cellar business. In the first half of the nineteenth century, it was widely accepted in New York that oyster cellars, like dance halls and many taverns, were run by blacks. Cato's Tavern, a popular drinking spot for leading politicians four miles north as travelers entered Manhattan, was also run by a black man. Working-class black New Yorkers often converted their rental apartments into oyster cellars and dance halls on the weekends. Another African American niche in New York was running summer outdoor cafés called pleasure gardens, specializing in tall, cool drinks and ice cream.

Downing had followed returning troops to Philadelphia at the end of the War of 1812. There he met his wife. When he got to New York, he rented an apartment to live in at 33 Pell Street and bought a small skiff, which he rowed across the Hudson to the oyster beds in New Jersey, tonged for oysters, and then rowed back with a load to sell before dark. His son George described him as an unusually energetic man. His customers increased every year and he acquired a reputation for excellent "fat" oysters. In 1825, Downing opened his oyster cellar at 5 Broad Street.

He had five children, all born in New York City and educated at the African Free School, a school system established by abolitionists, with whom he was involved for decades.

For businessmen who preferred discussing their affairs rather than having them, Downing's was the favorite oyster cellar, conveniently located near the Customs House, the banks, the Merchants Exchange, and important stores. It stood on the same street where the first oyster cellar had opened in 1763, a street long associated with selling oysters.

Between 1830 and 1860, Downing's was a place where oysters were eaten and deals were made. The senior partner of a leading banking house described the New York merchant's life:

> To rise early in the morning, to get breakfast, to go down to the counting house of the firm, to open and read letters—to go out and do some business, either at the Custom house, bank or elsewhere, until twelve, then to take lunch and a glass of wine at Delmonico's; or a few raw oysters at Downing's, to sign checks . . .

Downing's was also a popular spot for politicians. Like other oyster cellars, it was marked by a red balloon over dank sidewalk steps, but the interior of Downing's eschewed the seedy, vulgar look of the oyster cellars farther uptown and was decorated with mirrored arcades, damask curtains, gilded carvings, sparkling chandeliers, and plush carpeting.

Downing made oyster cellars respectable, at least his, which was a family restaurant where a man could bring his wife. Downing's was the one oyster cellar that respectable women could go to, provided they were accompanied by their husbands. Prostitutes were the only unescorted women ever seen in restaurants, and only in restaurants that allowed prostitution. One oyster cellar came to terms with the alleged moral ambiguities of leaving women alone with oysters by founding a women-only oyster cellar, the Ladies Oyster Shop, a forerunner of the Ladies' Fourteenth Street Oyster House in the 1880s, on 4 East Fourteenth Street just off Union Square. It reflected a growing movement. A Ladies' Bowling Alley was also opened.

In 1835, Downing expanded, renting the basements of the two neighboring buildings. Numbers 5 and 7 Broad Street held the basement restaurant and Number 3 became an oyster storage cellar with running salt water. Though he now raked in too much money to be raking oysters, Downing was known to prowl the harbor in the dark of night looking for the best deals on the best oysters. He would sometimes rent a skiff, row out in the harbor to intercept an incoming sloop or schooner, board her, and buy the best of the catch. Then he would row back to the market, which was an auction, and bid on the vessel's remaining oysters, which he had no intention of buying. When the vessel reached market the price for his leftover catch would already be high. The oyster captains liked Downing, and when they came to his cellar he would make sure that they were treated as well as the leading politicians and businessmen.

Downing's offered a wide variety of oyster dishes, but the standbys were raw, fried, and stewed. His son George described steamed oysters at Downing's:

Ladies and gentlemen with towels in hand, and an English oyster knife made for the purpose, would open their own oysters, drop into the burning hot concaved shell a lump of sweet butter and other seasoning and partake of a treat. Yes, there was a taste imparted by the saline and lime substance in which the juice of the oyster reached boiling heat that made it a delicate morsel.

Food writers always emphasized that smaller oysters could be used for stewing, fritters, or pies, but frying was to be done with large oysters. This is an excellent recipe for frying from the time of Downing's that most health-conscious people today will miss out on.

⚜ Fried Oysters

Take large oysters from their own liquor into a thickly folded napkin to dry them off; then make a tablespoonful of lard or beef fat hot, in a thick bottomed frying pan, add to it a half salt-spoonful of salt; dip each oyster in wheat flour, or cracker rolled fine, until it will take up no more, then lay them in the pan, hold it over a gentle fire until one side is a delicate brown; turn the other by sliding a fork under it; five minutes will fry them after they are in the pan. Oysters may be fried in butter but it is not so good; lard and butter half and half is very nice for frying. Some persons like a very little of the oyster liquor poured in the pan after the oysters are done, let it boil up, then put it in the dish with the oysters; when wanted for breakfast this should be done.

—MRS. T. J. CROWEN,
*The American System of
Cookery*, 1864

Oyster stew is a very old concept that seems to have changed slightly with each generation. In the heyday of Downing's, the second quarter of the nineteenth century, which many food historians consider to be the best age of American cuisine, Eliza Leslie, a Philadelphian, was recognized throughout the still-young country as the most reliable authority. She made a batter with eggs for frying oysters, which might be better than Mrs. Crowen's later recipe, but Miss Leslie fried in butter, which Mrs. Crowen justly criticized. Butter cannot be heated to a high enough temperature for true frying. But then again, it always tastes good. This is Miss Leslie's recipe for stewed oysters. Her admonishment against flour-thickening refers to a horrible practice of the early nineteenth century in many places, including New York.

> Put the oysters into a sieve, and set it on a pan to drain the liquor from them. Then cut off the hard part, and put the oysters into a stew pan with some whole pepper, a few blades of mace and some grated nutmeg. Add a small piece of butter rolled in flour. Then pour over them about half the liquor, or a little more. Set the pan on hot coals, and simmer them gently about five minutes. Try one, and if it tastes raw cook them a little longer. Make some thin slices of toast, having cut off the crust. Butter the toast and lay it in the bottom of a deep dish. Put the oysters upon it with the liquor in which they were stewed.
>
> The liquor of oysters should never be thickened by stirring in flour. It spoils the taste, and gives them a sodden and disagreeable appearance, and is no longer practiced by good cooks. A little cream is a fine improvement to stewed oysters.

> —ELIZA LESLIE,
> *Miss Leslie's Directions for*
> *Cookery*, 1851

Twentieth-century *New Yorker* writer Joseph Mitchell, who interviewed many oystermen over stew, observed: "It isn't easy to carry on a conversation while eating oyster stew," which would have been useful advice for those who arranged amorous trysts in New York's oyster cellars.

CHAPTER EIGHT

Making Your Own Bed

—

I have never seen any city so admirably adapted for commerce.

—CAPTAIN FREDERICK MARRYAT,
A Diary in America, 1837

B y 1842, about $6 million worth of oysters were being sold every year to restaurants, fish stores, and street vendors in New York City. Most of these oysters entered the Manhattan market from barges tied up on either the Hudson or East River. These barges were wholesale houses, storage bins, and packinghouses. Typically an oyster barge was a two-story wooden vessel with a curved deck for drainage. On one end, oystermen would tie up their boots and unload, while on the other, pedestrians and wagons from the street would pull up to buy oysters.

The oystermen could not afford to purchase waterfront property for an oyster market, but as early as 1805, oyster sloops started tying up at Coenties Slip, on the East River, just above Broad Street. These sloops served as oyster depots where the catch could be culled, sorted, packaged, and sold. Coenties Slip was a commercially choice spot, close to where the mouth of the East River met the harbor. As the port of New York grew, the oystermen were under considerable pressure to cede the spot to larger commercial interests. Finally, in 1845, the oyster boats moved to Catherine Slip, farther up the East River and close to the Catherine Market, or to Vie or Bear docks on the Hudson near the Washington Market. Because sloops did not have enough deck space for preparing oysters and lacked cabin space for conducting business, they were gradually replaced by canal barges.

By midcentury, oyster dealers were having special barges built, sometimes called arks or scows. The first had small decks, only twelve feet by thirty feet. By the 1880s, at least thirty barges were tied up along the Manhattan waterfront, and they had become two-story structures up to seventy-five feet long and twenty-four feet wide. They would be tied up together in a row, fixed to the waterfront by a gangplank the width of the barge, so that they looked like a row of two-story shopfronts except that they bobbed up and down in the current.

This row constituted a floating wholesale oyster market, with shuckers and cullers and barrelers working on deck and deals being negotiated upstairs. They were often painted pink, though yellow and green were also common. They often had ornate overhanging roofs and balconies. Across the top, in embellished nineteenth-century lettering, would be painted the name of the company. J. & J. W. Ellsworth, Fraser, Houseman, Silesby, and Still were all leading New York oyster companies. The 1840s and fifties, when the oyster barge developed, coincided with the emergence of large oyster companies in New York. Each barge flew a large American flag over the sign.

A midnineteenth century wholesale ad showing oyster barges tied up in the East River.
COLLECTION OF THE NEW-YORK HISTORICAL SOCIETY

The merchants decorated their barges with bunting, pennants, and other ornaments for the opening of oyster season in September and sometimes for national holidays.

The upper-floor office was fairly elegant, with an ornate oak desk and leather chairs. Also on this floor was the storeroom where oysters were kept in cedar tubs and beside them oak bushel baskets and barrels. On the lower deck, seated in a row on three-legged stools, sat shuckers, usually tough, burly men. In front of them the deck was covered with oysters, with more lying in seawater in the hold below. The hold was deep, and so well designed that as long as the hatches were closed, the oysters would stay cool in summer and could not freeze in the coldest winter. An oyster barge was usually designed to hold about seven hundred bushels at a time. A bushel averaged about 250 or 300 oysters, but a basket held only 150 extras and could carry 15,000 seed oysters. At the peak of the oyster industry in the late nineteenth century, at any moment at least six million oysters were on barges tied up at the waterfront.

Wagoneers would lead their teams onto the sloping gangplanks and position them for loading. While retail trade was going out the gangplank, wholesale trade was coming in the rear from the masted sloops that docked behind the barges. Sure-footed strongmen called carriers hoisted heavy baskets of oysters on their shoulders, walking a narrow plank from sloop to scow, the board bowing under the weight of their load as they walked like practiced tightrope artists across the bouncing plank.

Between twenty-five and forty oyster carriers worked on each river, and their job was exclusively to carry oysters, earning ten cents for every thousand toted. A thousand oysters was considered to be seven small and four large baskets. A successful carrier was said to earn thirty dollars, a respectable salary at the time, but to earn the thirty dollars a week he would have to haul five thousand oysters a day in a six-day week—thirty-five small baskets and twenty large ones every day. A "small" one-bushel basket of oysters weighed eighty pounds and a barrel contained three bushels.

Some sloops would leave after unloading, but many local sloops would tie up all night at the barges and leave at first light for the oyster beds. Sloops came in not only from different parts of New York Harbor but from Long Island, Connecticut, Rhode Island, even Cape Cod and the Chesapeake Bay.

According to a May 10, 1853, *New York Herald* article, the nine barges moored at Oliver Slip near the Catherine Market annually earned a half-million dollars in oyster sales, and the dealers who bought their oysters sold them for about a million dollars every year.

But, according to the same article, a larger market with twelve barges opposite the Washington Market did far more business.

In 1871, a New York newspaper offered this description:

When the wind changes, the fleet comes up the bay, and then there is a busy scene in the neighborhood off pier No. 54. The dock and its approaches are covered with cartmen, wagons and horses, stevedores, and oyster dealers. The vessels are fastened to the wharf by means of strong hawsers, and the hatches are off fore and aft. In the hold are men filling baskets rapidly, and others stand on deck, rail, and pierstring, ready to pass them to the cart being loaded. All is rush, bustle and trade, flavored with copious dashes of profanity. In front of the scow-warehouses are men continually employed on these days, filling barrels with oysters and heading them up. Inside of the scows dozens of men are opening, while others can them, ready for transmission by rail to Canada, country hotels, and restaurants. All day long, until the cargoes, which are always bespoken, are landed, the work goes on, and when they are discharged the vessels are sent away immediately for more.

It is noteworthy that even in the 1870s, the cartman, a solitary man with a one-horse open-bed carriage, was still an important component in New York City street commerce. It is clear from an 1812 commercial directory of Manhattan that in the early part of the century, cartmen had been the single most plentiful source of employment in New York City. Anyone who had goods to move hired a cartman. They were a ubiquitous and controversial element of perilous Manhattan traffic, notorious for rushing their carts closely past pedestrians, allegedly singling out attractive women to terrorize. Washington Irving satirically commented, "Saw a cartman run down a small boy on Broadway today. What of it? Served him well. Shouldn't have been there in the first place."

Cartman rates were fixed by law—the rates of cartage. Oysters were one of the better-paying loads. In 1858, a cartman could charge thirty-one cents for each load of oysters. This was not as good as the seventy-five cents allowed for furniture, but was better than a load of bricks, three bales of cotton, five barrels of beef, twenty bushels of salt, or a load of wheat, each of which was only twenty-five cents.

The commercial demands for Manhattan waterfront space kept growing. An oyster barge lacked the prestige, influence, and eco-

Photo by Berenice Abbott of oyster barges (houses) on South Street and Pike Slip on the East River under the Manhattan side of the Manhattan Bridge.

MUSEUM OF THE CITY OF NEW YORK

nomic value of a transatlantic steamer. As more steamers came to New York Harbor, the city kept having the rows of barges moved to new locations. On the Hudson, still known for most of the nineteenth century as the North River, markets that had been on the Vesey Street pier were moved to Spring Street, then West Street, then Christopher Street in Greenwich Village, which from 1865 to 1898 was the central oyster market of Manhattan. Then the barges were moved up to Tenth Street, then to the East River, and their final site in 1912 was near the Manhattan Bridge, though a barge owned by Geo. Still Inc. was tied up in the East River near the Brooklyn Bridge until the early 1940s. From 1898 to 1913, the foreign commerce of the port increased by 131 percent, but wharfage space increased by less than 25 percent. In 1914, the New York Merchants Association declared that the biggest problem facing the city was congestion in the harbor.

Though constantly pushed to another pier by larger industries, during the course of the nineteenth century the floating oyster market became an ever-greater economic force as the oyster trade became more concentrated. According to *The New York Times* in 1883, at least two hundred sloops tied up every day to unload on Manhattan oyster barges. In addition they were receiving oysters by steamboat from Connecticut and the Chesapeake Bay. On September 9, 1883, *The New York Times* quoted one of the larger oyster dealers:

"This consolidation of the oyster interests is one of the most important steps that have ever been taken by the trade," said Mr. J.W. Boyle. "It is proposed to pool our issues, hire a hall, and organize an Exchange, just as produce merchants and stock brokers have done. It won't be long before all of this is accomplished. The oyster business is growing so tremendously that it will be necessary to unite in order to protect it."

Most of these ambitious ideas never became reality because though a huge volume of oysters was sold, the prices remained low, limiting the economic importance of the industry. Most of the jobs in the trade were not even full-time. The key to the wholesale oyster business was moving bulk. Frequently visitors to New York would comment on the low oyster prices. With the exception of crises such as the meager harvest in January 1857, prices remained remarkably stable throughout most of the nineteenth century. In the 1880s, top-quality oysters, which took at least three years to grow, an acre of beds yielding only five hundred oysters in a harvest, were selling for between $1.00 and $1.50 a basket. An 1881 report on the oyster industry said that prices of New York oysters had not greatly changed over the past fifty years. George Augustus Sala wrote in his 1883 travel memoir, *America Revisited*, "[In New York] oysters in every size and variety of flavor are as cheap as oranges are at Havana—that is to say they may be bought for 'next to nothing.' " By 1896, oysters sold wholesale for three for a penny by the bushel.

Once New York oystermen changed from wild to planted oysters, the big New York oyster became a rarity because the economics were on the side of smaller oysters. Cullens, small low-grade oysters, sold for four or five dollars for a thousand oysters. If left growing in the beds another half year, they became boxes, which sold for seven to eight dollars for a basket containing 150 oysters. It took another eighteen months for a box to grow into an extra, but extras were worth fifteen to twenty dollars for a thousand. For oysters planted in the East River, the greatest profit came from high-quality box oysters. Faster-growing oysters such as Rockaways were most profitable as small cullens, used for stewing or fritters. This is because seed planted in Jamaica Bay reached market size in only four to six months. The same seed would have to grow for two to three years in the East River to reach the same size.

The low price of an oyster had to include the revenue of every stage in the New York oyster business—the oystermen's packinghouses, the oyster barges, the markets, the stands, cellars, and restaurants. The price of an individual oyster was kept low by dealing in enormous volume. Someone who rowed in a skiff and harvested the beds with tongs tried to land ten bushels every day. But if he used a sail-powered sloop, he tried to get almost thirty bushels. A steam dredger had to buy fuel and tried to bring in sixty bushels. If a shucker wanted to earn a living, he had to open thousands of oysters every day. A good shucker would spend no more than three seconds opening an oyster.

Every oyster region had its own tools and techniques for shucking oysters. The Massachusetts "stabber"—later adopted in New Jersey—was inserted in the bill end, while the hinge side was wedged on the bench with the left hand. The abductor muscle was cut first from the deep shell, then from the flat one. This was a fairly easy way to do it, but New Yorkers considered it too time-consuming.

The side knife was used in restaurants because it preserved the shell in good condition for serving. A good shucker could use a side knife quickly. The oyster was held in the left hand, deep shell down and hinge end away. The side knife was slipped between the shells—and this, as anyone who has ever opened oysters knows, is the great trick because it is not always easy to distinguish which fissure on an oyster shell is the real opening. The skilled shucker knew and immediately slipped the blade between the shells and sliced upward, cutting the abductor muscle from the top shell, which was then flipped aside with a turn of the wrist. That same wrist motion went full circle and brought the blade back under to free the oyster from the bottom shell. Done right, this was all accomplished in one fluid motion. Still, it was too much trouble for oysters destined for stews, pickling, or canning.

In New Haven, they had no time for these niceties and employed a hammer and a two-inch wedge of iron on an angle from a block of wood—"a cracking block." One whack of the hammer and the bill end of the oyster was snapped off, leaving an easy opening for a knife.

New York shuckers employed a number of techniques depending on the place and the purpose, but the most famously New York approach was the New York oyster knife used on the barges. Unlike the Massachusetts stabber, the side knife, or any of the others, the New York knife had no wooden handle but was a single piece of steel with a square end to crack the oysters open and a blade end to cut it from the shell.

In New England, New Jersey, and the South, enormous packing plants hired hundreds of full-time shuckers. But in New York, shucking was largely a seasonal job for longshoremen, deckhands, and other marine workers. It was estimated in 1881 that rarely were there more than 150 shuckers working at any one time in New York City.

Since shuckers worked side by side—three on a barge or hundreds in a packing plant—and the emphasis was always on speed because they were paid by the piece, it became popular for shuckers to amuse themselves with contests. There were many competitions in the New York oyster industry—the fastest run from Staten Island to Chesapeake and back with seed oysters, the fastest from Prince's Bay to Manhattan markets, the fastest to shovel seed overboard, the fastest tonger.

Shucking was an industry-wide competition that grew into regional contests—Manhattan against Long Island, or New Jersey versus New York, or New York versus New England, which was always a popular rivalry, or best in the Northeast, or North versus South. A contest between the two supposedly fastest shuckers on the Atlantic coast took place annually in a different place every year. When Manhattan was hosting it was held in Grand Central Terminal. The contests drew large crowds and heavy betting and were covered by major newspapers.

In 1885, one champion opened 2,300 oysters in two hours eighteen minutes and nineteen and a half seconds. But his competitor opened 2,500 in two hours twenty-three minutes and thirty-nine and three-fourths seconds. Even this, at slightly faster than seventeen oysters a minute, did not come close to the oysters-per-minute record. In the late 1870s, Rhode Island and New York champions went down to Philadelphia to take on the champions from the South. Billy Lowney, who opened oysters in the Robert Pettis shop in Providence, led the North, defeating the Southern champion by opening 100 oysters in three minutes and three seconds, establishing a new world record for 100 oysters. Most people could not pick up and put down 100 oysters in that amount of time. That was 100 oysters without breaking any shells, because in competition only unbroken oysters were counted.

Oyster-opening competitions continued and are still held today. But in the nineteenth and early twentieth century, they were annual events. In 1913, in Keyport, a New Jersey oyster center on Raritan Bay, the national championship was again decided. The competition came down to three men, one from Connecticut, one from Virginia, and one from Keyport. The Connecticut opener used the precision side-knife technique, while the other two used hammer and knife. According to local press they were the fastest openers in the world. The

Virginian had recently established a world record of opening forty-one gallons in one day's shift—more than ten thousand oysters.

Such contests were seen as evidence that shuckers' pay, based on enormous volume, was reasonable since they could easily open such quantities. The Keyport contest was covered by *The Oysterman and the Fisherman* magazine, which reported:

> The recent oyster opening contest held in Keyport, New Jersey was watched with considerable interest by those who are paying high prices to shuckers. The result of the contest was remarkable. The record time was 20 minutes and 23 seconds, and the number of oysters opened in this length of time was 500. The first prize was $300. The wholesale dealers of New York City pay their shuckers $1.00 for every thousand oysters opened. If we assume that this shucker could keep this record up for a working day of 10 hours, he would earn about $14.00, and if he worked six days a week, he would earn $84.00 per week, and the enormous salary of $336.00 per month. We do not wonder therefore that the New York oyster dealer thinks the cost of shucking is too high.

That was the shucker's workweek—ten hours a day, six days a week—and this was like calculating that if a sprinter can run a hundred yards at a certain speed, why not run a marathon at the same speed? The shucker could perform at a remarkable speed for twenty minutes, but if attempting to work a ten-hour day at that speed, he or she would soon collapse in exhaustion. Most shuckers opened between 500 and 750 oysters in an hour. An exceptionally fast shucker could open 1,000 oysters an hour. In the 1880s, when New York City shuckers were paid ten cents for opening a thousand oysters, most earned about three dollars a day. No modern invention has proved as efficient as a good shucker with an oyster knife.

The floating oyster markets were the middlemen between the oyster producers and the eleven central food markets located near the docks where products from around the state, the country, and the world were landed. By 1860, more than 12 million oysters were sold in New York markets annually. New York was the oyster-trading center of the world.

Twentieth-century New Yorkers used to go to Paris and marvel at the huge outdoor Les Halles central market until it was torn down in 1969 and replaced by a truckers' market on the southern edge of town. Few remember that New York markets were also lively all-night fairs for the general public. But by the twentieth century, the New York markets had lost their energetic social nature, their all-night restaurants and stands. The last were the Fulton, which was turned into an exclusively wholesale fish market and finally closed in 2005, and one of the oldest, the Washington Market, which was reduced to a produce market that was finally cleared to make way for the World Trade Center in 1968, a year before Paris closed Les Halles. Like the Collect, the markets were removed rather than cleaned up after decades of complaints about their condition. The Manhattan markets were moved to Hunts Point on the northern edge of the city, a site suitable for trucks but not city life. New Yorkers made exactly the same decision as the Parisians made, to move the markets despite their social value, away where the cities would not have to deal with their garbage and truck traffic.

But until the twentieth century, such sprawling, bustling outdoor food markets were so characteristic of New York that, like Les Halles in Paris, no tourist would come to the city without at least once experiencing a New York market. In 1836, James Fenimore Cooper commented that "It is difficult to name fish or fowl, or beast that is not to be obtained in the markets of New York." This was probably not surprising for a city whose two most famous attributes were commercial prowess and gluttony.

When the British took over in 1664, there were already three markets near the East River. Quickly after independence the city decreed a Market Act that regulated its markets, including forcing them to shut down one day a week on Sunday.

By the dawn of the nineteenth century, the six leading markets were well established, four of them close to the piers of the East River where food was received from Long Island, New Jersey, Connecticut, and Pennsylvania farmers and fishermen. Once steam-powered ships came into use, the markets began receiving shipments from the South, which meant greens and produce in the winter months.

The Water Street Market was a favored destination of Long Island producers. The Fly Market at Maiden Lane was known for meat and fish. But by the nineteenth century, this market was already old and decrepit and the boats that landed fish had to tie up by a pipe where raw sewage was dumped into the water.

In 1816, the city decided to build a new market, "a spacious market on an enlarged scale and suitable to the taste, opulence and standing of the Metropolis of the Union." The location, at the East River end of Fulton Street, was by the piers that were originally attractive because farmers could ferry in their goods and not have to pay cartmen to carry the goods through town. But it was the all-night ferry to and from Brooklyn that would make the Fulton Street Market a late-night institution in nineteenth-century New York. Also, many

New Yorkers lived within a short walk of the market. The immediate area was filled with decrepit wooden buildings ripe for slum clearance, yet another antique neighborhood neglected until it was so unlivable that the prevailing solution was to level it and put something else there. The city held an architectural contest for the new market's design, which was won by an Irish-born New York architect, James O'Donnell, whose plan the city council immediately began revising. The city did not actually level the neighborhood for the new market until 1821. As always, it was claimed that few people actually lived there and it remains a mystery what happened to them after their neighborhood was torn down. There was some controversy about tearing it down, which was solved by a fortuitous accident. A mysterious fire in a sailors' boardinghouse cleared most of the block.

The building was in a neoclassical style that most Londoners would have found slightly behind the times by the 1820s. A generation after the Revolution, while New Yorkers dogmatically asserted their Americanness and the two nations were still frequently teetering at the brink of war, a tendency remained to imitate the British in many things.

The market had three connected arcades, an E-shaped configuration, each capped by a two-story brick pavilion on the end. One hundred and two butchers rented stalls in the new space—eighty-six in the arcades and sixteen in the far more expensive cellar stalls. There were fruit and vegetable purveyors, fish and fowl mongers, and of course oyster stands, stalls, and cellars. The deputy clerk of the market, Ezra Frost, was given a second-story space in which to live. When the market first opened it was written about as though it were a wonder never before encountered in New York. On opening day a newspaper reported that the market was "ornamented with the handsomest exhibition of beef, mutton, pork, etc., ever presented to the

OYSTER STANDS IN FULTON MARKET.—[DRAWN BY A. R. WAUD.]

Oyster stands in the Fulton Market from Harper's Weekly, *October 20, 1870.*

public." *Harper's* reported, "It's a butcher's store, a fruiterer's stall, an oyster counter, a coffee shop, a poultry yard, a fish monger's estate. It's everything in one."

The Fulton Street Market was celebrated by locals and visitors as the place to get late-night oysters, like onion soup at Les Halles. Midnineteenth-century New Yorkers ate oysters everywhere from September until May; if not in the markets or the cellars or the restaurants, they bought them from street carts. The Fulton Market also sold soft-boiled eggs served in the shell with an empty wineglass to pour them into and a spoon with which to eat them. Visiting Europeans delighted in the oysters but found the eggs to be one of those American peculiarities.

Not only were oyster stands opened at the market but also coffee shops and restaurants. Sweet's was a famous restaurant that opened in 1847. Dorlon's was an extremely popular oyster bar. In 1866, an anonymous book, reportedly written by "members of the New York press," was published with the title *The Night Side of New York: a Picture of the Great Metropolis After Nightfall.* It said that Dorlon's was the liveliest place at the Fulton Market at least until midnight:

> If you delight in seeing the mysteries of shellfish cookery this is the place for you to feast your eyes. See how featly that slim youth with the check-sleeves and close cropped hair tosses up a stew. The young gentleman who obligingly opens oysters is the master of this profession. He is a graduate of the Fulton market; and that giving him precedence, nothing more remains to be said. . . .
>
> At some of the tables you will observe that solid, business-like men are having their oysters on the half-shell, accompanied by foaming "tobies" of nut-brown ale. These are probably residents of Brooklyn whose business lies in New York and keeps them in the city until the night is well advanced, and Dorlon's is their favorite place of stopping in on their way to the ferry.

Originally the Fulton Market was dominated by butchers, reflecting the fact that nineteenth-century New Yorkers, like most other Americans, were predominantly red-meat eaters. But more than one hundred butchers proved to be too many and they drove one another out of business. As the stalls of failed butcheries became available, the market decided to rent them to fishmongers. Because the other merchants disliked the fish sellers, complaining of fishy smells and malodorous melting ice, the fish stalls were constantly being moved to out-of-the-way locations. Yet they were the survivors. Fulton Street fish merchants were the only outdoor market businesses to withstand New York history and continue into the twenty-first century. That would not have been predicted in the nineteenth century when meat and oysters, usually sold separately from fish, were the two leading attractions. An 1855 *Tribune* article on the Catherine Market, a few blocks north of the Fulton Market along the East River, stated:

> Next to the meat-trade, a more extensive business is done in oysters and clams than in any other article of food in the market. The stands, of which there are five, are situated at the southerly side of the street, occupying the entire front of the fish-market. Each dealer sells on an average about $100 worth of all kinds every day, making a total of $3,000 a week. The fish are generally sold out of the shell, and a large proportion are cooked.

The same article reported that the Catherine Market, far smaller than the Fulton or Washington, sold $524,000 worth of products every year and that out of that, $156,000 was taken in from oysters and clams. Four-fifths of the molluscs sold in New York markets were oysters.

For both fish and oysters, an important component of the marketplace was ice, which was gathered in the winter, stored in icehouses, and distributed throughout the year. Providing ice for New York City was an almost $4-million-a-year industry. It was dominated by five companies, of which the Knickerbocker Company, with 283 acres of winter ice on Rockland Lake a few miles from the Hudson near Sing Sing, was the largest. During the ice harvest it employed five thousand workers. It had twenty icehouses receiving five hundred thousand tons of ice in the winter. Icehouses were wooden structures with double walls with the space between them packed with sawdust. The houses were divided into partitions that were also insulated with sawdust. The ice would be stored there until taken into the city by barge down the Hudson. An ice company could lose several hundred tons from a mild winter. Earlier in the century, New York ice companies had supplied Southern ports as well, but by the second half of the nineteenth century, they were kept busy just supplying the city and its markets. New England took over the Southern ice trade.

A peculiarity of New York was that marketing was most commonly done, not by servants and not by wives, but by the male heads of household. They would even carry the groceries home by themselves. It was common to see a wealthy, well-dressed, distinguished gentleman walking down the street with a chunk of raw meat or a bird or a fish in his hand. One man explained to a curious British visitor, "The man who was ashamed to carry home his dinner didn't deserve any."

The grand, well-turned-out gentlemen shoppers could not avoid seeing that the same markets they frequented were also visited by impoverished people who picked through garbage looking for edible scraps.

As the nineteenth century went on, the area around the markets became increasingly crowded with wooden shops, many selling dry goods. Merchants set up under awnings, outdoor stalls, and sheds, often selling oysters. By the time of the Civil War, the Fulton Market had lost its elegance and was a crowded, dirty, bustling, and dilapidated carnival. The neighborhood was also changing. By the time of the Civil War, few residents remained. They were either driven out by the market or swept up in the tide moving uptown. The lack of a neighborhood noticeably reduced the number of shoppers, though there were still the passengers to and from Brooklyn on the nearby ferries. The market increasingly turned from street traffic toward restaurants, hotels, shipping companies, and boardinghouses. By 1882, the sixty-year-old building was torn down and replaced with a new brick ornate Victorian structure, which featured a museum of maritime curiosities with an aquarium and a marine-biology laboratory in one of its turrets. This was the work of Eugene G. Blackford, a fish merchant and one of the great promoters of the fish market at Fulton Street. Within the market building he built fish tanks of marble, hardwoods, and glass in which to display living samples. But this building, too, would be torn down in time, as would its successor.

The downtown markets, especially Fulton by the ferry, established New York's tradition of being an all-night town. The Brooklyn Ferry service never stopped and the market remained packed with people throughout the night. It became one of the places to go late, a place to go at 2 A.M. The women in the fruit stalls closed down at 10 P.M., but the basement bars and the cake and coffee shops along the East River remained lively.

The gas lighting was dim and the air often misty from the river and this gave an eerie smudgy haziness to the busy market where deer and squirrels and opossums and wild turkeys were hanging from beams. Black dancers from the slums demonstrated tap dancing on street corners. In *The Night Side of New York*, what it calls the "ghostly appearance" of the Fulton Street market at night is described:

> Shadowy butchers, or watchmen employed by the butchers to look after their property, are seen flitting slowly here and there among the rows of carcasses with which the alley ways are lined.

Particularly praised by these nocturnal newsmen were the oyster stands that served raw, roasted, and fried oysters as well as other shellfish:

Here and there you pass on toward the Beekman Street front of the market, little oyster establishments are in full operation under the arcade. The glowing braziers look very comfortable this chilly night and it is not easy to resist the urgent invitation of the artist who is engaged in frying scallops for a night customer, who sits inside the little stall.

The journalists complained that the Civil War had doubled prices. A plate of shellfish now cost forty cents, whereas before the war it had been twenty cents. They also complained that Dorlon's charged twenty-five cents for an oyster stew, whereas just up the street at Libby's it was only twenty cents. "But," they hastened to add, "the shellfish in the Fulton market are superb."

By the 1870s, journalists were denouncing the markets. In October 1877, *Scribner's Monthly* stated, "There are ten public markets in New York City and not one of them is worthy of the extent of business done or deserving of praise on economic or sanitarian grounds."

The journalists in 1866 had commented on "the reeking exhalations that arise from the heaps of oyster shells and garbage with which the gutters are dammed." They and the *Scribner's* article a decade later singled out the Washington Market along the Hudson as the shabbiest. Yet this was the largest market in Manhattan. *Scribner's* reported 950 stands paying the city $250,000 annually, a considerable boon to the city treasury. In 1869, the entire health expenditure of the city budget was less than $200,000. Like the Fulton Market, the largest contingent at the Washington Market were the butchers. A narrow street separated the wholesale and retail sides of the market. Another 450 stands operating in the wholesale West Washington Market paid another $110,000 to the city yearly. The retail side alone took in more than $100 million a year. It had started in 1814 as a place for farmers from New Jersey to cross the Hudson and sell their butter and eggs. Late in the century, the sign was still hanging labeling it THE GRAND COUNTRY MARKET.

"The two buildings have been called bad names so often by the daily press," wrote *Scribner's*, "that we need not repeat the charges of inadequacy and uncleanliness made against them." The journalists of 1866 called the Washington Market "the terrible old huddle of abomination, and purulence and slime. The structures were so ramshackle they seemed near collapse." *Scribner's* said "plastering and patching cannot save it from downfall much longer." The grounds had become the home of large wharf rats. It was also infamously the hangout of

Washington Market in 1866 from Harper's Weekly.

thieves and pickpockets. The roads leading into the market were deep in mud, and in an age of long, full skirts, this could have been reason enough to leave the marketing to men.

But for all this, the market's detractors acknowledge that it had exceptional food. *Scribner's* reported, "New Yorkers endure all the inconveniences of a streetcar ride from Manhattanville or Harlem that they may have the traditional benefits of Washington Market in replenishing their larders." It described the market:

> There are avenues with crimson drapery,—the best beef in prodigious quarters; and avenues with soft velvet plumage of prairie game from floor to ceiling; farther on a vegetable bower, and next to that a yellow barricade of country butter and cheese. You cannot see an idle trader. The poulterer fills in his spare moments in plucking his birds, and saluting the buyers; and while the butcher is cracking a joint for one purchaser he is loudly canvassing another from his small stand, which is completely walled in with meats. All the while there arises a din of clashing sounds which never loses pitch. Yonder there is a long counter, and standing behind it in a row are about twenty men in blue blouses, opening oysters. Their movements are like clockwork. Before each is a basket of oysters; one is picked out, a knife flashes, the shell yawns, and the delicate morsel is committed to a tin pail in two or three seconds.

It was not necessary to go to a market to find an oyster stand unless one was overtaken by the urge late at night. They were located throughout the city, as commonplace as hotdog stands today—street carts or dilapidated little shacks with a window through which the

Nicolino Calyo's 1840 watercolor of a New York City oyster stand.
COLLECTION OF THE NEW-YORK HISTORICAL SOCIETY

oysters were passed. They were particularly common along the East River. Oysters were a penny each and a stew was ten cents. There, longshoremen, cartmen, sailors, and fishermen were the regular clientele. But the oyster stands at the markets were thought to be particularly good. Cornelius Vanderbilt, a native Staten Islander who accrued a fortune from maritime transportation, got his start shipping Staten Island oysters to the Washington Market.

While most of the city was quietly sleeping, business at the Washington Market would actually pick up after midnight and reached its height just before the first purple-and-orange light broke over the East River and the rest of New York started to wake up.

While products were unloaded at the waterfront, wagons arrived all night on ferries from Jersey City, Paterson, Elizabeth, Newark, as well as the towns of the Hudson Valley, loading up and leaving before daybreak, because the New York City markets supplied not only the city but the outlying areas. Next would come the wagons from the city stores, and the last, just before dawn, were the buyers from hotels and restaurants and still a few early-morning retailers, women with large wicker baskets.

The market favored by the city's poor was along the East River at Catherine Street, which, though shabby, was in better condition than the Washington Market. It was a much quieter market, with only eighty vendors who called out to passersby, hoping to get some needed business. They serviced mostly the residents of nearby tenements, who ate very little most of the week. But the poor had a tradition of feasting one day a week and on Saturdays the Catherine Market was overflowing with retail shoppers. The emphasis in the Catherine Market was on low prices and the shoppers would barter with the vendors. The Catherine Market vendors reflected the ethnic diversity that was characteristic of New York, with Jewish, Irish, and Chinese salespeople. This market died down after midnight, when the city's poorest would quietly arrive, hoping for affordable final prices for whatever had not sold. Other markets included the sizable Center Market, with 161 stands, and Clinton, with 158, and the smaller 78-stand Tompkins, 70-stand Jefferson, 66-stand Essex, and even a little 37-stand Union Market.

Scribner's noted with irony that the only really good market building was at the Manhattan Market, which was about to close. The market building's nine spires made of colorful slate and ground glass stood over the Hudson—the only ornament on the Hudson water-front. The market had been built by a joint stock company that by the 1870s was collapsing and most of the 767 stands were empty.

It would all vanish in time. Bridges would put an end to the all-night street traffic of the ferries, and larger steamships would dock in the deeper water of the Hudson, abandoning the East River as a working waterfront. In time more food would enter the city by truck than ship, and the logic of harbor-front markets would be gone. But in the nineteenth century, there was no better New York experience than to go down to one of the markets late at night and eat oysters.

Charles Mackay told this story about oysters in lower Manhattan:

It is related of an amiable English earl, who a few years ago paid a visit to the United States, that his great delight was to wander up and down Broadway at night, and visit the princi-pal oyster saloons in succession, regaling himself upon fried oysters at one place, stewed oysters at another, upon roasted oysters at a third, and winding up the evening by a dish of oys-ters, à l'Anglaise. On leaving New York to return to England, he miscalculated the time of sailing of the steamer, and found that he had an hour and a half upon his hands.

"What shall we do?" said the American friend, who had come to see him off.

"Return to Broadway," said his lordship, "and have some more oysters."

CHAPTER NINE

Ostreamaniacal Behavior

—

The pigs in the street are the most respectable
part of the population.

—HENRY DAVID THOREAU
in a letter from New York to
Ralph Waldo Emerson, 1843

anhattan was the field for the bloodiest engagement of the Civil War that did not involve Confederate troops.

Five Points, the most infamous slum in America, was ruled by
street gangs such as the Swamp Angels, who earned their name by at-
tacking from out of sewers, the Daybreak Boys, who were ten and
eleven years old, the Dead Rabbits, who went into battle with their
namesake impaled on a pike. They fought sweeping, pitched battles
on the streets of Five Points. These gangs could muster one thousand
fighters or more for a street battle. In 1857, the Dead Rabbits seized
City Hall and held it for an hour while slaughtering their gang oppo-
nents in front of the building.

By the time of the outbreak of the Civil War, Manhattan had built five hundred miles of city streets, but three-quarters of them had no sewage. The city's population, 813,669, was a little more than half foreign-born. One-fourth of the New York population had been born in Ireland. Seemingly following the example of the Collect, the city created slums for immigrants to move to. In the 1840s, as gas lighting was being introduced all over the city, huge gas tanks were built near the East River just above Fourteenth Street, which was considered an unused area. After they were built, no one wanted to live near them because the gas tanks leaked, and so impoverished Irish immigrants settled into the area. Eighty percent of police arrests were of immigrants, which gave a sense of an ongoing war between the immigrant poor and the police. In the year 1862, the police arrested eighty-two thousand people—a tenth of the population of New York.

In March 1863, the Conscription Act was passed by the U.S. Congress. All men between the ages of twenty and forty-five were required to register, and if drafted were required to serve for three years. Adding to the outrage of the poor, the act provided an exemption for the very wealthy; anyone could buy their way out of the draft with $300. Few New Yorkers, few Americans, could raise this sum. It was about a third of a year's wages for an oyster shucker. A wealthy man could also hire someone to serve in his place, which was considered— by the rich—a civic-minded thing to do. The fathers of Theodore Roosevelt and Franklin Delano Roosevelt, industrialist Andrew Carnegie, banker J. P. Morgan, and future presidents Chester A. Arthur and Grover Cleveland all hired substitutes. Even Abraham Lincoln, himself over the draft age of forty-five, set an example by hiring a substitute. George Templeton Strong paid his proxy soldier $1,100 and wrote, "My *alter ego* could make a good soldier if he tried. Gave him my address and told him to write to me if he found himself in the hospital or in trouble, and that I would try to do what I properly could to help him."

A few New Yorkers such as meat producers, industrialists, and the oyster producers benefited from the war. The main competitors of New York oysters, Chesapeake oysters, were no longer available. The military did not allow oyster sloops on the Chesapeake Bay for fear they would somehow be used to help the Confederacy. Closing down the bay meant New Yorkers not only took over the Chesapeake share of the market but went into the business of supplying seed oysters. Staten Island planters, ironically the same oystermen who had saved their beds by planting Chesapeake seeds, especially profited. Their prices almost doubled during the war, and the demand never slackened. The Union Army had always been a good customer. In 1859, the quartermaster general wrote that more money had been paid out that year for oysters than for meat. Much of that had been canned or pickled, but even during the war, troops on occasion were treated to fresh New York oysters.

But with the general New York population there had been little enthusiasm for the war at the outset and it had grown even more unpopular. Most New Yorkers did not regard slavery as a serious transgression and thought abolitionists were fanatics. In 1850, George Templeton Strong, a Lincoln supporter, had written in his diary:

My creed on that question is this: That slave holding is no sin.

That the slaves of the Southern States are happier and better off than the niggers of the North, and are more kindly dealt with by their owners than servants are by Northern masters.

That the reasoning, the tone of feeling, the first principles, the practices, and the designs of Northern Abolitionists are very particularly false, foolish, wicked, and unchristian.

There was a huge and enthusiastic rally in Union Square in 1861 to see off the troops, but few had predicted what a slaughter this war would be. From the very start the news in New York was bad. New York troops fought in the first engagement and New Yorkers were shocked to learn they had been routed by the Confederates at a place called Manassas, Virginia, with an unimaginable 460 federal troops killed and 1,582 wounded. A New York soldier wrote in his diary, "Tonight not 100 men are in camp. . . . A hundred men are drunk, a hundred more are in houses of ill fame, and the balance are everywhere. . . . Colonel Alfred is very drunk all the time now." Horace Greeley of the *New York Tribune*, who had urged Lincoln to let the South secede, and had then urged him to march on Richmond, now urged him to give up the fight and negotiate terms.

Other slaughters followed. In one battle in 1862 at a place called Shiloh, 3,477 men died, almost as many as had died in the eight years of the American Revolution. Later that year, more than twelve thousand Union troops were killed or wounded in one day at Antietam. Every day New Yorkers read the lists of dead and wounded in the newspapers. In September 1862, photographer Mathew Brady opened an exhibit in New York of work by his assistants Alexander Gardner and James E. Gibson entitled *The Dead of Antietam*. Photography was new, and few had ever seen such images of war. Because the camera exposed slowly and was a large cumbersome box with glass plates for negatives, it could not function in the heat of battle. Instead it recorded battlefields covered with the staring, twisted, mutilated dead. *The New York Times* reported, "Mr. Brady has done something to bring to us the terrible reality, the earnestness of war."

By the summer of 1863, as New York prepared for conscription, General Robert E. Lee's army was in Pennsylvania, not far away, and many New Yorkers were calling for Lincoln to negotiate a peace settlement. A masterpiece of warped logic became widespread in New York: All of the carnage and suffering of the Civil War was the fault of black people for being slaves. As blacks fled north and challenged New York immigrants for the worst jobs, the poorest immigrants, especially the Irish, turned bitterly against those they regarded as the newcomers. The idea of fighting to free blacks so they could migrate north and steal their jobs was infuriating to these impoverished New Yorkers. Were they all to be slaughtered because of *them*? Blacks were beaten on the streets of New York, even lynched. Avenue A was particularly infamous for lynchings.

On Sunday, July 12, 1863, the first conscripts, the names drawn the day before, were listed in the New York papers along with the New Yorkers among the twenty-three thousand Union dead or wounded at Gettysburg. On Monday morning, more names were being drawn as a mob attacked the conscription office, destroyed the files, tore down the building, and went out on the streets looting and burning. According to *The New York Times*, "They talk, or rather they did talk at first, of the oppressiveness of the Conscription Law, but three fourths of those who have been actively engaged in violence have been boys and young men under twenty years of age, and not at all subject to the Conscription." What had happened was that the slums and their street gangs were finally exploding.

The metropolitan police force fought back with 2,297 men and were often badly outnumbered. An estimated fifty thousand to seventy thousand people took part in the riot, with some gangs rallying ten thousand fighters. A thousand citizens armed with handguns and clubs were sworn in as auxiliary but still could not contain the mobs. The police chief was beaten to death. The mob attacked the wealthy in their homes and smashed stores and looted. Two disabled veterans were killed. They attacked black homes, boardinghouses, orphanages, and schools. Women gang members were said to be the most vicious against blacks and captured policemen, torturing them with knives, gouging out eyes and tongues, or spraying a victim lashed to a tree with oil and setting him on fire.

Rioters fought the police in the streets, in buildings, in parks, and on rooftops. More than one hundred buildings were burned down. After four days of fighting, regiments of infantry and cavalry pulled from the battlefield at Gettysburg, sunburned from their days fighting under the July sun, arrived in New York and the street gangs were no match for these battle-hardened veterans.

In the end, of 161 Five Pointers conscripted, 59 received exemptions, 11 hired substitutes, two paid the $300 fee, and 88 simply failed to report. Only one Five Pointer draftee served, Hugh Boyle, who went in at the end of 1864, served in the war until it ended five months later, and then, on his way to join occupation forces in Texas, deserted.

After the war, the memory of the 1863 draft riot left the people of New York with a lingering fear of the slums, the immigrants, and the poor. The seventeenth- and eighteenth-century claim that Manhattan was a healthy spot had long been forgotten. The city was notoriously unhealthy and much of that bad health was centered in the slums. In 1863, the year of the riots, one in every thirty-six New Yorkers died. The same year, one in every forty-four Philadelphians died and the same for Bostonians. Even in London and Liverpool, with their Dickensian slums and poverty, only one in every forty-five died that year.

In 1865, the bleeding nation, with its more than six hundred thousand dead and another almost half million wounded, was reeling from the Civil War. But in New York there was also fear of fetid slums and terrifying epidemics. In reality, smallpox, cholera, and typhoid epidemics did not cause the high fatality rate. More people died of nonepidemic diseases such as tuberculosis, diarrhea in children, bronchitis, and pneumonia. But it was the sudden sweep of a fatal disease, the epidemic, that incited the fear and imagination of New Yorkers.

Cholera would periodically attack cities all over the world, an unseen deadly force. Death came within a few days, and mortality rates were as high as 90 percent of all patients stricken with the disease. Terrified populations would search for causes. In New York, it was often traced to a ship that came from an infected port city. New Yorkers would brace themselves when they learned of cholera outbreaks in European cities.

What caused such pestilence? In New York, the principal suspects were foreigners, poverty, slums, immoral living, and alcoholism. It was often thought not that the poor were victimized by disease, but rather that they caused it. The modern-day assault of AIDS was not the first time an epidemic led to the stigmatization of its victims. In nineteenth-century New York, victims of cholera, yellow fever, and typhus were commonly looked down upon. Then, in the fall of 1854, several prominent citizens came down with cholera and died. A major epidemic had begun among the privileged. "There is a strange flare up of this epidemic just now, among people of the more 'respectable' class," George Templeton Strong noted in his diary on October 24. He was to personally witness a few fatal cases among his circle of friends.

The epidemic was a tremendous shock. Since it could not be blamed on the filth and moral degradation of the slums, perhaps it was being caused by oysters. And so what became known as "the oyster panic" began.

Numerous frightened New Yorkers began theorizing that the cholera resulted from eating bad oysters. Not surprisingly, there was a marked drop in oyster sales, especially among merchants who sold to the rich, such as Downing. Strong quoted, in his words, "the former venerable Ethiop" insisting, "If any gentleman can prove he died of the oyster I works in, I'll pay his expenses to Greenwood," the Brooklyn cemetery. In Downing's defense, Strong assured in his October 31 diary entry, "There is no serious increase of cholera cases, and probably no foundation for distrust of oysters, raw, broiled or roast." Strong was very wrong. It is now known that a chief cause of cholera is food that has been infected by sewage, and that raw shellfish is a particularly likely way to contract the disease.

In 1855, New York City mayor Henry Wood, responding to the oyster panic the previous year, moved to rigorously enforce the generally ignored laws restricting oyster sales. In 1839, a law had been passed reviving an old law about months lacking *R*. It outlawed the sale of oysters in New York from May 1 to September 1. This had created a festive moment in restaurants and markets when the oyster season reopened in September. Municipalities were free to lengthen the off-season, and the Great South Bay had stayed closed until September 15 and the Brookhaven beds didn't open until October 1. But by 1855, when Mayor Wood began rigorously enforcing the law, most New Yorkers had nearly forgotten about it. By then, New Yorkers were not panicked anymore and they laughed at the old-fashioned law. *Ballou's Pictorial* in the fall of 1855 wrote of oystermen who had started spelling the month "Orgust" so that it would have an *R*. Even then this was already an old joke.

The debate about the *R* months continued throughout the century. In September, at the opening of the 1883 season, a satirical *New York Times* editorial said, "There are eager lovers of the oyster who will eat 'fries' and 'broiled' up to 12 P.M. on the 30ᵗʰ day of April, but no good man will touch an oyster after the hour has struck." The article suggests that the unlucky Italians can't eat oysters in January because *Gennaio,* the Italian name for January, has no *R.* "On the other hand, the Arab of the desert can eat oysters in certain Mohammedan months which contain an R, while in the corresponding Christian months the gracious R is wanting."

It was mainly with a view to oysters that Julius Caesar reformed the calendar. He found that what the almanach called the Summer occurred late in the Autumn, so that in the months in which oysters were peculiarly desirable no "r" existed. He therefore pushed back the "r"less months into the heat of summer and enabled the Roman to feast on oysters on the true first of September. Moreover he invented leap year merely for the purpose of adding another oyster day to February. It was by these two grand strokes of genius that Caesar won the enthusiastic support of the Roman oyster dealers and endeared himself to every Roman whose taste for oysters had not been destroyed by the artificial and unwholesome dishes affected by the rich and dissolute members of the Pompeiian party.

In 1864, a New York citizens' association undertook a block-by-block inspection of the city. In 1865, it published its three-hundred-page report, which was widely distributed and resulted in the formation of a Metropolitan Board of Health. The goal of the report, which was largely sponsored by the wealthy, was to clean up the sanitary and moral conditions in the slums that caused diseases. The report pointed out that "The mobs that held fearful sway in our city during the memorable out-break of violence in the month of July 1863, were gathered in overcrowded and neglected quarters of the city."

It also reported that "everything is thrown into the street and gutters all times of the day. The slums still had overflowing outhouses. . . . Filth of every kind was thrown into the streets, covering their surface, filling the gutters, obstructing the sewer culverts, and sending forth perennial emanations which must generate pestiforous diseases." Scientists did not yet know the causes of most diseases, but most educated New Yorkers were convinced that somehow the problem was slums—the source of disease and crime and violence. Always in the back of New Yorkers' minds was the 1863 draft riot. Finally, in 1887, the city turned to its usual solution and began buying up and tearing down the Five Points neighborhood.

The unheeled, limping nation was quickly spreading westward. The cattle industry that fed the Union Army, the largest army to date in history, continued to grow. Industry that armed the Union Army in booming cities such as Cleveland continued its expansion. The railroads that moved the army continued branching into the West. Even before the war, in 1857, New York had been linked to St. Louis by train. After the war, New York oysters became a common feature of the restaurants in St. Louis hotels.

Ships were faster, and the Atlantic seemed smaller. The three thousand miles between New York and Liverpool had taken President Martin Van Buren five weeks in 1832. In 1850, the S.S. *Atlantic* of the New York & Liverpool United States Mail Steamship Company broke the record of its competitor, Cunard's Royal Steam Packet Company, by crossing from Liverpool to New York in ten days sixteen hours. Two years later, her sister ship became the first to cross from New York to Liverpool in less than ten days. After the war, ten-day crossings became commonplace.

New York City, the great port for this expanding nation, became a city of wealth and extravagance, with a brash sense of its own importance. War profiteers who had made fortunes settled in and began showing off. It was labeled the Flash Age. New York City had been known not only for its slums but for its beauty, its lawns and gardens and trees, including those in Battery Park, designed to be seen from the sea in the foreground. A pear tree on Third Avenue and Twelfth Street planted in 1660 by Peter Stuyvesant lasted until the early 1860s. It was a city of Georgian homes. Union Square, named not after the Northern cause but because it joined so many avenues and streets, was a flower market in the springtime.

After the war, the city grew from a charming port to a major commercial center. An enormous number of brownstones were built, denounced for modern architectural banality by the old guard. Steel- and ironworks, created for military contracts that ended with the war, turned to making cast-iron buildings, raising the skyline above what had been a three-story town. In 1870, the seven-story Equitable Life Assurance Society Building at Broadway and Cedar Street created a sensation with what the *New York Post* called "The new way of getting up stairs," a steam-powered elevator, which encouraged the designing of taller buildings. In 1873, the first streetcar rails were laid, though the public was so skeptical of the invention—the car deriving electricity from one of the rails—that horse-drawn coaches continued to congest Broadway.

For all the new brownstones, living space was becoming even more scarce to a growing population. Folding beds that doubled in the day as a bookcase, a wardrobe, or a desk became a popular New Yorkism. Manhattan still had hills and marshes and wetlands. But waterfront marshes were being filled in with granite and earth from the center of the island.

New York had become a commercial center connecting the new American West and the old Europe. In 1830, the port of New York had handled 37 percent of the United States' foreign trade. In 1870, it was handling 57 percent.

Travelers who visited New York before and after the war were amazed by the difference. British journalist George Augustus Sala, who had been a harsh critic on his 1863 visit—also a Confederate sympathizer—returned, and in *America Revisited,* published in 1883, he wrote, "Manhattan is, at the present moment, perhaps with one exception, as enjoyable a metropolis as could be found in the whole world over." The one exception was that he did not like the way, after it snowed, the streets became mired with sloppy, dirty slush. This problem remains unsolved.

Dickens also noted the change when he returned in 1867–68. He said he felt as though he "might be living in Paris," staying at the Westminster on Irving Place with its French staff. "The number of grand houses and splendid equipages is quite surprising," he wrote. Only in his fifties, the venerated author was in poor health and seemed elderly. He had been receiving offers to perform readings of his work in the United States since the end of the war and now had arranged a tour from which he was hoping to earn a considerable sum in ticket sales. He was an even bigger star than he had been on his first trip and was thought to be a brilliant reader. In New York, more than five thousand waited in line for hours to buy tickets and a man was arrested with thousands of forged tickets. Performances were sold out, with standing room let in at the last moment. But there were still bruised feelings from some who had attended the Boz Ball. George Templeton Strong wrote:

> Charles Dickens' first Reading last night at Steinway Hall is said to have been admirable. It doubtless was so, but I am in no fever to hear him. I remember the *American Notes* and the American chapters in *Martin Chuzzlewit*, which were his return for the extravagant honors paid him on his first avatar twenty-five years ago. I also remember that both books, especially the former, were filled with abuse and sarcasm against the slaveholding republic, and that during our four years of death-struggle with slavery, Mr. Dickens never uttered one word of sympathy with us or our national cause, though one such word from the most popular living writer of prose fiction, would have been so welcome, and though it would have come so fitly from a professional "humanitarian." I fear Mr. Dickens is a snob of genius, and that some considerable percentage of his fine feeling for the wrongs and sorrows of humanity is histrionic, but perhaps I do him injustice. Anyhow, I should like to hear him read the *Christmas Carol:* Scrooge, and Marley's Ghost, and Bob Cratchit.

Dickens was alone—he had separated from his wife and left her back in England with her suet dumplings, and, aware of the hostile feelings in the American press, did not want to show his new mistress. When not performing, he kept to his quiet French hotel and dined by himself at Delmonico's, eating and drinking well, according

Dickens being introduced at the banquet.
FROM AN 1868 PERIODICAL

to the waiters. It was a kind of elegant New York existence that would not have been possible twenty-five years earlier in the rough little town of oyster cellars and dance halls.

Dickens spent four months in the United States and gave seventy readings, earning himself almost £20,000, considerably less than American scalpers made off his readings. This just added to his bitterness about a country whose failure to conform to copyright law had already denied him a considerable income. Yet before he left, New York just had to throw him another banquet. This time it was given by the New York press at Delmonico's, as were all grand occasions at the time in New York. The banquet cost $3,000, overtaking the Boz Ball and the City Hotel dinner but considerably less than the 1871 bill for a Delmonico's dinner to celebrate politician William

"Boss" Tweed's daughter's wedding for $13,000. At the Dickens affair, tickets were sold for $15. Horace Greeley hosted the proceedings and the guests included many of America's notable journalists from Boston to Chicago. It was intended to be a dinner for 175, but 204 diners managed to get tickets.

Dickens arrived an hour late, limping in with the help of a cane. The *New York Herald* commented that the menu offered "oysters on the half shell, sure, but these were the only things that were not dignified with some literary name." There was *"crème d'asperges à la Dumas," "agneau farci à la Walter Scott,"* and *"côtelettes de grouse à la Fenimore Cooper."* Those platters of oysters at the start were the only touch of the old New York and even they were labeled in French. The entire menu was in French—correct French—and the seventy-three dishes that had been served at the City Hotel had been cut to about half that number.

Women were not invited to the Dickens dinner. Even influential women writers were denied tickets despite the committee having invited members of the New York working press. When Jane (Jennie) Cunningham Croly, a fashion and theater critic for the *New York World,* applied for a ticket, the New York Press Club simply laughed, despite the fact that her husband, David Croly, managing editor of the *World,* was chairman of the dinner committee and supported her claim. Laughing at journalists always comes with risks, and Jennie Croly angrily reported this rebuke to other prominent women journalists, who in turn also applied for tickets, including Fanny Fern, one of the highest-paid newspaper writers in New York. Fern was a pseudonym for Sara Willis Parton, the wife of James Parton, another member of the committee. But Croly and Parton found that they were powerless to help their wives. The women retaliated by forming their own club that did not allow men. There was at the time not a single women's club in New York—not even a garden club or bridge club or church club. The men, who had men-only clubs excluding women for every occasion, continued to laugh.

While men were planning the Dickens dinner, women were planning their club, which they named Sorosis, a botanical term meaning "agglomeration." This, in fact, was one of the first women's clubs in the United States and it met twice a month in a private room at Delmonico's, which gave the restaurant a progressive reputation at a time when women were not allowed to dine without men in public. Sorosis discussed issues of the day, championed women's issues, including pressuring Columbia University to admit women, and entertained distinguished visiting women such as Louisa May Alcott. Despite relentless gibes by men, the club became a famous fixture of Delmonico's and once a year Delmonico's hosted the Sorosis banquet, to which men were invited. The women would perplex the men by dressing in stunning gowns and leaving them to wonder why such beautiful women would act in such unfeminine ways.

But even Delmonico's did not allow unescorted women in their public dining rooms. A woman by herself, like the women in the oyster cellars, was considered of low morals, a prostitute. Emma Goldman, the radical anarchist who arrived in New York in 1889, defied these rules and was often mistaken for a prostitute. Victoria Woodhull, a socialist who advocated free love and opposed marriage and later ran for president, insisted on being served in Delmonico's and, when the management refused, went outside and brought in a driver from a horse cab and ordered tomato soup for both of them. In the 1880s, Delmonico's showed its fashionably progressive credentials by allowing unescorted women to dine during the day up until dinner service.

The New York of the second half of the nineteenth century was a city overtaken by oystermania. It was usual for a family to have two oyster dinners a week, one of which would be on Sunday. It was one of the few moments in culinary history when a single food, served in more or less the same preparations, was commonplace for all socio-economic levels. It was the food of Delmonico's and the food of the dangerous slum. The oyster remained inexpensive. Shucked oysters were sold by street vendors for twenty-five cents a quart. The poor person might eat raw oysters from a street stand or have a stew at the market—it was cheap enough—or a wealthy man might get the same raw oysters to start his meal or the same stew for a fish course at the most expensive restaurants. At Delmonico's, a serving of six or eight oysters, depending on the size, cost twenty-five cents. Or it would not be uncommon for the wealthy man to eat oysters from a street vendor at the Washington Market or in an oyster cellar. The next night he might be attending an extravagant banquet in honor of some notable and be served oysters again.

Even the New York press indulged in great logic-defying flourishes and hyperbole in their laudatory tributes to oysters. In 1872, in an article on the American oyster boom, *Harper's Weekly* magazine made this observation:

> The delicious bivalve was familiar to the ancients. . . . Their indulgence, however, never encouraged tyranny or degenerated into despotism, as did the love of peacock's tongues; nor were they ever known to share the demoralizing tendencies necessarily incident to the unrestrained consumption of *pâté de foie gras.*

The elegant restaurants published cookbooks with oyster recipes. But there was also a movement in the second half of the nineteenth century toward cooking schools and cookbooks for working-class and poor women. There, too, oyster recipes played a prominent role.

Juliet Corson was born in the Roxbury section of Boston in 1841 and opened the Free Training School for Women at age thirty-three, before she learned how to cook. She hired a French chef, thought to have been the celebrated Pierre Blot. Two years later she was living on St. Mark's Place in Manhattan giving cooking classes in her home. She called her classes the New York Cooking School and had one thousand students a year. In everything Corson did, she addressed her social conscience. The New York Cooking School tried to charge enormous fees to the rich while asking only a nickel a lesson of the middle class. The poor could attend for free. When New York's economy declined in the 1870s, she self-published controversial pamphlets such as "Fifteen cent dinners for Families of Six" and "How can we live if we are moderately poor." One of her numerous cookbooks, titled *Meals for the Million: The People's Cookbook*, has eight oyster recipes including this one for oyster fritters, a popular inexpensive dish because it could be made with the smallest, lowest-grade shucked oysters.

The oysters should be examined for bits of shell, and their liquor strained. Then make a batter by mixing two cupfuls of flour, the yelk [sic] of one raw egg, a tablespoonful of salad oil, a dust of cayenne pepper, and sufficient oyster liquor to make a batter just thick enough to sustain the drops from the mixing spoon; plenty of fat should now be heated until it is smoking; the white of the egg should be beaten stiff and gently stirred into the batter when the fat is hot, together

with the oysters, either whole or chopped, and it should be
put into the hot fat by the large spoonful, and fried brown;
the fritters when done should be laid on brown paper for a
moment to free them from grease, and then served hot.

Her numerous books to help people of modest income almost always included recipes for oysters, though not always in the copious
quantity suggested in books for the upper classes. For heated oysters
in the shell, she suggests only four or five per person. Her 1885 *Family Cook Book* included these among its ten oyster recipes.

❈ Cold Half-shell Oysters

Thoroughly wash 25 oysters, keeping half the shells entire;
arrange them on a platter, or on several small dishes,
putting into each shell an oyster, together with a dust of
cayenne and a squeeze of lemon juice. Serve with salt and
brown bread and butter for luncheon or supper. They are
frequently served with thin bread before the soup at dinner.

❈ Hot Half-shell Oysters

Open the oysters as directed in the recipe "Oysters on the
Half-shell;" arrange the deep shells on a baking pan, set
them in a very hot oven, or before a hot fire, until they are
perfectly hot; then put into each one half a teaspoonful of
butter, a dust of cayenne, and a raw oyster; put the pan in
the oven for one minute, turn the oyster over once in the
butter, and then serve them on the shells at once, putting

four or five on a plate before each person. The success of the
dish depends on the rapidity with which it is prepared.
Brown bread and butter, or crackers, are served with the
oyster, either for luncheon or supper.

Pierre Blot, who probably taught Corson to cook, approached
most things American and especially New York with a tourist's enthusiasm. His 1869 *Handbook of Practical Cookery* was intended to be
a guide to American food and emphasized American products and
ways. He paid particular attention to Indian traditions and offered
such insights as the Indian custom of bleeding fish before cooking,
which, he said, made for whiter flesh. He authenticated his clam-
chowder recipe by asserting that it was given to him by a Harlem
River boat captain. Reflecting the time and place, Blot's book included a dozen recipes for oysters. He flatly stated that "The American oyster is unquestionably the best that can be found." But, as the
following recipe for oysters in silver shells indicates, his oyster recipes
were not aimed at the poor.

Put a quart of oysters and their liquor in a saucepan, set it
on the fire, take off at the first boil, and drain. Set a
saucepan on the fire with two ounces of butter in it; as soon
as melted, add a teaspoonful of flour, stir, and, when turning
rather brown, add the juice of the oysters, about a gill of
gravy, salt and pepper; boil generally for about ten minutes,
stirring now and then. While it is boiling, place the oysters
on scallop-shells, or on silver shells made for that purpose,
two or three oysters on each, turn some of the above sauce
on each, after it has boiled; dust with bread-crumbs, put a

little piece of butter on each shell, and bake for about twelve
minutes in a warm oven.

A dozen silver shells served thus make a sightly and
excellent dish.

The two most common gastronomic observations made about
nineteenth-century New York were that the oysters were cheap and
that the people ate enormous quantities not only of oysters but of
everything. In 1881, exiled Cuban independence leader José Martí
wrote of the newly fashionable Coney Island resort:

> The poor people eat shrimps and oysters on the beach, or pas-
> tries, and meats on the free tables provided by some of the ho-
> tels for such meals. The wealthy squandered huge sums on
> purple infusions that pass for wine, and strange, heavy dishes,
> which our palates, delighted by the artistic and the light,
> would surely find little to our taste. These people enjoy quan-
> tity; we enjoy quality.

This was not much improvement over the observations of James
Fenimore Cooper, who in the 1830s had called Americans "the gross-
est feeders of any civilized nation known." Despite such complaints,
New York in the 1880s was a far better place to eat than it had been
when the century had begun. It was still led by America's premier
restaurant, Delmonico's, which was ever larger and more grand as it
moved along with the fashionable people, uptown. In 1846, 21–25
Broadway became the Delmonico Hotel. In 1855, Delmonico's opened
on the corner of Broadway and Chambers. In 1860, it took over the

Grinnell Mansion at Fifth Avenue and Fourteenth Street, an enormous house of elegant ballrooms and spacious dining rooms. In 1876, Delmonico's followed the uptown trend to Twenty-sixth Street and Fifth Avenue, and in 1897 moved again to Fifth and Forty-fourth Street.

It was unthinkable for anyone even modestly affluent to visit New York and not dine at Delmonico's. Anyone of note that the city wanted to celebrate was thrown a Delmonico's banquet. In 1861, Delmonico's served a banquet in honor of Samuel T. Morse. From his table he sent the first cablegram to Europe. In forty minutes an answer came back to applause from the 350 guests. After the war, most of the leading generals, including Grant, Sherman, and McClelland, as well as President Johnson, were thrown Delmonico's banquets. These feasts usually began, in true New York fashion, with an oyster dish. Sometimes, as in the November 5, 1863, ball for the commanders of the visiting Russian fleet, the menu would begin with two oyster dishes. A November 1882 buffet for forty in honor of Charles Dana, owner-editor of the *New York Sun,* started with oysters béchamel—a white sauce invented by a seventeenth-century Frenchman for salt cod—and "*huîtres farcies,*" stuffed oysters. The select dinner for General Grant and twelve guests in March 1873 began with raw oysters on the half shell, which was listed simply as "*huître,*" followed by soups, hor d'oeuvres, trout, lamb, duck, fois gras, a few other treats, and desserts, followed by a supper for eighty that began with "*huîtres béchamel aux truffes,*" oysters in white sauce with truffles. The menus for these events were sometimes engraved on silver pages or printed on satin or sometimes bound in leather.

Charles Ranhofer, the Alsatian who was chef at Delmonico's from 1862 until 1894, knew his audiences. In a banquet for a Frenchman, he would serve only raw oysters, for which he gave the following instructions on how to bring the oysters to the table with the hearts still beating:

> Open the oysters carefully by inserting the blade of the knife between the shells and prying them open so as to avoid breaking and leave them in their deep shells with the liquor. Serve six or eight according to their size with a quarter of a lemon for each guest. Crackers or slices of very thin bread and butter can be served at the same time. The clams are to be treated exactly the same. A hot sauce or a shallot sauce made with finely chopped shallots mixed with salt, pepper and vinegar, or else a pimentade sauce can be eaten with the oysters. They should only be opened when ready to serve and sent to the table on finely broken ice.

⚜ *Pimentade Sauce*

Cut up into quarter inch squares a quarter of a pound of lean veal and two ounces of onions, a quarter pound of raw, lean ham, then add a small clove of crushed garlic, put all these into a saucepan with some butter and let cook slowly. Fry some sweet Spanish peppers in oil after removing the skins; also some green peppers having both finely chopped, add these to the ham, veal and onions and then add a little good gravy and espagnole sauce, also a little tomato purée. Boil all together, season properly, skim off the fat and serve.

But for the non-French, there was a traditional New York appetizer, pickled oysters, but with a new French name, *huîtres marinées,* which he served to the officers of the Russian fleet in 1863:

Blanch some large oysters, drain them after the first boil
and keep the liquor; boil some vinegar with cloves, whole
pepper, whole allspice, half an ounce of each for every quart
of vinegar, and add a little mace; put two-thirds of the oyster
liquor with one-third of the vinegar, and also the oysters
into hermetically closed glass bottles, and keep them in a
cool place. Serve on side dishes with sliced lemon and sprigs
of parsley set around.

He also offered Americans a long list of cooked oyster dishes including oysters with curry, oysters on skewers, fried oysters à la Horly,
oysters fried with butter or lard. The other oyster dish served in 1863
at the ball for the Russian fleet was oysters à la poulette, which New
Yorkers used to call oyster fricassee:

Reduce some velouté sauce with oyster liquor, season with
with salt, pepper, and nutmeg, and thicken with egg yolks
diluted in a little cream, incorporate into it a piece of fresh
butter, some strained lemon juice and chopped parsley.

Ranhofer, the most influential New York chef of the second half
of the nineteenth century, was a practitioner of French classical cuisine, the cooking of Europe's top hotels at the time, the cuisine de-
fined by Auguste Escoffier. Typical of this cuisine, Ranhofer's recipes
are almost always more complicated than they seem. Just to follow his
directions for raw oysters on the half shell, the cook needs to know
how to make pimentade sauce, and to make pimentade sauce, the
recipe for sauce espagnol, the standard brown sauce made from thick-
ening stock, must be known, and in turn the cook needs to know how
to make a good stock. To make the fricassee, the cook must know

how to make a velouté, and for this, too, a knowledge of the making of stocks is required. The cook also has to know the right temperature, low, to thicken with egg yolks, and how to finish a sauce with a piece of butter—also stirred at a low temperature. The above fricassee is also just a sauce to pour over poached oysters. Ranhofer's instructions for poaching oysters:

> Set a saucepan on the hot fire, and place the oysters in it with their own liquor, being careful to stir them about at times to prevent them adhering to the bottom; when firm to the touch, drain them from their liquor.

But occasionally he offered a simple dish such as his Philadelphia-style oysters, which of course, he and fashionable New Yorkers called *huîtres à la Philadelphie:*

> Put two ounces of butter into a pan, and let it cook until nut brown, then add to it twenty oysters well drained and wiped: fry them until they assume a light color on both sides, then pour in a quarter of a pint of oyster liquor, salt, and pepper. Serve at the same time thin slices of toasted bread, or else pour the oysters over slices of toast laid in a deep dish.

This was one of Ranhofer's secrets. New Yorkers knew they could go to Delmonico's and get some basic New York dishes like the fried oysters served in the markets, even if it was ascribed to some distant place called Philadelphie. In 1893, Ranhofer published *The Epicurean,* his twelve-hundred-page, four-thousand recipe "Franco-American Culinary Encyclopedia," which, though it made its way into few household kitchens, became a bible for American restaurants and hotels. Though it has thirty oyster recipes, its oyster section states that an oyster is "sexless," which is incorrect, and that it cannot live out of water, which it can for a considerable number of weeks if kept cool, which is how fresh New York oysters were able to reach faraway places. Showing his French roots, Ranhofer ventured the opinion that cooked oysters, which composed the majority of his oyster recipes, were not as digestible as raw ones. The following is one of his more impressive recipes for a lightly cooked oyster appetizer that could be served instead of raw oysters on the half shell.

⚜ Oysters Tartare (huîtres tartare)

Blanch some large oysters, drain them, well, and season
with salt, pepper, fine herbs, shallots cut into very small
dice, and blanched capers, minced pickled cucumbers and
lobster coral chopped up very fine. Have some thin slices of
bread cut oval shaped the size of an oyster, fry in butter,
place one oyster on each and cover every one of these with
the chopped garnishing, finish by covering all with a
mayonnaise jelly.

⚜ Mayonnaise Sauce Jellied

Use an ordinary Mayonnaise with oil, pouring into it slowly
some cold liquid jelly. A jellied mayonnaise may also be
prepared by whipping the jelly on ice and incorporating into
it at the same time some oil and vinegar, exactly the same
as for the egg mayonnaise.

Ranhofer also invented baked Alaska to honor the U.S. purchase of that territory. There were several other Delmonico's dishes that became American classics such as Delmonico potatoes and Delmonico steaks. People would bring ideas to the restaurant. In 1895, after Ranhofer retired, Richard Harding Davis, the journalist who did much to romanticize the image of foreign correspondents, fresh from Latin America, introduced Delmonico's to the avocado. The fruit was one of Davis's few verifiable facts from Latin America. Three years later he would popularize the Spanish-American War and by then Delmonico's had popularized the avocado in New York.

Ben Wenberg, a fruit merchant who traded in the Caribbean and a Delmonico's regular, in 1876 showed Charles Delmonico a new lobster dish that he demonstrated in a chafing dish. Delmonico called it lobster à la Wenberg. But soon the two had an irreparable disagreement and Delmonico refused to use his name. In a fit of intentional dyslexsia, Delmonico inverted Wen-berg to New-berg. Ranhofer established the dish and it became known all over America as lobster Newberg.

Lobster Newberg became an instant classic with many spin-offs, including the inevitable oyster Newberg, this one from the 1894 book *Fifteen New Ways for Oysters* by Sarah Tyson Rorer, a food writer and magazine editor who was one of the founders of the *Ladies' Home Journal*. Notice the quantity of oysters:

Drain fifty oysters; pour over them a pitcher of cold water. Have ready a granite pan, smoking hot; throw in the oysters; add two ounces of butter, a teaspoonful of pepper. Stir carefully with a wooden spoon until the oysters are smoking hot. Have ready the yolks of two eggs beaten with six tablespoons of cream; add quickly—do not boil; then add a tablespoonful of sherry and serve on nicely browned toast.

The oyster craze had also taken London and Paris. Happily for the American oyster business, European beds were becoming exhausted. By the midnineteenth century, the increased popularity of oysters had led to the stripping of natural beds around the world that had until then been thought to be inexhaustible. In 1861, oyster merchants in the Zeeland region of the Netherlands had handled three million oysters, one million gathered by Zeelanders and the rest by Scots and Englishmen whose native beds had already become distressed. By 1864, the same dealers got only fifty thousand oysters to trade. The same decline was also occurring in France. It had also happened in New York, but by the second half of the century, New Yorkers had become skilled cultivators.

Like New Yorkers, the late-nineteenth-century French were consuming oysters at a staggering rate, perhaps more staggering because they were almost all being eaten raw. It was said that oysters were served four times a day—breakfast, lunch, dinner, and supper. But recipes for cooking oysters were long held to be a gastronomic atrocity in France, whereas in New York only one in three retail oysters was sold in the shell. Most of the others were stewed, stuffed, fried, roasted, put in soups or sauces, or in some way cooked.

The French had long been oyster fanatics. Not only was there the legend of Napoléon's prebattle oysters, but Diderot, Rousseau, and Voltaire are all believed to have eaten a few dozen oysters when in search of inspiration. And having won France's greatest battles and launched its most original ideas, oysters, it is not surprising to learn, had also fueled its revolution. Danton and Robespierre found that whenever the revolutionary spirit began to wane, several dozen on the half shell would spur them on again. Some would say they ate too many oysters. It is not certain which, if any of these often-repeated legends are true, but sometimes as much can be learned about a people from their myths as from the verifiable facts.

In the seventeenth century, the French regulated the mussel industry but not oysters, believing in their unconquerable fertility. But unlike the British, by the early eighteenth century they could see their mistake and began regulating natural beds. In the nineteenth century, faced with disease, flukes of nature, bad luck, and overfishing, they realized regulations were not enough, and they began developing cultivation.

It was unfortunate for the British that Jean Jacques Marie Cyprien Victor Coste, who probably in any case had too many names to be trusted by most Englishmen, had gotten into a heated and arcane dispute in 1838 with a leading English zoologist, Richard Owen, over the reproduction of kangaroos. As a result, Coste, the most important nineteenth-century scientist on the subject of oysters, was regarded with great distrust and dislike by the British scientific establishment. Coste died in 1873, but his work, along with a stroke of good fortune, did save French beds. In 1868, an entire cargo of Portuguese oysters, *Crassostrea angulata*, was dumped in a storm near the mouth of the Gironde. A cousin of the American oyster, they were more durable than the European oysters, and as those declined, the Portuguese took their place.

According to Henry Mayhew's London Labour and the London Poor, originally published in 1851, 500 million oysters were sold every year in London's Billingsgate Market. If all 500 million had been consumed in London, that would have meant an average of 185 oysters a year eaten by each Londoner, including children. But of course some Londoners ate more than their 185 and some none at all, and a great many oysters from Billingsgate were shipped out of the city. Still, London was an oyster-eating town. They had a market similar to the New York oyster barges. Theirs floated up the Thames and tied up together at a London wharf known as "Oyster Street." The first to go were the scuttlemouths, large heavy oysters with thick shells and surprisingly small meat. They came from the Sussex coast and were dredged from the Channel, where the French dredged them, too, and called them "horse hooves," *pieds-de-cheval.* They sold fast because they were cheaper than the quality oysters from the Thames estuary, a short boat ride from the London market. In 1864, it was calculated by the *Times* of London that 700 million oysters were being consumed annually in London and that all totaled, the English ate 1.5 billion oysters a year.

The two most famous English oysters, Whitstable and Colchester, the ones so often compared to New York oysters in colonial times, were both in decline. The Whitstable Oyster Company had grown from 36 oystermen in 1793 to 408 in 1866. The Colne oyster fishery in Colchester grew from 73 in 1807 to 400 in 1866, a number that did not include the many apprentices. In fact, by 1844 its five hundred vessels employed two thousand men. Soon there were more oystermen than beds in Essex and they began moving farther off in search of new oyster beds, which they also cleaned out. With increased pollution and excessive exploitation, the beds began to decline. Further destruction was caused by the arrival of two foreign pests, the oyster drill and *Crepidula fornicata,* which creates muddy conditions.

In another oyster center, Falmouth, on the coast of Cornwall, seven hundred men worked three hundred boats in the extensive inlets of Falmouth Bay. It was a profitable oyster center regulated by "close times" when the beds would be replenished by moratoriums on shellfishing. In 1866, it was decided by regulators ingesting new science that oysters were so fecund that they would continue replenishing the beds and oystering could not possibly take enough to affect the total population. It was a popular theory in the age of Darwin, inexhaustible nature. In 1863, a Royal Commission on Sea Fisheries headed by England's preeminent scientist, Thomas Huxley, was formed to investigate what appeared to be the disappearance of a number of varieties of commercial fish. After two years of investigation, the same commission that assured the public that it was scientifically impossible to overfish cod also assured them that a healthy oyster bed could not be cleaned out. It agreed that the "supply of oysters has greatly fallen off" but explained:

> This decrease has not arisen from overfishing, nor from any causes over which man has direct control, but from the very general failure of the spat, or young of the oyster; which appears, during the year in question, to have been destroyed soon after it was produced. A similar failure of the spat has frequently happened before, and probably will often happen again.

Nineteenth-century Darwinian naturalism often taught that the forces of nature are so great and intricate that man cannot possibly impact on the result. By 1876, only ten years after the regulations were dropped, the Falmouth oyster beds had only forty boats and forty working oystermen and still each boat could only find sixty to one hundred oysters in a day. Before 1866, an average daily take of a Falmouth boat was between ten thousand and twelve thousand oysters.

Oystering in the Channel Islands went from four hundred vessels to a few part-time oystermen. By 1886, annual English oyster production was down to 40 million oysters, which at the time was about five weeks' consumption in New York City.

In 1882, as the fall oyster season opened, the *London Daily News* reported:

In the present dearth of oysters, turning what was once a season of joy, into one of regret, a pang of envy will seize the gormand who reads of the great oyster beds formed and in process of formation in that arm of the sea between Long Island and continental New York known as the Sound of the East River. Oyster farming in that favored region is carried out on a stupendous scale, which dwarfs the puny efforts of the Old World to insignificance. There are among the oyster-culturists of the Sound proprietors owning beds with an area of 4,000, 6,000, and 10,000 acres apiece and the bedding of the oyster is an operation on which considerable care, skill, time and labour are employed. The American oyster, which, when fresh torn from its natural bed, is a very different animal from the unhappy bivalves after an ocean voyage, lends itself very readily to cultivation and grows with extraordinary rapidity. In this country we are too apt to confound size with coarseness as the Zulus do fat with dignity, but the better advised Americans know by agreeable practice with Blue Points, Shrewsburys, Mobile Bays and other favorite oysters that the bigger they are the better they are and for every kind of roasting, broiling, steaming, and stewing immeasurably superior to any to be obtained in Europe. The East River farmers are gaining knowledge by experience, and have already discovered facts, which, if known, are practically ignored in Europe, to wit, that oysters thrive far better in deep than in shallow water, and prefer a bottom artificially made of oyster shells to any other. While they are eagerly laying down spat "full fathom five" beneath the surface, English and French oyster-growers appear to cling fondly to the shallow puddles in which oysters take an unconscionable time in growing to maturity.

This ignores the fact that the American oyster is a completely different, faster-growing species than the European oyster. But what is significant is the extent to which the British were turning to American oysters. New York oyster producers had long been shipping to Europe. Before the Civil War, Colonel Harmon Thorne was known to give receptions in Paris featuring fried oysters from Downing's. Downing's was a New York trademark. This would be like a Paris reception today serving smoked fish from a famous New York deli. Downing also sent oysters to Queen Victoria, in appreciation for which the Queen sent him a gold chronometer watch.

But in the second half of the nineteenth century, foreign markets, especially the English, were no longer an occasional outlet but an important part of the New York oyster trade. In 1883, a year after the *London Daily News* article appeared, *The New York Times* noted:

The oyster men now do a heavy business in furnishing oysters for the European market. It has all grown up within the last five years. Five years ago I sent ten barrels to Liverpool as an experiment and had the greatest difficulty imaginable in disposing of them. There seemed to be a prejudice against things American and in order to sell them men had to be employed to peddle them around the streets in hand baskets. That was only five years ago. The statistics show that during the year 1882, 5000 barrels a week were shipped to Europe and sold after they reached there. The English people have acquired a taste for American oysters and are obliged to admit their superiority over their natives.

Oysters were being shipped from New York not only to Liverpool, Bristol, Cardiff, and Glasgow, but also to Le Havre, Bremen, and Hamburg. Bluepoints, not an obvious choice for shipping because of their thin shells, became a European favorite as they had long been in New York. Though not large by New York standards, they were known for their flavor, and their round thin shell that looked more like a European oyster than most New York varieties. Struggling to supply the demand for the brand name, producers in the 1870s attempted to pass off as Bluepoints Southern oysters that they tossed into the Great South Bay for a year. But the European market was demanding, and it rejected Bluepoints that were not truly native to the area.

The leading merchants realized that such practices were damaging the reputation of their most valuable product. One of the leading New York City houses grew concerned that Chesapeake oysters were being sold to England as Bluepoints. An agent for the house intercepted a shipment of Bluepoints, opened the barrels as they were being loaded, and found that they were mostly "Virginias." It was a new age of communications and the agent was able to telegraph Liverpool so that British authorities were waiting for the shipment when it landed. The oysters were confiscated, though it is not clear what happens to a healthy confiscated oyster. The American shipper was charged under British law with mislabeling, which carried considerable fines. The New Yorkers were not accustomed to such stringent consumer protection and the American agent argued that the oysters had spent a little time in the Great South Bay and they had thought that this was all that was required to label them Bluepoints. That the Americans don't know any better is always an argument of some currency in England, and the charges were dropped.

New York's oyster markets were also supplying the nation. After the rail link was established from Atlantic to Pacific, the transcontinental railroad, a project passed by Congress during the war but not completed until 1869, New York had the continent for a market. This was true not only for all the goods brought into New York's port from Europe and other points in the world, but also for local oysters. Every Christmas, thousands of barrels of oysters labeled Saddle Rock or Bluepoint, the best marketing names, were shipped to Denver, San Francisco, and other Western cities.

The agents who bought oysters for shipping were called packers, and they sailed the New York waters on sloops with a crew and a basket hanging from the masthead. The basket was the sign that this vessel was buying. Oystermen would row out to the sloop with oysters packed in two-bushel tubs and the packers would buy their product for cash and ship it around the world. In the winter, a packer would dispense several thousand dollars a day in cash and then retreat to his "shanty"—a seaweed-packed shed along a beach. There his crew would sort the oysters by size. Since New Yorkers have always been willing to pay for size, the crew would set aside the largest few to be sold in the city. They would separate the middle- and small-size oysters, unpopular in the city, and pack them in flour barrels, the traditional New York oyster container since colonial times, to be shipped to Europe, where oyster lovers did not have the New York obsession with size. Sometimes packers would buy out an oyster planter's crop a year in advance at an agreed-upon price. Occasionally a packer would even advance money to a planter to finance his developing of a new bed whose oysters the packer would be guaranteed.

The late nineteenth century was sometimes called the Gilded Age, the age of the robber barons who ruthlessly amassed fortunes building banks, railroads, steel and other industry without fair-practice regulations, a unionized labor force, or a fair share of the tax burden. Nor did they have regulations or restrictions on what they discharged into the earth, into the air, or into the water, including the Hudson, Raritan, Newark, and other rivers that flow into New York Harbor. *The History of New York,* an 1884 book by Benson J. Lossing, warned:

> New York, unfortunately, is becoming to a large degree a city of only two conspicuous classes, the rich and the poor. The great middle class, which constitutes the bone and sinew of the social structure, have been squeezed out, as it were, by the continually increasing pressure of the burden of the cost of living in the city.

In 1898, New York became the second largest city in the Western world after London, when Manhattan merged with Brooklyn, already the third largest U.S. city, Queens, the Bronx, and Staten Island. Many Manhattanites laughed at the notion that a resident of anyplace but Manhattan could be called a New Yorker. New York City had a population of about 2.5 million and consumed as many as a million oysters a day, which would be the equivalent of every New Yorker consuming more than a dozen oysters every month—along with startling quantities of lobsters, steak, champagne, and cigars.

The wealthy came to Manhattan and spent ostentatiously. A new kind of restaurant appeared in New York to serve them the seafood they were polluting. They were called lobster palaces. They could just as easily have been called oyster palaces except that one doesn't name a palace after a twenty-five-cent item.

Julian Street, a popular journalist of the epoch, wrote an article for *Everybody's Magazine* titled "Lobster Palace Society" in which he compared the people of standing and the people without it. When a truly consequential guest dined at a lobster palace, he didn't pay but simply signed the bill. It would be settled later on a monthly basis. "Check-signing is one of the most impressive rites," said Street. On the other hand, what could be worse than what Street called "getting the rope." A velvet rope separated the maître d' from the dining hall, and if he chose not to seat someone, the rope stayed closed. This was Street's satire of the death of a lobster-palace habitué, whom he calls "Mr. Feldman."

> While Mr. Feldman lives, he lives very high, and when he comes to die, he does it so quickly that he actually interrupts himself in the midst of ordering another bottle. His colour changes. If he was purple, he turns mauve; if cream-coloured, a lovely shade of pale green. An attentive waiter catches him as he starts to flop over on the wine cooler. He has stopped ordering, so his friends know he must be dead.

The Waldorf-Astoria was one of the palaces frequented by J. Pierpont Morgan. Business deals were made at the bar, and a million dollars could change hands in an all-night baccarat game in one of the private rooms. In the dining room, with white-tie attire required, dinner began with enormous quantities of oysters and then moved on to a half-dozen more courses.

The most famous of the lobster-palace gourmands was James Buchanan Brady, popularly known as Diamond Jim for the gems with which he adorned himself—"them that has them wears them," he would say of diamonds. He was a New Yorker from a working-class Irish family, raised in a tough Irish neighborhood on Manhattan's Lower West Side. His first job was as a baggage handler for the New York Central at the Spuyten Duyvil station at a time when railroads were the most prominent and fastest-growing industry in America.

As he worked his way up, Brady became enamored of Chauncey Depew, the New York Central president and reputedly one of the best-dressed men in New York. Brady started going to Depew's tailors and haberdashers, even though he could barely afford them. "If you are going to make money, you have to look like money," he said. And that is what he did as the salesman for a company that made a handsaw for cutting rails, a technological marvel in an age of expanding rail lines. He became its most successful railroad-equipment salesman, known for his dogged courting of clients. He started at the lobster palaces, taking clients there on an expense account. His favorite was Rector's, occupying a two-story building with a yellow facade on the east side of Broadway between Forty-third and Forty-fourth streets. Rector's had sixty waiters and eight captains, and of all the palaces, this was the one known for hosting out-of-town millionaires, the nouveaux riches whose copper mines, railroad lines, and steel mills had just paid off in legendary fashion.

Unlike most of the lobster palaces, which had French names or mythically New York names such as Astor, Knickerbocker, or Gotham, Rector's garish hall of mirrors was simply named after its owner. Charles Rector was a Civil War veteran into whose home, by chance, the fatally wounded Abraham Lincoln had been carried. His brother had died at Fredricksburg. His father owned a famous hotel and restaurant along the Erie Canal. After the war, Charles Rector worked for George Pullman, one of the railroad barons, and was put in charge of the first Pullman hotel dining car to cross the North American continent. He then started Rector's Oyster House on Clark and Munroe streets in Chicago, one of the famous Chicago houses that brought in Eastern oysters by rail. He was the first to ship in fresh oysters in the shell, Rockaways. He was also the first to bring live lobsters to Chicago. In 1899, Rector relocated to New York. All the Western barons who came to New York already knew Rector from Chicago. The restaurant had the reputation of serving the same-quality food as Delmonico's without the old-school formality and with slightly more reasonable prices.

In an age when men wore diamonds in their evening clothes, when they turned out at night sparkling, Brady sparkled a little more, his stones a little bigger. It was estimated that he owned $2 million in evening jewelry. Some of his large stones were mounted in platinum in the shape of bicycles, automobiles, trains, and planes—"the transportation set." It was also estimated that he gave away, mostly to "lady friends," another $2 million in jewels. He would give out $1,000 party favors.

Brady would also make companies overnight. He gave a chocolate maker $150,000 to expand after eating a five-pound box. "Best goddamned candy I ever ate." He was a legendary glutton. A teetotaler, he was said to begin a meal with a gallon of orange juice and six dozen Lynnhaven oysters. The choice of Lynnhavens was typical of his gourmandism. A Chesapeake oyster, it was considered bland but had the distinction of being extremely large. He would then reputedly move on to crabs, turtles, ducks, steaks, maybe a partridge, and perhaps a twelve-egg soufflé for dessert.

When he learned that everyone in Paris was talking about a sole-and-oyster dish at the Café Marguery, he demanded that Charles Rector add it to his repertoire. Rector yanked his son, George, out of Cornell and sent him to Paris to get the recipe. After eating the dish at Rector's, Brady said, "George, that sole was marvelous. I've had nine helpings and even right now, if you poured some of the sauce over a Turkish towel, I believe I could eat all of it." Rector assumed this was praise. This was the dish as served at Rector's:

❧ *Fillet of Sole Marguery à la Diamond Jim*

Have 2 flounders filleted. Place bones, skin, and heads in stewpan. Add 1 pound inexpensive fish cleaned and cut into small pieces, ½ cup thinly sliced young carrots, and a small chopped leek, 3 sprigs of parsley, 10 whole peppercorns, 1 small bay leaf, 1 sprig of thyme, 1½ quarts cold water. Bring to a boiling point very slowly and simmer until liquid is reduced to one pint, then strain through fine cheese cloth. Place filets in buttered baking pan and pour over one cup fish stock. Season with sprinkling of salt and pepper, and place in moderate oven (325° F) 15 to 20 minutes. Carefully lift fillet from pan and arrange on hot ovenproof serving platter. Garnish with 1 dozen poached oysters and 1 dozen boiled shrimps which have been shelled and cleaned. Pour remaining fish stock into baking pan in which fillets were

poached and simmer gently until quantity is reduced to 3 or
4 tablespoons, no more. Strain into top part of double boiler
and add 4 tablespoons dry white wine, ¼ pound butter. Cook
over hot water, stirring until butter is melted. (Have very
little water in the lower part of double boiler, just enough to
create a gentle steam.) Add 4 egg yolks which have been well
beaten. Stir continuously until sauce is the consistency of
a medium cream sauce. Pour this creamy sauce over fish
fillets, oysters, and shrimps, and place under broiler flame
until nicely glazed or lightly browned. Allow one fillet per
serving.

More impressive than his jewelry was the woman seen on his arm,
the actress Lillian Russell, billed as "the English Ballad Singer." In
fact, she was Helen Louise Leonard of Iowa and had in common
with Brady both fame and humble origins. Despite an enduring
friendship through various marriages for both of them, a man as in-
tent on show as the obese and bejeweled salesman Brady must have
enjoyed being regularly seen with someone often regarded as the
world's most beautiful woman. They would be flooded in lights at the
entrance to Rector's, the red and round Diamond Jim and the curva-
ceous and radiant Miss Russell announced by a Hungarian Gypsy vi-
olin band and the bow of the headwaiter as they were ushered in away
from the view of the masses and into the view of the privileged. Press
photos were sometimes labeled "beauty and the beast."

George Rector called the two his twenty-five best customers, and
according to him and popular legend, they ate enormous meals. In an
age of fleshiness, Russell was admired for her shapely pudginess,
though it expanded more every year. Supposedly Brady said, "I always

make it a point to leave just four inches between my stomach and the edge of the table and then when I can feel 'em rubbin' together pretty hard I know I've had enough."

Or was it all just a myth?

Oscar Tschirky, who ran the dining room at the Waldorf, remembered being a young immigrant in 1883 when he happened to be passing Delmonico's as a young trim Lillian Russell was rushing in:

> I remember the smooth flow of her blue gown, the exotic effect of her golden hair, but most of all the banked-down fire that smoldered in her beautiful face. She was the loveliest woman I had ever seen.

The next day he applied for a job as a busboy in Delmonico's. Years later, when Tschirky was the waiter in charge of Delmonico's private rooms, Diamond Jim Brady came in to have a private dinner with Lillian Russell and he waited on them. The waiter found Brady, with his diamond stickpin, diamond-headed cane, and diamond rings, "warm, friendly, and jovial." He knew Brady's reputation and was ready with oysters by the dozen and double portions of everything. But he was shocked and a bit crushed to discover that Miss Russell ate even more than Diamond Jim.

Tschirky, who went on to serve him many times in Delmonico's and later when he ran the dining room at the Waldorf, said that he usually ate what he ate that first night: one dozen raw oysters, a filet mignon with a green vegetable, and a slice of apple pie or watermelon when in season. The only thing he drank was orange juice. In the nineteenth century, one dozen oysters was considered a modest portion. Russell also ate a dozen oysters, but then she ate soup, fish, a main dish, a roast, two vegetables, sherbet, game, salad, ice cream, cake, and coffee. All accompanied by vintage wines. She was one of those American eaters Europeans used to write about. He was not.

Tschirky called it "the surprise and disillusionment of my life."

It could have been that the round and sad-faced Brady had taken up dieting. It was well known, from the spectacle it created, that he and Russell attempted to trim down by taking up the new New York craze, bicycling. The chain-driven bicycle with two equal-size wheels was developed in the 1880s and soon Central Park and city streets were filled with cyclists. It was said that so many bicycle lamps glowed in Manhattan streets at night that the streets appeared to be "filled with fireflies." City newspapers were brimming with angry editorials about "blazing"—reckless bicycling—though it seemed doubtful that New York's most celebrated elephantine couple were blazers. Feminists and suffragettes including Susan B. Anthony were excited about bicycles as a mode of transportation that fostered sexual equality and female independence. In fact, Russell took it up first, pedaling through Central Park dressed in white with fellow actress Marie Dressler. Afterward, they would defy sexual decorum by smoking cigarettes behind drawn curtains. When pounds started disappearing from Russell, Brady took up the sport, ordering a dozen gold-plated bicycles made with diamond-encrusted handlebars for him and her friends to be seen pedaling through the park.

Despite Tschirky's recollection of Diamond Jim, George Rector insisted in his memoirs that Brady ate Homeric quantities. He certainly looked as if he did and so did Russell. She was so tightly trussed it seemed all the fleshiness of her body had been pushed up to her soft and fleshy arms. As one chronicler of Delmonico's, Lately

Thomas, quipped, New Yorkers always wanted to see her and they got to see "more and more."

Theirs was a legend that fit the times—a tale of excess. It was the Gilded Age and there was a tendency to gild just about everything, including the proverbial lily. It was the age when it was no longer enough to serve a raw oyster in its shell. It became the fashion to commission ornate oyster plates, often hand-painted and custom-made, from leading china makers. Gilded porcelain would, of course, be better. Originally, oyster plates had one deep well, like a soup bowl, for a bed of ice on which to put the oysters. But soon they were made with a half-dozen wells, shaped like the interior of an oyster, in highly ornate patterns preferably with a maximum of gilding. The only problem with these plates was that they could not hold enough oysters to keep many diners happy and would require constant refilling. And it is true that oysters have the unusual quality of not filling or bloating, even when large quantities are consumed. One book, *The Oyster Epicure*, published in New York in 1883, quotes a man who has just dispatched ten dozen on the half shell, "Something must be wrong with me! I have eaten 120 oysters and upon my word of honor, I don't think I am quite as hungry as when I began."

Tschirky, who admitted that he really couldn't cook, collected his recipes without acknowledgment from people who could, the leading chefs of New York, during his many years first at Delmonico's then as maître d' of the Waldorf-Astoria. The Waldorf-Astoria was known for its oysters, though it is only remembered today for a salad. Though most modern diners would choose dry white wine with oysters, Tschirky recommended the sweet, musty, complex, and costly wines of Sauternes, specifically an 1878 Château-Rieussec.

His oyster science, like that of many of the great chefs he stole from, was somewhat faulty. He identified all oysters as *Ostrea edulis,* the fading flat oyster of Europe. He considered Bluepoints to be the best oysters, though he didn't seem to realize that they, along with all the other East Coast oysters, were *Crassostrea.* This was his oyster-bisque recipe:

> Place about thirty medium sized oysters in a saucepan together with their own juice, and poach them over a hot fire, after which drain them well. Then fry a shallot colorless in some butter together with an onion, sprinkle over them a little curry and add some oyster juice, seasoning with salt and red pepper; pound the oysters to a good firm paste, moisten them with a little of their juice, and strain them through a fine tammy-cloth; warm them over the fire, but do not let them boil; add a small quantity of thickening of potato flour mixed with a little water (about a tablespoon for each quart of the mixture), and when about to serve, incorporate some cream and fine butter, garnishing with some chopped oysters and mushrooms, mixed with bread crumbs and herbs; add a little seasoning of salt, pepper and nutmeg, some raw egg yolks and roll this mixture into ball-shaped pieces, place them on a well buttered baking sheet in a slack oven and poach them, then serve.

In his 1912 article on lobster palaces, Julian Street wrote, "Let us dry our tears, go to the Café de l'Opéra and listen to the *haute monde* of the Tenderloin eat soup." The Tenderloin, where many of the lobster palaces were located, was between Forty-second and Twenty-fourth streets, between Fifth and Seventh avenues. Known for its corruption, it was sometimes called "Satan's Circus," while the original name, tenderloin, came to mean a bribe paid to the police.

No one can say exactly who ate the hundreds of millions of oysters that were sold in New York markets, but New Yorkers seemed to be able to consume as many oysters as were available. More came to the city every year. By 1872, New York City had cornered a third of the annual $25 million U.S. oyster trade. New York operators planted hundreds of thousands of bushels of seeds to keep up with the demand. On September 10, 1883, *The New York Times* reported:

> One of the dealers was asked whether he did not think the oyster business was increasing in volume to such an extent as to imperil the future of the oysterbeds. He replied that there was, in his judgment, some fear that before many years, the demand, if it continued to increase as it had been doing in the past five years, would be greater than the supply. The oyster could not last forever any more than the lobster, and the latter were becoming scarcer every year.

CHAPTER TEN

Ostracized in the Golden Age

—

*A splendid desert—a domed and steepled solitude, where the
stranger is lonely in the midst of a million of his race.*

—MARK TWAIN'S
description of New York for the newspaper
Alta California, May 19, 1867

By 1880, New York was the undisputed capital of history's greatest oyster boom in its golden age, which lasted until at least 1910. The oyster beds of the New York area were producing 700 million oysters a year. That is without including the oysters of New Jersey, Connecticut, Rhode Island, or eastern Long Island, all of which were sold in the New York City markets.

On almost every block of Manhattan, oysters were for sale from streetside stands, belowground cellars, and aboveground palaces. In addition to all this, New Yorkers ate them at home. Lida A. Seely, in her 1902 book *Mrs. Seely's Cook Book: A Manual of French and American Cookery with Chapters on Domestic Servants, their Rights and Du-*

Early twentieth-century New York City oyster stand
MUSEUM OF THE CITY OF NEW YORK

ties, and Many Other Details of Household Management, offers this advice on giving dinner parties:

> As soon as a guest is seated, and has taken his napkin and bread from his plate, the butler puts down on it another on which are oysters, clams, or melon, according to the season, neatly arranged on a small doily. Oysters and clams should be served on plates of cracked ice, six or eight on each plate, with a quarter of a lemon in the centre. Although the former are said to be better if eaten from their deep shell, for formal dinners they look rather prettier on their flat upper one. The plates should be placed in the plates already in front of each guest, after the

napkins have been lifted. As the butler puts down the oysters
or clams, the footman should follow with a small silver tray on
which are black cayenne, liquid red pepper, and grated horse-
radish. Brown-bread sandwiches, cut very thin and spread with
unsalted butter, are also handed with this course.

Seely was born in Canada in 1854 with the name Eliza Campbell.
After marrying a man named Holly Seely, she moved to Manhattan
and set up what was called an intelligence office on Twenty-second
Street just off Fifth Avenue. An intelligence office, a growing business at the time, was an employment agency for butlers, maids, cooks,
chauffeurs, valets, and other domestic servants. In 1900, about 1.8
million women, 90 percent of the female workforce in the United
States, were domestics. It was, as it still is, one of the most sensitive
and difficult employee–employer relationships, and Lida Seely
earned a reputation for her skill, tact, and empathy.

The book urged employers to allow servants their privacy and
never spy on them and entreated servants to overlook their employers'
moments of ill temper. With its wealth of detail, *Mrs. Seely's Cookbook*
is a social document of that Gilded Age before the Depression, an age
that coincided with the last great era of New York oysters. In 1890,
when the word *millionaire* still had meaning, there were only 4,074 of
them in the entire United States, of which 1,103 lived in Manhattan. In
the recipe section of her book, Mrs. Seely offers more than twenty oyster recipes. These recipes tended to call for copious amounts of bivalves. "Have at hand thirty-five oysters," begins one recipe.

⚜ Stuffed Oysters

Have at hand twenty-eight large oysters and some chicken
forcemeat prepared as follows: Scrape and pound the breast

of an uncooked medium-sized fowl, then rub it through a purée sieve. Mix one-quarter of a cup of cream or milk with one-eighth of a cup of fine bread crumbs. Cook them slowly until they form a smooth paste. Then add the chicken, the white of one egg, one tablespoonful of butter, one half teaspoonful of salt, a bit of white pepper. Mix all together thoroughly and set away to cool. Dry the oysters thoroughly and season them with salt and pepper. Roll them in bread crumbs. Arrange the forcemeat in half as many pieces as you have oysters, cover with the remaining oysters. Press them together so they will stick. Take one whole egg and the yolk left from the forcemeat. Beat it well, season with a little salt. Dip each oyster in the egg, then roll them in bread crumbs. Fry in hot fat until a good color. Drain on brown paper and serve very hot with Madeira sauce in a separate dish.

"Pigs in Blankets" was a very popular turn-of-the-century dish.

Have at hand oysters, salt, pepper, sliced fat bacon. Clean and season some nice large oysters with salt and pepper. Wrap each oyster in a slice of thin bacon, pinning it with a toothpick. Cook them until the bacon is crisp.

Many of the waters of the New York City area were still oyster producing. In 1883, *The New York Times* identified Bluepoint, today the closest New York City has to a local oyster, as the farthest oyster away, shipments reaching the city only once a week. The principal New

York beds were Shrewsbury and Keyport, New Jersey; Prince's Bay, Staten Island; Jamaica Bay; the Great South Bay; City Island; Cow Bay; Hempstead Harbor; North Port; and Port Jefferson on the East River.

Industrialization was encroaching on New York City beds. The natural beds around Hell Gate and in the Harlem River were abandoned in the 1870s because they were too close to industry. But oystermen were still working farther up the Harlem River and commuters on the Harlem and New Rochelle railroad passed in plain view of the Harlem River oyster rakers. Some Westchester and Bronx beds were still in use, notably East Chester Bay, the waters of City Island. There was also oystering along the Bronx coastline until 1889, when the dredging of the Harlem Ship Canal, allowing passage for larger ships, took away the wetlands, the shellfish beds, and the traditional look of that coast.

After the Civil War, Staten Island oyster prices went back down to their prewar level. The response was to produce more oysters. A handful of families had become wealthy on oysters—a kind of Staten Island oyster aristocracy who named streets after themselves and built grand mansions facing the Kill van Kull. The Virginia oysters of Prince's Bay, now some generations from Virginia, continued to be highly prized, as were the native Staten Island "Sounds," which competed with Bluepoints and sometimes replaced them when the Long Islanders did not maintain their quality in the European market.

Staten Island oysters bound for Europe, with at times as much as a third of the catch for London alone, would be sent across the water to New Jersey packing plants in Keyport and Perth Amboy. Keyport also did a prosperous business supplying the beach resorts on the Jersey shore. In the late nineteenth century, oysters were the most popular snack on all the New York area beaches, including Coney Island

and Rockaway. In 1867, a German immigrant named Charles Feltman had invented a cart for keeping sausages warm so they could be
sold on the beach at Coney Island. The sausages grew in popularity
after 1875 when he started selling them on a roll as they had done back
in Nuremberg. By 1882, the eighty Frankfurt vendors on Coney Island beach and Feltman's 1,200-waiter restaurant were giving oysters
some competition, but for the ten-cent price of a hotdog, the bather
could get a whole plateful of oysters.

In the late nineteenth century, both the technology and the market existed to clean out New York oyster beds in a few energetic sea-
sons. The economics were growing tougher because steam-powered
dredges were greatly increasing the harvest. Each time a dredge was
hauled across a bed, it hauled up seven to eight bushels of oysters. By
1880, the use of steam power was estimated to have increased the
amount of oysters brought to market twelve times from the catch
when oyster fleets had been purely sail-powered.

Laws were passed to moderate the natural industriousness of men
who earned their living by harvesting huge quantities of a low-priced
product. Steam power was now commonplace, but steam-powered
dredging was banned in much of New York, and even in the case of
dredging from a sail-powered sloop, the size of the dredge was re-
stricted to a maximum of thirty pounds. Queens County barred all
dredging except in Oyster Bay and Cow Bay.

So long as tonging rather than dredging was used, it seemed the
beds could go on forever. A round of tonging stirred up the bed, exposed new surfaces, and promoted new attachments and a fresh crop.
Some argued that dredging would do an even better job of this and
that it was a mistake to ban the practice.

But it became clear that cultivation had its own kind of overfishing problem. Because of the Civil War, New Yorkers had abandoned

their reliance on Southern seed oysters to plant their beds. Selling tiny seed oysters became a growing business, especially in the Great South Bay. Boats from as far away as Rhode Island and Massachusetts came to the Great South Bay to gather seed for their own beds. The bay was also a major source of seeds for Rockaway and Staten Island beds. In its cheapest form, seed was sold the way it was caught. The tiny oysters were clumped in with rocks, shells, and dead sea life. This sold for twenty-five cents a bushel in the 1880s. But often a skiff would hire boys to sit on deck as the oystermen were tonging and cull through the matter that came up with the oysters, spreading it out on the boards placed across the gunwales. The seed they culled sold for as much as sixty cents a bushel. But starting in the 1870s, seed became increasingly difficult to find in the Great South Bay. By the 1880s, with five hundred sailing vessels coming every year with a basket hoisted up the mast, young oystermen in the Great South Bay had no memory of the days when seed was easy to come by.

Old practices were becoming newly controversial, including the New York custom of "drinking" oysters. After oysters were harvested, rather than taking them directly to market, the oystermen would "float" them in holding tanks in the mouths of freshwater rivers and streams. This made the oysters whiter in color and plumper in appearance, although this plumpness was a bloating that may have made the oysters less flavorful. An article in *The New York Times* in 1910 called drinking "adulteration." It argued, "Adulteration of oysters on the half shell, freshly opened, might be thought as difficult as adulteration of unpeeled fruit." The *Times* reported that the U.S. Department of Agriculture had been looking into the question because oysters were classified and priced by their size, and an oyster could become bloated into a different price category. The Department of Agriculture argued that four quarts of shucked oysters placed in one quart of water would quickly become five quarts of oysters if the oysters had been drinking fresh water prior to shucking. The consumer would not know that one of those quarts was water.

Surprisingly few consumers, most of them European, complained that the practice also watered down the flavor. But there was another growing issue. The freshwater sources of the New York estuary system where the oysters were drinking were the most polluted waters. Industry dumped waste into rivers. Already by the eighteenth century, Gowanus Bay, where the Dutch had praised foot-long oysters, had been closed to oystering because of raw sewage. By the midnineteenth century, Jamaica Bay's famous Rockaway beds were closed because of the tons of raw sewage dumped there from nearby Long Island towns. Such contaminated freshwater openings to the sea were exactly where oystermen chose to have their catches drink.

Sewage along with other New York garbage and waste was taken out to sea on scows and dumped. Some of it washed back into the city, even clogging parts of the harbor, and as early as the 1854 oyster panic, many people were denouncing this practice, especially when the waste, including dead animals, washed up in the popular beach resorts in the summertime. A growing belief that the foul smells were poisonous disease-causing gas led to the formation of the Metropolitan Board of Health in 1866. In 1870, this was taken over by the New York City Board of Health, which in 1886 built the first chemically treated waste-water facility in the United States on Coney Island. But by 1910, 600 million gallons of untreated sewage were dumped into New York City water every day. When at the beginning of the twentieth century, floating bathhouses opened on the shores of Manhattan every summer for swimming and recreation, sewage could be seen among the swimmers and sometimes children would emerge covered in filth.

Cholera is a disease caused by bacteria, *Vibrio cholerae*. Although bacteria, the oldest form of life on earth, was first discovered in the seventeenth century, it was not until the late nineteenth century that its role in diseases was understood. Only a few years after the oyster panic, the French chemist Louis Pasteur promoted his theory that diseases were caused by germs. But it was only a theory—referred to as "the germ theory"—until the German bacteriologist Robert Koch started proving the connection. In 1884, after documenting the infection process of numerous other diseases, he demonstrated how *Vibrio cholerae* caused cholera. In 1885, cholera bacteria were recovered from harbor water during an epidemic in Marseille. The long-suspected connection between oysters and typhoid became clearly established in the 1890s. It was also determined that sewage bred the *Salmonella bacillus,* which public-health authorities could identify in the water and in oysters and which was the cause of persistent outbreaks of typhoid.

In one decade, the medical view of the world changed. The culprits of urban epidemics switched from poverty, immigration, and immorality to bacteria, sewage, and shellfish. The "germ theory" that had been debated and often rejected in medical schools up until the 1880s became, by 1890, the established scientific thinking.

Though typhoid did not have nearly the mortality rate of cholera, it was a prolonged ailment that sometimes resulted in death. It swept rapidly through urban areas because infected people, especially if involved in handling food, could pass it on. The most famous example was Mary Mallon, Typhoid Mary, who became infected in 1904 while working as a cook in a typhoid-stricken household in Oyster Bay, Long Island. She continued as a cook in numerous households and was apprehended in 1907 while cooking for a Park Avenue home. So began a history of being institutionalized, released, caught cooking, and once again apprehended. She was thought to have been responsible for at least fifty cases of typhoid, three fatal, including a serious outbreak at a women's hospital.

Public-health officials began to understand that oysters, because they feed by filtering water, are a reflection of the quality of the water in which they live. They can be used to measure pollutants such as DDT and have even been used to measure radiation. At the turn of the century, oysters showed that New York was producing too much sewage to be able to dump it all into the sea without consequences.

London, whose valuable oyster beds were in the estuary of the Thames, had the same problem. In 1896, a British medical inspector, Dr. H. Timbrell Bulstrode, toured the principal oyster beds of England and Wales and reported in detail on the relationship of sewage drains to oyster beds. Scares in prominent oyster beds, such as Whitstable in 1903, seriously diminished the demand for oysters in Britain. France also had scares about infected oysters, and between 1898 and 1901, the demand for oysters in France was cut in half. But while British demand continued to decline, the French, always the more courageous eaters, soon resumed their old ways.

In New York, once the typhoid scares began, the practice of drinking oysters was banned by the Pure Food Department in Washington. But the large New Jersey oyster packers fought the decision.

The 1905 Christmas edition of the *Keyport Weekly*, a publication that was a great booster of the local oyster industry, argued:

> The oysterman contended that the "floated" oysters were better, kept longer and were more tender than those not thus treated. The discussion led Professor Julius Nelson of Rutgers College, Biologist of the New Jersey State Agricultural Experiment Station and a scientist of the highest standing—himself at first opposed to the oystermen's contention—to investigate the problem. . . . He made an exhaustive study of the question, and the result was that for once that practical man knew more than the scientist and the oystermen's contention was upheld in every detail and the Pure Food Department has withdrawn the ban. The freshened oyster is better, cleaner, tenderer, purer, free from sand, etc. and the unfloated article has practically passed from the market. The only possible danger is from oysters floated in polluted waters, and as all such grounds are now under the supervision of both the State and local boards of health such a thing is well nigh an impossibility, especially with a reputable firm.

This was characteristic of the thinking of many people in 1905. They believed that now that the government had learned how to measure pollution, they didn't have to worry about it anymore. But what those health boards found was that there was almost no unpolluted fresh water available for floating oysters. And so the practice was once again banned, a development cheered by *The New York Times*. At the opening of the season in 1909, the paper reported that "the sickly bleached color is disappearing from oysters" because the practice of "drinking" had been, at last, stopped.

By 1880, the oysters known as Yorks, from York Bay, the shallow water along northern New Jersey, were no longer available. The water of York Bay was so fouled with sewage and discharges from Jersey City factories that the oysters were safe to use only as seed. Most of the seed oysters planted in Raritan Bay were from Newark Bay, while oysters from the lower Passaic were shipped by the carload to the Pacific to be planted in California.

It began as an experiment in 1873 when Joseph Ellsworth, owner of one of the more prominent oyster firms, with a barge in Manhattan and an office at the Washington Market, sent a train boxcar full of Newark Bay seed oysters to San Francisco. The best and cleanest dime-size oysters were selected. These oysters needed to grow in the Pacific for only two years, in part because, as the Reverend Samuel Lockwood wrote in an 1874 *Popular Science Monthly* article, Californians were "more easily suited on the question of size than the people East."

Californians were accustomed to smaller oysters and New Yorkers theorized that cold Pacific waters stunted them early in their growth, but it might be that the *Crassostrea gigas* is a smaller oyster than its East Coast cousin, the *Crassostrea virginica.* The tendency was to blame it on the water. Lockwood said, "The native Californian oyster is a puny affair and it is to be feared that the Eastern oyster will degenerate in Pacific waters." But Ellsworth hoped that the transplanted New Jersey product would thrive and grow rapidly off the California coast. It did and it also lost what a 1902 commission investigating New Jersey oysters called "the unpleasant flavor it derives early in life from the polluted Newark waters." This was at a time when the Passaic River, once regarded as the best fishing river in New

Jersey, was so foul that it emitted acrid fumes that blistered the paint off nearby houses. Riverside residents were abandoning their homes to escape the stench. In 1901, J. & J. W. Ellsworth, which had built a packing plant in Keyport two years earlier, shipped 110 carloads of Newark Bay seed across the country to planters in California. Nine days after being taken from Newark Bay, the oysters were settled in upper San Francisco Bay.

By 1900, the market-size oysters of the Passaic River and Newark Bay, whose fresh waters were used for drinking oysters, were too polluted to be eaten. The beds became important sources of seed oysters, especially for shipping to California, but also for replanting the Keyport beds. Polluted Newark Bay was regarded as among the most valuable seed source in New Jersey at a time when seed was starting to become difficult to find.

This transplanting of species that began in the late nineteenth and early twentieth century quickly became commonplace. It became a contest, like those in nature, in which the hardiest triumphed and the hardiest were clearly the *Crassostrea*. Europeans replaced many struggling *Ostrea edulis* beds with the more durable Portuguese oyster, the *Crassostrea angulata*, and with the American *Crassostrea virginica*. *Ostreas* are found naturally on the Pacific coast of North America, such as the *Ostrea lurida*, the Olympia oyster. But West Coast beds were planted with the more temperature-resistant East Coast *Crassostrea virginica* and the more disease-resistant Asian *Crassostrea gigas*, the Japanese and Korean oyster. The highly adaptable *Crassostrea gigas* has also been transplanted in Taiwan and China and has been introduced to New Zealand, Tasmania, Chile, the west coast of Canada, France, and Britain. The Chinese produce huge quantities of *Crassostrea plicatula*, which some biologists think is a misnomer and that the oyster is of a separate genus they have called *Alectryonella*.

Saccostrea, the Sydney rock oyster, is Australian and thrives in warm water. *Crassostrea rhizophorae,* the mangrove oyster, is common in the Caribbean and Central America, including Venezuela and Colombia, though the oyster industry remains small in these countries. There are also different *Crassostrea* species in Brazil, Sierra Leone and Senegal, the Philippines, and Thailand. There are also unique oysters such as *Tiostrea lutarea,* the New Zealand bluff oyster.

What all of this means is that while a certain diversity of genera is maintained, most of the oysters eaten in the world today are *Crassostrea.* No one is particularly upset about this, although there is justifiable mourning for the passing of the European *Ostrea,* not just because Europeans like to obsess about foreign takeovers but because most of Europe's greatest and most famous oysters, like the French belon and the British Colchester, are *Ostrea edulis,* a species that produces a meaty creature with an incomparable fresh, briny flavor.

The European flat oyster ranged from the Mediterranean to the British Isles and into Norway, even north of the Arctic Circle. But it has been destroyed by overharvesting and disease and it now exists in only a few places, including Maine, where belons have been transplanted but taste different in their new environment.

It was not only oysters that were being threatened in New York Harbor. The tremendous variety of fish in the harbor and its rivers, like oysters, provided the livelihood of many New Yorkers. By tradition a poor family, short of money, could always gather oysters or catch a fish for dinner. It was an advantage of being poor in New York. When the British took New York from the Dutch, they had visions of developing a New York fishing industry because the harbor was filled with mackerel and cod. The Hudson River was particularly rich in both fresh- and saltwater species, including striped bass, shad, and sturgeon. The sturgeon provided a caviar industry whose product graced New York bars—a free salty snack to encourage drinking. The harbor had lobster, though they were getting scarcer. The succulent larvae of blue-claw crab, the celebrated Chesapeake residents, drifted into the summer harbor, and those that weren't eaten by fish became crabs that scudded their way up the Hudson to Albany. In the summer, while the oysters were spawning, small crustaceans, the grass shrimp that like the brackish waters of the oyster, appeared, and in the saltier sea, little sand shrimp tempted hungry fish. Translucent anchovies arrived and spawned daily, tantalizing the toothy bluefish, Spanish mackerel, and fluke, which chased them into the harbor.

In the midnineteenth century, sportsmen came from throughout the Eastern United States to fish in New York Harbor. Sporting publications featured articles about angling in the harbor. *The American Angler*, the first American magazine exclusively devoted to sports fishing, began publishing in 1881 in the angling capital, Manhattan. Most of the best fishing spots could be reached by rowboats rented for twenty-five cents an hour at the end of Whitehall Street. Governors Island was known for bluefish and weakfish, Ellis Island was the place to land twenty-pound stripers, though just north of Staten Island was another striped-bass spot. Weakfish was best off of Brooklyn just above the Narrows. New Yorkers were noted for trolling by rowing while dragging the line held in their mouth. When a sudden strike yanked their teeth, they would drop the oars and grab the line.

But many Manhattanites, especially poor ones in search of dinner, fished from the shore. Sea drums, grown to enormous sizes, fed off the oyster beds close to the Manhattan shore. The record drum, seventy pounds, was taken in the Harlem River. But the Battery was also a good spot. Shark fishing was a popular sport. Despite the growing popularity of summer bathing, the harbor was full of huge sharks. It seemed the bathers never talked to the fishermen.

Until the mideighteenth century, most New York commercial fishing was done with a hook and handheld line from small sloops. In midcentury, New Yorkers began imitating the New England cod fishery, launching one- and two-man rowboats, dories, from larger vessels. The city's large and expanding immigrant population was mostly Catholic, and by Church orders ate fish on Fridays. The dories began long-lining—baiting as many as 350 hooks on a single line dragged off a dory. Much of the fishing fleet, which remained under sail into the twentieth century, was docked near the Fulton Market, where they landed their catch.

But by the end of the nineteenth century, finfishing, too, was feeling the effect of the water having been treated for centuries as a city dump. Sturgeon catches, which had been more than one million pounds a year, giving the fish the nickname Albany beef, started to dramatically drop from pollution, which also ended the caviar industry. Fish trapped in shallow water found themselves suffocated in oil spills. "Shad have been driven out of the Hudson," *The New York Times* reported in 1924. Soon almost every species had met the same fate. Lobster and bluefish started disappearing. Those that survived, including some oysters, were too contaminated to eat. The sharks stayed off of Sandy Hook to avoid the city's foul waters.

At the turn of the century, the public did not complain about the sewage nearly as much as the dye wastes discharged into rivers, a relatively nontoxic form of pollution. In the 1880s, residents near the

Gowanus Canal complained of the smell but were more struck by the colors. Dye manufacturers turned the waterway a different pigment every day. The canal was nicknamed "Lavender Lake," and poor people in the surrounding neighborhoods would stand on the canal bridges with their asthmatic children, believing the rising rank fumes had healing powers.

But many people did get upset when the water started changing colors because it was visible. When sewage washed up on beaches, this also could be seen, not to mention smelled, and it became an issue. In 1914, the city began closing most of its public beaches in all five boroughs. Coney Island, which had a treatment plant, remained open. Sometimes the smell alone was enough to anger the public, because they believed bad smells were toxic, but it took a really bad stench to rile them.

Newtown Creek, which wanders the Queens–Brooklyn border and empties into the East River across from Manhattan, gave off such a stink that nearby residents in all three boroughs were forced to keep their windows closed in the summer. In 1891, the locals formed a committee to sniff out the culprits. Known as the Fifteenth Ward Smelling Committee, they sniffed their way down the canal and compiled a list of culprits that included a fertilizer company, a chemical works, and a "dead animal wharf." John Waldman, a contemporary biologist, compared traffic on the entire Mississippi and the four-mile Newtown Creek between 1915 and 1917 and found the freight tonnage to be almost equal, though the Newtown Creek cargo had twice the value. In 1872, John D. Rockefeller chose the creek to be America's first oil-refining site. By the turn of the century, the refinery had dumped or accidentally spilled enough petroleum and by-products to effectively kill the creek.

Oystermen and fishermen—anyone who worked on the water—

knew that the harbor water was not clean and it was getting worse. But they did not see the problem as critical until the linkage between typhoid and oysters was established. This had a growing impact on the oyster business. New York restaurants became increasingly concerned after a 1909 British case that was widely reported in New York, in which a British court ordered a hotel in Chatham to pay $1,320 to a Royal Navy lieutenant who claimed to have gotten typhoid fever from eating their oysters. New York restaurateurs wondered if such cases would not soon be filed against them. New York chefs, notably Albert Leopold Lattard of the Plaza hotel, started emphasizing recipes that involved cooking oysters thoroughly rather than serving them raw. There was a growing outcry in New York City against what *The New York Times* called "sewage fed oysters."

That same year, New York City hosted a conference of the Na-

An article in an 1891 issue of Harper's Weekly *shows the city's street-cleaning department loading garbage onto barges to be dumped in the harbor.*

tional Association of Shellfish Commissioners. The thirteen states present represented 88 percent of the world's oyster production. At the time, New York State had a $10 million investment in an oyster industry that produced about 1.4 billion oysters a year, a significant industry considering some New York oysters were getting a reputation for tasting like petroleum. Given the things New York Harbor could taste like, critics may have been kind. New York City was still the oyster capital even though the city's production was now little more than half that of the late nineteenth century.

The year 1909, when the city hosted the conference, was one of the last good years for New York City oysters. The industry was being strangled. Once the typhoid connection had been established, the big oyster houses, the Manhattan wholesalers who provided all the venture capital to keep the industry growing, became reluctant to further invest in New York City beds.

In 1915, the city closed down all the shellfish beds of Jamaica Bay because of contamination from sewage. In the summer of 1916, another outbreak of typhoid was traced to eating oysters from beds in the lower bay that had been contaminated by a New Jersey sewer line that emptied into the Kill van Kull where it met the upper bay. This was a considerable distance from the oyster beds, but the tides carried the sewage there.

On January 27, 1920, *The New York Times,* reporting on the findings of a state commissioner's report, warned that "Oysters, once plentiful and considered a frugal repast, are gradually being classed as luxuries and will soon become a delicacy." The cause of this depletion in the oyster supply was simply stated as "pollution of waters in which oysters ordinarily spawn."

The news was getting worse and worse, not necessarily because the pollution was getting worse but because the ability to measure it was getting better. In January 1921, the New York City Health Department again closed the oyster beds of Jamaica Bay, which had been sending 80 million oysters or more to market every year. *The New York Times* announced the closing with a lead article at the top center of the front page and the headline JAMAICA BAY, FOUL WITH SEWAGE, CLOSED TO OYSTER BEDS; 300,000 BUSHELS GONE. The water was fouled with sewage, which should not have been surprising since no fewer than forty trunk lines of the city sewage system emptied into the bay. But in explaining the decision, the Health Department said that in addition to the risk posed by sewage, several cases of typhoid had been diagnosed in the area and they cited the case of Typhoid Mary to remind the public of the risk of contagion. The city warned that Jamaica Bay produced between a quarter and a third of the oysters in New York City markets and that there might be a shortage that year. The city even contacted the French government to say that they might need to start importing oysters and asked that their health department send reports on French oyster cultivation.

An experimental oyster purification plant, which attempted to clean out contaminated oysters, was built near Jamaica Bay in Inwood. Salt water was pumped into holding tanks through which was also pumped a "sterilizing agent," hypochlorite of sodium, produced by electrolysis of the seawater. But a 1922 report of the Bureau of Prevention of Stream Pollution cautioned that this was effective only if the oysters were not excessively contaminated and the report also pointed out that the seawater used "must not be grossly contaminated with sewage or other filth. . . ."

The emerging data on pollution led to closing the beds, but it did not lead to a cleanup of the pollution. In 1924, an outbreak of typhoid was traced to drinking water from Englewood Brook in the Palisades Interstate Park that was polluted from sewage. But finding the source did not end the problem. EXPECT MORE TYPHOID, said a *Times* head-line. Sixty-eight New York City cases were traced to the Englewood Brook incident, which was caused by a blocked sewer that could have been fixed in half an hour for about five dollars in expenses. The *Times* was right. In three weeks the number of cases had climbed to 124.

A *New York Times* editorial on July 25, 1924 stated:

The agitation about polluted streams in the Palisades Inter-state Park calls attention to the general neglect of the waters in and about New York. The wonder is not that a number of cases of typhoid have been traced to a certain stream, but that there has not been more illness caused by contaminated water. It has been estimated that no less than 14,000,000 tons of sewage go into the Hudson River alone each year. The harbor and coast waters within a radius of twenty miles of New York are full of refuse of all sorts. Thanks to the ruling that garbage from the city is to be dumped further out at sea than last year, the amount of filth on the beaches has been less noticeable this summer. But waters which ten or fifteen years ago were clear are now clouded with impurities coming from waste matter of all sorts—garbage and sewage, as well as the dis-charges from factories and the oil from ships.

Articles regularly appeared in all the New York papers about pol-lution and, from time to time, about one oyster bed or another being closed. In 1927, the last of the Raritan Bay beds was closed, marking the end of oystering in New York City. New Yorkers, who had begun by polluting a little pond called the Collect, had now befouled the en-tire estuary of the Hudson River. The pollution also killed off clamming, lobstering, and both commercial and sportfishing. A New Yorker could no longer wade out or row out from shore and catch dinner. New York families could no longer earn a living harvesting the sea they lived next to.

New Yorkers continued to eat oysters, though not as many, and oyster bars remained popular, though not on the same scale. New ones opened all the time, like the Oyster Bar in Grand Central Terminal that debuted in 1913. But they weren't serving local oysters. New York chefs still prided themselves on their oyster dishes, though they were not made with New York City oysters. In 1951, Louis de Gouy, the master chef of the Waldorf-Astoria, published a 170-page recipe collection on oysters alone, *The Oyster Book.* This was the first book by a major food authority dedicated exclusively to oysters since the slim 1894 book *Fifteen New Ways for Oysters* by Sarah Tyson Rorer of Philadelphia, one of the founders of the *Ladies' Home Journal.* But a New Yorker could not walk to the corner and buy a roasted East River oyster.

Though goods continued to be shipped in and shipped out on container vessels in plain sight and the city lived off that commerce, it had lost its direct connection to its own vast and once sweet-smelling sea.

Enduring Shellfishness

—

La aurora de Nueva York tiene
cuatro columnas de cieno
y un huracán de negras palomas
que chapotean las aguas podridas

(Dawn in New York has
four columns of mud
and a hurricane of black doves
wet from the stagnant water.)
—FEDERICO GARCÍA LORCA,
Poeta en Nueva York, 1929–30

It is difficult not to ask the question: *Are ten million or* more people not too many to be living on one estuary? In 1790, when the first U.S. census was conducted, 49,401 people were living in what were to become the five boroughs of New York City. By 1930, when all the oyster beds had been polluted and shut down, the population was 6,930,446, almost double what it had been at the start of that century. In the seventy years since then, perhaps in recognition that the space was nearly filled to capacity, the population grew by only about half a million. New Yorkers have long regarded their city as unnatural, in contradiction with nature. They talk of leaving the city "to see some nature." Perhaps it is not just unnatural but a threat to nature. Perhaps that many people just won't fit. After all, that is not what estuaries were designed for. Ten million people produce far too much garbage.

The original attempt at a solution to the dilemma of New York's garbage, leaving it on the streets to be eaten by wandering pigs, had, along with the sewage problem and the soap and meat-slaughtering industries, quickly turned sweet-smelling New York into a notoriously foul place. By the time of American independence, New York City stank, and it continued to be redolent of garbage and sewage into the twentieth century. The solution to both problems was to dump it into the sea. In 1885, New York built the country's first trash incinerator on Governors Island. Trash incinerators began to compete with ocean dumping. But unfortunately it was now the age of coal, and the incinerators, like the plants that generated the city's electricity and the industry that sprang up in the area, was coal-fired. Even the heat in apartment buildings came from burning coal. New York was veiled with clouds of black smoke.

In 1934, the city, losing a Supreme Court case, agreed to stop dumping its garbage at sea because too much was washing up on beaches. The city then turned to landfills, of which there were eighty-nine the year of the Court decision. Thousands of acres of the estuary's environmentally precious wetland became trash heaps. The dumps leached a pollutant composite known as leachate that inevitably seeped into the already polluted harbor. In 1948, responding to the growing amount of garbage and the ban on ocean dumping, the city established a 2,100-acre landfill at Fresh Kills in Staten Island. Unlike earlier sites, an attempt was made to seal off the seepage from Fresh Kills, and methane gas was extracted and used to heat fourteen thousand Staten Island homes. But with twelve thousand tons of garbage arriving every day by barge and truck, Fresh Kills is filled to capacity. The tallest mound in Fresh Kills is the highest promontory on the Atlantic coastline of the United States.

The reality is that millions of people produce far too much sewage to coexist with millions of oysters. Raw sewage continued to be dumped into the harbor despite the Coney Island treatment plant being modernized in 1935. Modern sewage-treatment plants such as the one in Coney Island and fifteen others built in the subsequent fifty years produced a by-product called "sludge," a pollutant, though less toxic than raw sewage, that was dumped only twelve miles out to sea.

In 1951, *The New Yorker* published an article by Joseph Mitchell titled "The Bottom of the Harbor," which began:

The bulk of the water in New York Harbor is oily, dirty, and germy. Men on the mud suckers, the big harbor dredges, like to say that you could bottle it and sell it for poison. The bottom of the harbor is dirtier than the water. In most places, it is covered with a blanket of sludge that is composed of silt, sewage, industrial wastes, and clotted oils.

Black gunk, devoid of oxygen, but flatulent with other gases that bubble to the surface, lies in thick underwater swamps in places hundreds of feet deep. Mitchell claimed that the sludge was accumulating in some spots at a rate of a foot and a half a year. It was particularly thick around Liberty Island, once Great Oyster Island with its famous beds. Some of the thickest deposits of this sludge were in the less salty backwaters where oysters used to like to live. The Gowanus Canal had become notorious. In the warm months the sludge there would start decomposing and releasing gas bubbles that rose to the surface, according to Mitchell, with some bubbles the size of basketballs. People would stand along the piers of the canal and watch the soupy black water boil and spit.

On Staten Island, the wooden mansions with lacy fretsaw ornaments now looked out on New York's muckiest water in the Kill van Kull. Thirty years after the oyster ban, most of these mansions had been abandoned and were slowly disintegrating. In Sandy Ground, too, where the asphalt roads were cracking, exposing the original oyster-shell pavement, the large handsome houses built by the newly prosperous African Americans who had escaped Southern poverty, now faced the fetid waters of Arthur Kill. It was not only the water that was contaminated. During the unrestricted industrial boom of World War II, the smelting plants in New Jersey on the opposite bank of the kill heaved up clouds so toxic, they destroyed the strawberry farms across the water.

New York City continued to dump sewage sludge at its selected site twelve miles out to sea until 1987. Popularly known as the "Dead Sea," it was a lifeless sixteen-square-mile zone. In 1977, New Yorkers heard a huge explosive sound and many were certain that the methane gas bubbling up from the Dead Sea had finally exploded. But the air force came forward and admitted that the sound was caused by a sonic boom from one of their jets.

Miraculously, these waters, even in the midtwentieth century when they were their most foul, were not devoid of life. More than thirty species of fish entered the harbor every spring, summer, and fall. Even tuna still came to New York. And there were mackerel, herring, whiting, porgy, blackback flounder, and others by the millions. Mossbonkers alone, the New York menhaden, would some years invade the harbor by the hundreds of millions. But there were some notable absentees, including the once-immense beds of natural oysters. The beds were largely dead, though a few rugged individuals survived. The destruction of the oyster population may explain why the drum population was decimated. The oyster-eating black drum, hated by Staten Island oyster planters, have been missing since shortly after the oyster beds were closed. It almost seems as though they respected the ban and moved on to other waters to eat oysters. The red drum has also become rare.

When the oyster beds were closed, the Staten Island planters had been allowed to take their oysters and transplant them in cleaner Long Island water. But they could not gather up every last one, and the ones that they missed started their own families of dozens of oysters huddled together in a clump. The surviving shellfish were too contaminated to be eaten, but they were there, and because they were there, some older New Yorkers who used to harvest them found it hard to believe they could not be eaten. The New York City Health Department and the state conservation department enforced the ban. But if a few former oystermen wanted to drift over the oysters with tongs or rakes and grab a bushel for old times' sake, they had only to choose their moment. In a dense fog or on a black, moonless night, a rowboat could make its way out and take oysters or clams, which were also banned for the same reason. These poachers would eat the old catch in all the old ways, clam chowder, oyster stew, and worst of all, from the medical point of view, raw on the half shell. According to Mitchell in 1951, "Every once in a while, whole families got horribly sick."

Some were more careful. They checked water temperatures. If the temperature dropped below forty-one degrees for three or four days, they would take some oysters. At forty-one degrees, oysters stop feeding. Four days of this "hibernation," it was believed, were enough to completely purge the oysters of the germs they may have taken in. Then the old-timers would snatch a clump and safely eat them raw— a Proustian moment with the "harbor oysters" of their youth.

In his 1951 article, Joseph Mitchell interviewed a Staten Islander named Poole who said of his native harbor, "It's getting worse and worse. Everything is getting worse. When I was young, I used to dream the time would come when we could bed oysters in the harbor again. Now I'm satisfied that that time will never come. I don't even worry about the pollution anymore. My only hope is they don't pollute the harbor with something a million times worse than pollution."

"A million times worse than pollution" happened. The silt and sludge alone would have been enough to kill oysters, which would sink in it and suffocate. But the industrial wastes consisted of heavy metals, including seven thousand pounds of zinc, copper, lead, chromium, and nickel that entered the city sewer system every day. Staten Island's Arthur Kill, once famous for its oyster beds, had become known for its oil spills. An oil by-product, polynuclear aromatic hydrocarbons, which are worse than they sound, poisoned the harbor's water. Pesticides from agriculture were carried in the rain to the river, including chlorinated hydrocarbons—DDT, dieldrin, endrin, and heptachlor. DDT, like heavy metals, moves up the food chain, becoming more lethal in larger fish and animals. And between the 1940s and the 1970s, General Electric dumped hundreds of thousands

of pounds of polychlorinated biphenyls, PCBs, into the Hudson. Things got worse in the 1960s and seventies. Asbestos and solvents were added to the mixture. The Diamond Shamrock Company made Agent Orange, the defoliant that poisoned Vietnam and also New York Harbor, filling the mouth of the Passaic River with dioxins.

The rivers that filled the harbor with fresh water, making oyster beds grow, were now filling the harbor with deadly chemicals. Four rivers, the Raritan, Hackensack, Passaic, and Hudson, empty into Raritan Bay. Concentrations of six heavy metals were found in the 1980s in the central muddy portion of the bay. They had entered the water from the many factories built on the Raritan River during World War II. With the sentiment "anything for the war effort," these industries were allowed to freely dump into the river, and the practice continued after the war. In 1978, Raritan Bay was found to have the highest concentration of copper ever reported in any estuary, as well as a concentration of hydrocarbons. Fish in the bay were found to be laced with PCBs. The fish were often misshapen by a pollution-caused disease known as "fin erosion disease." In the late 1960s, more than twenty species suffered from the disease, the fins slowly deteriorating and falling off. Twenty percent of all harbor bluefish suffered from it. In the 1970s, tomcod were found to be suffering from an epidemic of liver cancer, and Harlem River catfish are still mysteriously going blind.

In defiling the Hudson, industry had befouled a relatively small river of 315 miles in length, but it also happened to be one of the most treasured spots in North America. The river is home to more than two hundred fish species—a stunning assortment of both fresh- and saltwater fish, like an aquarium that displays the wildlife of several lakes, a river, and the ocean in the same tank. Among the residents of the Hudson River are largemouth bass, herring, carp, white perch, yellow perch, menhaden, shiners, darters, sunfish, tomcod, and even some subtropical fish such as the mullet and the jack crevalle, which are more typical of Florida than of the Northeast. The Caribbean needlefish and pompano as well as mangrove snapper have been found in the lower Hudson. The lower half of the Hudson is a tidal estuary where typical river species such as trout and pike swim past ocean species including sea horses, dolphins, bluefish, shark, and an occasional intrepid whale. Two species of sturgeon that are classified endangered, striped bass and shad, despite man's abuse, have stubbornly continued to return each spring through the Narrows and up the Hudson to spawn a new generation of seagoing fish in the river's fresh waters. Their numbers were critically reduced in the 1970s and eighties, but the populations have been increasing significantly. These three fish have been not only industries but part of New York lore and culture.

The Hudson River and the waterways at its mouth have evoked passion in many who lived around it. In the nineteenth century, the steep wooded banks of the valley with its softly refracted light fostered one of the most important schools of American painting. And while it is always an inexact science to locate the birthplace of a political movement, an argument can be made—and New York environmentalists do not hesitate to make it—that the American environmental movement began with the urge to save the Hudson.

Many of the first voices of American environmentalism, including Teddy Roosevelt, spent time by this river that had so astounded Henry Hudson. By the 1890s, there were movements to save upstate forests from lumbermen and in 1901 to save some of the Hudson's most spectacular scenery from stone quarries.

In 1963, Consolidated Edison announced its intention to blast a six-million-gallon reservoir at Storm King Mountain to build a power plant. This mountain, about fifty miles north of New York City, was celebrated for its beauty and was a favorite subject of the painters of the Hudson River School. Con Edison's logic was simple: New York needed the electricity. Their slogan was "Build we must." This was the same logic that had led to the destruction of so much of New York in the past two centuries, including the oyster beds. Black smoke in the sky, sewage in the water, it had all been accepted as necessary. But in the mid-1960s, many from the Hudson Valley, from New York City, from all over the country, were determined not to let Con Ed deface one of the most celebrated sights along the Hudson. National attention was focused on the fight. Con Ed stockholders sent dividend checks to Scenic Hudson, an organization trying to stop the project. It took years, but in the end the environmentalists won.

Encouraged by their victory, environmental groups took on some of the country's largest utility companies, oil companies, industries, town halls, city halls, federal agencies. In 1971, Anaconda Wire and Cable Company, which had been dumping metals, oil, and solvents into the Hudson, was charged by the U.S. attorney with one hundred counts of violating the Refuse Act of 1899. The message was that the courts were going to enforce the law. The action had been started by a complaint from Fred Danback, a janitor who grew up in the Hudson Valley and was disturbed by what his employer was doing to the river. Anaconda paid a then-record fine of $200,000.

An old legal principle was being revived. The law had long recognized that government controls should prevent nuisances to the public well-being. Anaconda and many other companies were stopped from dumping in the Hudson, the Raritan, and the rest of the estuary system under the same legal principle applied in 1703 when the New York provincial government prohibited the burning of oyster shells within the city limits because of the smoke.

Another legal principle available to environmentalists was the concept that the public has a right to fish. This principle had been established over access to natural oyster beds, which both New York and New Jersey courts recognized as a public right for residents. A company that pollutes shellfish beds and poisons fish populations is, according to this legal argument, impeding the long-recognized right of residents to fish their wild waters.

In the 1970s, some forty acts of Congress were passed for the protection of the environment. Among the most crucial for the waters of New York was the 1972 Clean Water Act, which gave a deadline of 1985 for all bodies of water in the United States to be swimmable and fishable.

In the 1980s, the city proposed to do what it had been doing ever since Dutch times, creating more Manhattan real estate by filling in the coastal waters. In this case, it was a highway called Westway that was to cut into the Hudson River bed. The public outcry against construction at the expense of the Hudson River was so forceful and determined that the project was stopped. New Yorkers had changed. They had come to care about their waterways and the estuary in which they lived.

Bluefish are back, the striper are plentiful, and the sharks off of Sandy Hook are waiting for the water to get clean enough for their return. Sharks hunt by a keen sense of smell, and the harbor still does not smell quite right to them. But the Hudson is rich in fish, and for all its continuing faults, especially PCBs, it is now considered one of the healthier estuaries in the North Atlantic. Today, all of the Hudson River and almost all of the waters of New York Harbor are swimmable and most are fishable, as the Clean Water Act mandated, but the fish that are caught are not all edible. Health authorities do not recommend eating most New York Harbor fish, though some people do, with a great deal of the fish consumed by poor people who are probably eating poisoned food. Shad is an exception, because it spends its time in the Hudson so obsessed with sex that it does not eat. This is true of sturgeon also, but it is still too scarce to eat. The striped bass is plentiful but dangerously loaded with chemicals because it likes to eat after sex.

Environmentalists are in constant battles with the port of New York, which tries to give access to ever larger vessels by dredging the harbor deeper. It is dangerous to do anything that stirs up the harbor floor and its centuries of pollution.

In 1993, a study of the presence of toxins in New York City fish showed the worst to be the PCB-laden eels of the Newtown Creek. As for the Gowanus Canal, which empties onto Jasper Danckaerts's favorite oyster bed, it may not bubble up as it did in Joseph Mitchell's time, but it still does not have enough oxygen for fish or oyster beds. When oysters were left in the canal as an experiment to see if they would spawn, they not only died within two weeks but their shells were partially eaten away by acidic compounds in the water.

A careful examination of many historic oyster-bed sites, such as those in Jamaica Bay, shows an absence of life, though the beds contain empty shells of impressive size. But there are still oysters in the East River, Arthur Kill, and other spots in New York Harbor. Miraculously, a few were recently found growing in the Newtown Creek. They can be seen between the rocks at the seawall of the Battery in lower Manhattan. In 1986, a group called the River Project, wishing to both monitor and teach about the state of water quality in the estuary, established headquarters on a pier in the TriBeCa section of lower Manhattan. They found a few oysters living under the pier and have found more every year since.

The waters have been getting measurably cleaner and the levels of contamination in fish greatly reduced. Even the Gowanus Canal got a flushing system that made the water clear enough for fish to return.

William Brooks's warning from the nineteenth century is almost forgotten, that the water system that loses its oysters loses its self-cleaning system. A healthy oyster population filters and cleans bay water, makes it clearer, and lets light penetrate so that nutrients and habitats will grow. Cathy Drew, the executive director of the River Project, said, "We project that if the oysters were here in the numbers they used to be, they would clear the water in the harbor in a few days."

Since more and more oysters are slowly turning up, they might conceivably someday cover most of the estuary's shorelines again. But the harbor is still a long way from that quantity of oysters. In 1999, an artificial oyster reef made of shells was placed at an old historic oyster site, just south of Liberty Island. Several other shell oyster reefs have also been started and oysters do grow on them. Environmentalists have been recruiting volunteers to "oyster garden," that is, to grow a few oysters on private piers in various locations around the harbor and then donate these oysters to the oyster reefs. But the organizers, a group called Baykeeper, cautions that these oysters are for building up the reefs only and that there might be serious health risks for anyone who actually ate them. They state with optimistic bravado their goal that "Oysters will thrive from Sandy Hook to the Tappan Zee, and again be served on New York City restaurant tables."

Cathy Drew said, "In our lifetime, there's no hope we could eat them, because the water contains heavy metal. But we want them back to clean the water and to enrich the food web, which would attract other animals and birds to the area." Oysters filter the water of organic waste but can do nothing about heavy metals and PCBs.

Jonathan Swift famously commented on the courage of the unknown original gourmet who first popped a raw oyster into his or her mouth. It is hard to explain to those who don't do it by what strange impulse humans take these primitive creatures with their tiny hearts pounding and slide them down their throats. It certainly has been something New Yorkers did with passion. The best explanation is that a fresh oyster from a clean sea fills the palate with the taste of all the excitement and beauty—the essence—of the ocean. If the water is not pure, that, too, can be tasted in the oyster. So if someday New Yorkers can once again wander into their estuary, pluck a bivalve, and taste the estuary of the Hudson in all the "freshness and sweetness" that was once there, the cataclysm humans have unleashed on New York will have been at last undone. But that day is far off.

If we had had the ability to see deep into water, it would have all been different. New Yorkers dumped trash and sewage into the water because there it was out of sight. Suppose they could have seen it landing on the oyster beds. In the spring, the migratory fish return. Thousands of bumpy alligator-headed, primeval two-hundred-pound sturgeon; elegant silver-streaked striped bass, their stripes seemingly made for racing; and thick schools of radiant shad tear into the strong currents, while little baitfish, purposeless hangers-on caught up in all the exhilaration of the moment, struggle furiously along as best they can. They are all bumping shoulders, swatting tails, thousands and thousands of determined fish, putting their heads nose first into the same current, charging through the Narrows over to the oyster beds of Liberty and Ellis islands, while their sedentary partners, the oysters, wave their shells open and closed beneath them, pumping clean the water, the seething crowds above turning and racing toward Manhattan and the Hudson River, past the teeming and humming city, street by street to the picturesque upstate waters of their birth. Certainly anyone who could have seen that would have understood that the great and unnatural city was built at the site of a natural wonder, and that the lowly oysters working at the bottom were a treasure more precious than pearls.

Acknowledgments

I would like to thank Connie Rosenblum of the City section of *The New York Times* for asking me to write about New York City oysters for the newspaper. Researching that article opened up worlds to me.

I want to again thank my great editor, Nancy Miller, who works with such care and diligence and gives so much to my books. And to Charlotte Sheedy, my agent, who always intercedes for me with grace and humor. How lucky I am to have friends like Nancy and Charlotte and luckier yet to get to work with them.

I want to thank Deborah Copeland and Susan Birnbaum for all their hard work. Thanks to Cathy Drew for her interest and enthusiasm. And thank you, William Kennedy, who pointed me to his piece on "Jack and the Oyster," in which he criticized an Albany columnist for being too dull to use the phrase *ambivalent bivalvency*. And thank you, Charles Gehring, for your generosity in sharing your research and anecdotes on the bivalvency of early Dutchmen. And thanks to Bob Wallace in Wellfleet for his molluscular insights.

A special thanks to caffeine, without which this book could never have been completed, and lots of love to Marian, the deeper shell of our bivalve, who makes us happy as oysters—no reason to think clams are any happier just because they don't make attachments and can hop on one foot.

Bibliography

HISTORY

Albion, Robert Greenhalgh. *The Rise of New York Port, 1815–1860*. Hamden, Conn.: Archon Books, 1961.

Anbinder, Tyler. *Five Points: The 19th-Century New York City Neighborhood That Invented Tap Dance, Stole Elections, and Became the World's Most Notorious Slum*. New York: The Free Press, 2001.

Armbruster, Eugene L. *The Indians of New England and New Netherlands*. New York: G. Quattlander, 1918.

Asbury, Herbert. *The Gangs of New York*. New York: Alfred A. Knopf, 1927.

Barry, Gerald J. *The Marine Society of the City of New York 1770–1995: A Concise History*. New York: Sea History Press, 1995.

Bayles, William Harrison. *Old Taverns of New York*. New York: Frank Allaben, 1915.

Beebe, Lucius. *The Big Spenders: The Epic Story of the Rich, the Grandees of America and the Magnificoes, and How They Spent Their Fortunes*. New York: Doubleday, 1966.

Bellot, Alfred. *History of the Rockaways from the Year 1685 to 1917*. Far Rockaway, N.Y.: Bellot's Histories, c. 1918.

Boorstin, Daniel J. *The Americans: The Democratic Experience*. New York: Random House, 1973.

Bradley, David L. *Bradley's Reminiscences of New York Harbor.* Bayonne, N.J.: David Bradley, 1896.

Brown, Eve. *The Plaza 1907–1967: Its Life and Times.* New York: Meridith Press, 1967.

Bunker, John. *Harbor & Haven: An Illustrated History of the Port of New York.* Woodland Hills, Calif.: Windsor Publications, 1979.

Burke, John. *Duet in Diamonds: The Flamboyant Saga of Lillian Russell and Diamond Jim Brady in America's Gilded Age.* New York: G. P. Putnam's Sons, 1972.

Burrows, Edwin G., and Mike Wallace. *Gotham: A History of New York City to 1898.* New York: Oxford University Press, 1999.

Buttenwieser, Ann L. *Manhattan Water-Bound: Manhattan's Waterfront from the Seventeenth Century to the Present.* Syracuse: Syracuse University Press, 1987.

Cantwell, Anne-Marie, and Diana diZerega Wall. *Unearthing Gotham: The Archeology of New York City.* New Haven: Yale University Press, 2001.

Charpentier, Henri, and Boyden Sparkes. *Those Rich and Great Ones or Life à la Henri: being The Memoirs of Henri Charpentier.* London: Victor Gollanz Ltd, 1935.

Clute, J. J. *Annals of Staten Island.* New York: 1877.

Denevan, William. *The Native Population of the Americas in 1492.* Madison: University of Wisconsin Press, 1976.

Dickens, Charles. *American Notes. The Gadshill Edition: The Works of Charles Dickens in Thirty-Four Volumes,* Vol. XXVIII. London: Chapman & Hall, 1897.

————. *The Life and Adventures of Martin Chuzzlewit. The Gadshill Edition: The Works of Charles Dickens in Thirty-Four Volumes,* Vols. VI and VII. London: Chapman & Hall, 1897.

Dickenson, Richard, ed. *Holden's Staten Island: The History of Richmond County.* New York: Center for Migration Studies, 2002.

Every, Edward van. *Sins of New York: As "Exposed" by the Police Gazette.* New York: Frederick A. Stokes Company, 1930.

Foster, George C. *New York by Gas-light: and Other Urban Sketches.* Berkeley: University of California Press, 1990.

Gilfoyle, Timothy J. *City of Eros: New York City, Prostitution, and the Commercialization of Sex, 1790–1920*. New York: W. W. Norton, 1992.

Godfrey, Carlos E. *The Lenape Indians: Their Origin and Migrations to the Delaware*. Trenton: The Trenton Historical Society, 1919.

Grumet, Robert Steven. *The Lenape*. New York: Chelsea House, 1989.

Harrington, Mark Raymond. *A Preliminary Sketch of Lenape Culture*. Lancaster, Penn.: New Era Printing Company, 1913.

Hill, Marilynn Wood. *Their Sisters' Keepers: Prostitution in New York City, 1830–1870*. Berkeley: University of California Press, 1993.

Hine, Charles Gilbert, and William T. Davis. *Legends, Stories and Folklore of Old Staten Island: From Printed Records, Manuscripts and the Memories of the Older Inhabitants*. Staten Island: The Staten Island Historical Society, 1925.

Hodges, Graham Russell. *New York City Cartmen, 1667–1850*. New York: New York University Press, 1986.

———. *Root & Branch: African Americans in New York & New Jersey, 1613–1863*. Chapel Hill: University of North Carolina Press, 1999.

Homans, I. Smith. *An Historical and Statistical Account of the Foreign Commerce of the United States*. New York: Putnam, 1857.

Hone, Philip. *The Diary of Philip Hone, 1828–1851*. New York: Dodd, Mead and Company, 1910.

Jackson, Kenneth T. *The Encyclopedia of New York City*. New Haven: Yale University Press, 1995.

James, Barlett Burleigh, and J. Franklin Jameson, eds. *Journal of Jasper Danckaerts, 1679–1680*. New York: Barnes & Noble, 1913.

Jeffers, Paul H. *Diamond Jim Brady: Prince of the Gilded Age*. New York: John Wiley and Sons, 2001.

Juet, Robert. *Juet's Journal: The Voyage of the Half Moon from 4 April to 7 November 1609*. Newark: The New Jersey Historical Society, 1959.

Kalm, Peter. Edited by Adolph B. Benson. *Travels in North America*, Vol. I. New York: Dover Publication, 1966.

Kammen, Michael. *Colonial New York: A History*. New York: Charles Scribner's Sons, 1975.

Kaplan, Fred. *Dickens: A Biography*. New York: Avon Books, 1988.

Kraft, Herbert C. *The Indians of Lenapehoking.* South Orange, N.J.: Seton Hall University Museum, 1985.

Kross, Jessica. *The Evolution of an American Town: Newtown, New York, 1642–1775.* Philadelphia: Temple University Press, 1983.

Lopate, Phillip, ed. *Writing New York: A Literary Anthology.* New York: Washington Square Press, 1998.

Mackay, Charles. *Life and Liberty in America; or, Sketches of a Tour in the United States and Canada, in 1857–58.* London: Smith, Elder and Company, 1859.

MacKenzie Jr., Clyde L. *The Fisheries of Raritan Bay.* New Brunswick, N.J.: Rutgers University Press, 1992.

Marryat, Frederick. *A Diary in America: With Remarks on Its Institutions.* New York: Alfred A. Knopf, 1962.

Meckier, Jerome. *Innocents Abroad: Charles Dickens's American Engagements.* Lexington: University Press of Kentucky, 1990.

Morison, Samuel Eliot. *The Great Explorers: The European Discovery of America.* New York: Oxford University Press, 1978.

Mosley, Lois A. H. *Sandy Ground Memories.* Staten Island: Staten Island Historical Society, 2003.

Moss, Sidney P. *Charles Dickens' Quarrel With America.* Troy, N.Y.: The Whitstone Publishing Company, 1984.

Pitkin, Timothy. *A Statistical View of the Commerce of the United States of America.* New York: Johnson Reprint Corp., 1967.

Rosner, David, ed. *Hives of Sickness: Public Health and Epidemics in New York City.* New Brunswick, N.J.: Rutgers University Press, 1995.

Sala, George Augustus. *America Revisited,* two volumes. London: Vizetelly & Co., 1882.

Schecter, Barnet. *The Battle for New York: The City at the Heart of the American Revolution.* New York: Walker & Company, 2002.

Seitz, Sharon, and Stuart Miller. *The Other Islands of New York City: A Historic Companion.* Woodstock, Vt.: The Countryman Press, 1996.

Shorto, Russell. *The Island at the Center of the World: The Epic Story of Dutch Manhattan, the Forgotten Colony That Shaped America.* New York: Doubleday, 2003.

Skinner, Alanson. *The Lenapé Indians of Staten Island.* New York: American Museum of Natural History, 1909.

Smith, Thomas E. V. *The City of New York: In the Year of Washington's Inauguration, 1789.* Riverside, Conn.: Riverside Press, 1972.

Smith Jr., William. *The History of the Province of New York: From the First Discovery to the Year 1732,* two volumes. Cambridge: Harvard University Press, 1972.

Stokes, I. N. Phelps. *The Iconography of Manhattan Island,* six volumes. New York: Robert H. Dodd, 1915–28.

Street, Julian. *Welcome to Our City.* New York: John Lane Company, 1912.

Strong, George Templeton. *The Diary of George Templeton Strong,* four volumes. New York: Farrar, Straus and Giroux, 1974.

Taylor, Lawrence J. *Dutchmen on the Bay: the Ethnohistory of a Contractual Community.* Philadelphia: University of Pennsylvania Press, 1983.

Thomas, Lately. *Delmonico's: A Century of Splendor.* Boston: Houghton Mifflin Company, 1967.

Trager, James. *The New York Chronology.* New York: HarperResource, 2003.

Trollope, Fanny. *Domestic Manners of the Americans.* London: Penguin Books, 1997.

Van Rensselaer, Jeremias. *Correspondence of Jeremias van Rensselaer, 1654–1674.* Albany: University of the State of New York, 1932.

Van Rensselaer, Maria. *Correspondence of Maria van Rensselaer, 1669–1689.* Albany: University of the State of New York, 1935.

West Indische Compagnie. *Documents Relating to New Netherlands, 1624–1626.* San Marino, Calif.: The Henry E. Huntington Library and Art Gallery, 1924.

Williamson, W. M. *Adriaen Block: Navigator, Fur Trader, Explorer, New York's First Shipbuilder.* New York: Museum of the City of New York, 1959.

ENVIRONMENT

Boyle, Robert H. *The Hudson River: A Natural and Unnatural History.*
New York: W. W. Norton, 1969.

Cronin, John, and Robert F. Kennedy Jr. *The Riverkeepers.* New York: A
Touchstone Book, 1999.

Hagevik, George H. *Decision-making in Air Pollution Control: A Review of
the Theory and Practice, with Emphasis on Selected Los Angeles and New
York City Management Experiences.* New York: Praeger Publishers, 1970.

Johnson, Alan A., ed. *Water Pollution in the Greater New York Area.* New
York: Gordon and Breach, 1970.

Members of the New York Press. *The Night Side of New York: A Picture of
the Great Metropolis After Nightfall.* New York: J. C. Haney & Company, 1866.

Mitchell, Joseph. *The Bottom of the Harbor.* London: Jonathan Cape,
2000.

New Jersey Department of Environmental Protection, Division of Water
Resources. *Use Attainability Analyses of the New York Harbor Complex.*
Trenton: The Division, 1985.

New York (state) Bureau of Prevention of Stream Pollution. *Report of Bureau of Prevention of Stream Pollution Under the Supervision of Russel
Suter, Senior Assistant Engineer.* Albany: J. B. Lyon Company, 1923.

Smith, C. Lavett, ed. *Fisheries Research in the Hudson River.* Albany: State
University of New York, 1988.

United States Commission of Fish and Fisheries. *The Fisheries and Fishery Industries of the United States.* Section II, *A Geographical Review of
the Fisheries Industries and Fishing Communities for the Year 1880.*
Washington: Government Printing Office, 1887.

Waldman, John. *Heartbeats in the Muck: A Dramatic Look at the History,
Sea Life, and Environment of New York Harbor.* New York: The Lyons
Press, 1999.

Zupan, Jeffrey M. *The Distribution of Air Quality in the New York Region.*
Washington, D.C.: Resources for the Future, 1973.

OYSTERS

Blackford, Eugene Gilbert. *Report of the Oyster Investigation and Shell-fish Commission, for the Year Ending November 30th, 1887.* Troy: The Troy Press Company, 1888.

Brooks, William K. *The Oyster.* Baltimore: Johns Hopkins University Press, 1996.

Carpenter, O. G. *Oyster Cultivation in the World Famous L.I., New York, Oyster Beds.* New York: Long Island Oyster Growers, 1949.

Clark, Eleanor. *The Oysters of Locmariaquer.* Hopewell, N.J.: Ecco Press, 1964.

Fisher, M.F.K. *Consider the Oyster.* New York: Duel, Sloan and Pearce, 1941.

De Gouy, Louis P. *The Oyster Book.* New York: Greenberg, 1951.

Hedeen, Robert. *The Oyster: The Life and Lore of the Celebrated Bivalve.* Centreville, Md.: Tidewater Publishers, 1986.

Ingersoll, Ernest. *The Oyster-Industry.* Washington D.C.: Government Printing Office, 1881.

Kochiss, John M. *Oystering from New York to Boston.* Middletown, Conn.: Wesleyan University Press, 1974.

Laver, Henry. *The Colchester Oyster Fishery; Its Antiquity and Position, Method of Working and the Quality and Safety of its Products.* Colchester: Colne Fishery Board, 1916.

Mathiessen, George C. *Oyster Culture.* Oxford: Fishing New Books, 2001.

McCay, Bonnie J. *Oyster Wars and the Public Trust: Property, Law, and Ecology in New Jersey History.* Tucson: University of Arizona Press, 1998.

Neild, Robert. *The English, the French and the Oyster.* London: Quiller Press, 1995.

New Jersey Oyster Industry Investigation Committee. *Report of the Commission for the Investigation of the Oyster Industry.* Camden: Sinnickson Chew & Sons, 1902.

New York State Fisheries Commission. *Report of the Commissioner of Fisheries of the State of New York, in Charge of the Oyster Investigation.* Albany: State of New York, 1885.

Parks, Frederick J. *The Celebrated Oysterhouse Cookbook.* Allentown, Pa.: Park's Seafood, 1985.

Rorer, Sarah Tyson. *Fifteen New Ways for Oysters.* Philadelphia: Arnold and Company, 1894.

Rydon, John. *Oysters with Love.* London: Peter Owen, 1968.

FOOD

Barnes, Donna R., and Peter G. Rose. *Matters of Taste: Food and Drink in Seventeenth-Century Dutch Art and Life.* Syracuse: Syracuse University Press, 2002.

Batterby, Michael and Ariane. *On the Town in New York: The Landmark History of Eating, Drinking, and Entertainments from the American Revolution to the Food Revolution.* New York: Routledge, 1999.

Benes, Peter, ed. *Foodways in the Northeast.* Boston: Boston University, 1984.

Blot, Pierre. *Handbook of Practical Cookery, for Ladies and Professional Cooks.* New York: D. Appleton and Company, 1869.

Brereton, Georgina E. and Janet M. Ferrier, eds. *Le Mesnagier de Paris.* Paris: Le Livre de Poche, 1994.

Charpentier, Henri. *The Henri Charpentier Cookbook.* Los Angeles: Price/Stern/Sloan, 1970.

Chadwick, J. *Home Cookery: A Collection of Tried Receipts Both Foreign and Domestic.* New York: Charles S. Francis and Company, 1853.

———. *Ladies' Indispensable Companion and Housekeepers' Guide.* New York, 1854.

Collins, John. *Salt and Fishery.* London: A. Godbid and J. Playford, 1682.

Corson, Juliet. *Juliet Corson's New Family Cookbook: A Complete Cookbook for Family Use in City and Country.* New York: George Munro, 1885.

———. *Meals for The Millions.* New York, New York School of Cookery, 1882.

Crowen T. J. *The American System of Cookery: Comprising Every Variety of Information for Ordinary and Holiday Occasions.* New York: T. R. Dawley, 1864.

Diat, Louis. *Cooking à la Ritz.* New York: J. B. Lippincott, 1941.

De Gouy, Louis P. (See *Oysters*)

Drummond, J. C., and Anne Wilbraham. *The Englishman's Food: Five Centuries of English Diet.* London: Pimlico, 1994.

DuSablon, Mary Anna. *America's Collectible Cookbooks.* Athens: Ohio University Press, 1994.

Giacosa, Ilaria Gozzini. *A Taste of Ancient Rome.* Chicago: University of Chicago Press, 1992.

Glasse, Hannah. *The Art of Cookery Made Plain and Easy.* Totnes, Devon, England: Prospect Books, 1995.

Hieatt, Constance B., ed. *An Ordinance of Pottage: An Edition of the Fifteenth Century Culinary Recipes in Yale University's Ms Beinecke 163.* Totnes, Devon, England: Prospect Books, 1988.

Grant, Mark, trans. and ed. *Anthimus: On the Observance of Foods.* Totnes, Devon, England: Prospect Books, 1996.

———. *Galen on Food and Diet.* London: Routledge, 2000.

Guest, Flora Bigelow. *Soup, Oysters and Surprises.* London: The John Lane Company, 1918.

Hagen, Ann. *A Second Handbook of Anglo-Saxon Food & Drink Production & Distribution.* Norfolk, England: Anglo-Saxon Books, 1995.

Kirkland, Alexander. *Rector's Naughty '90s Cookbook.* Garden City, N.Y.: Doubleday, 1949.

Leslie, Eliza. *Miss Leslie's Directions for Cookery.* New York: Dover Publications, 1999.

Lewis, Amelia. *How to Live in Winter.* New York: Food and Health Publishing Office, 1881.

Peachey, Stuart. *The Book of Boiled Meats: Volume 1: Fish.* Bristol, England: Stuart Press, 1999.

Pliny the Elder. *Natural History.* London: Penguin Books, 1991.

Ranhofer, Charles. *The Epicurean: A Complete Treatise of Analytical and Practical Studies of the Culinary Arts.* New York: Dover Publications, 1971.

Riley, Gillian. *The Dutch Table: Gastronomy in the Golden Age of the Netherlands.* San Francisco: Pomegranate Artbooks, 1994.

Root, Waverley, and Richard de Rochemont. *Eating in America: A History.* New York: William Morris, 1976.

Rorer, Sarah Tyson. (See *Oysters*)

Rose, Peter G. *The Sensible Cook: Dutch Foodways in the Old and the New World.* Syracuse: Syracuse University Press, 1989.

Rundell, Maria Eliza Ketelby. *American Domestic Cookery: Formed on Principles of Economy, for the Use of Private families by an experienced Housekeeper.* New York: E. Duyckinck, 1823.

Seely, L. *Mrs. Seely's Cook Book: A Manual of French and American Cookery.* New York: The Macmillan Company, 1902.

Simmons, Amelia. *American Cookery: or the Art of Dressing Viands, Fish, Poultry and Vegetables and the Best Modes of Making Puff-Pastries, Pies, Tarts, Puddings, Custards and Preserves, and all kinds of Cakes, from the Imperial Plumb to Plain Cake, adopted to the country and all grades of life.* Bedford, Mass.: Applewood Books, 1996.

Tschirky, Oscar. *"Oscar" of the Waldorf's Cookbook.* New York: Dover Publications, 1973.

Waugh, F. W. *Iroquois Foods and Food Preparation.* Ohsweken, Ontario: Iroqrafts, 1991.

Wilkins, John, and Shaun Hill. *The Life of Luxury: Archestratus.* Totnes, Devon, England: Prospect Books, 1994.

ARTICLES

Blumberg, Deborah Lynn. "At the River Project, the World Is Their Oyster." *The Villager,* 73, no. 50 (March 14–20, 2004).

Brouwer, Norman. "The New York Fisheries." *Seaport: New York's History Magazine,* Winter/Spring 1990.

Claassen, Cheryl. "Summary of the Results of Research at the Archaic Dogan Point Site, Westchester County, New York." *The Bulletin* 107 (Spring 1994). New York State Archeological Society.

Hewitt, John H. "Mr. Downing and His Oyster House: The Life and

Good Works of an African American Entrepreneur." *New York History,* July 1993. New York Historical Association.

Kochiss, John M. "New York Oyster Barges." *The Log of Mystic Seaport,* Winter 1971.

Kollmer, Burton A. "The Yesterday of the Oysterman." *Staten Island Historian,* July 1940.

Lockwood, Reverend Samuel. "The Natural History of the Oyster." *Popular Science Monthly,* November 1874.

London *Daily News.* "American Oysters Praised." *New York Times,* September 10, 1882.

Melvin, Tessa. "Site of Artifacts Poses Quandary in Dobbs Ferry." *New York Times,* April 17, 1988.

National Historic Landmark Nomination for Old Barge Cafe (the last oyster barge) in New Haven Connecticut. National Register of Historic Places, 1994.

Schaper, Hans F., and Louis A. Brennan. "Shell Middens in the Lower Hudson Valley." *The Bulletin* 98 (Spring 1989). New York State Archeological Society.

———. "Oysters and Settlement in the Lower Hudson Valley." *The Bulletin* 106 (Fall 1993). New York State Archeological Society.

Schuyler, Robert L. "Sandy Ground: Archeological Sampling in a Black Community in Metropolitan New York." The Conference on Historic Site Archeology Papers. University of South Carolina, August 1974.

Walford Memorial Convocation. "Raritan Bay: Its Multiple Uses and Abuses." Sandy Hook Laboratory Technical Series Report no. 30, August 1984.

Whitridge, Arnold. "Dickens and Thackeray in America." *New York Historical Society Quarterly* 62, no. 3 (July 1978).

Zeisel Jr., William N. "Shark!!! And Other Sport Fish Once Abundant in New York Harbor." *Seaport: New York's History Magazine,* Winter/Spring 1990.

"The City's Oyster Market: Oystermen Combining at the Foot of Perry Street." *New York Times,* September 10, 1889.

"Extinction of Oysters in New York Now Feared." *New York Times,* January 27, 1920.

"An Early Attack by Typhoid." *New York Times,* July 11, 1924.

"The Great Oyster Placer: Millions of Dollars' Worth Found: Great Excitement Along the Shore." *New York Daily Tribune,* October 1, 1859.

"Grievances of Oystermen." *New York Times,* November 25, 1884.

"How New York Is Fed." *Scribner's Monthly,* October 1877.

"How the Oyster 'De Luxe' is Gathered." *New York Times Illustrated Magazine,* December 25, 1898.

"Jamaica Bay, Foul with Sewage, Closed to Oyster Beds; 300 Bushels Gone." *New York Times,* January 30, 1921.

"Mine Oyster." *Harper's Weekly,* Supplement, March 16, 1872.

"National Meeting Booms the Oyster." *New York Times,* May 6, 1969.

"The Oyster Season." *New York Times,* September 6, 1909.

"Shell Fisheries." *Keyport Weekly,* Christmas Edition, 1905.

INDEX OF

Recipes

INDEX

Page numbers in *italics* refer to illustrations.

MARK KURLANSKY is the *New York Times*
bestselling and James A. Beard Award–winning
author of *Cod: A Biography of the Fish That
Changed the World, Salt: A World History, 1968:
The Year That Rocked the World,* and *The Basque
History of the World,* as well as *Boogaloo on 2nd Avenue*
(his debut novel) and several other books.
He lives in New York City.